Meridians feminism, race, transnationalism

···

VOLUME 17 · NUMBER 2 · NOVEMBER 2018

AFRICAN FEMINISMS
Cartographies for the Twenty-First Century

Ginetta E. B. Candelario

Editor's Introduction

> Here, I deliberately call . . . Wambui by [her] first name, not to take away
> from the titles that carry [her surname] but to acknowledge [her] contribu-
> tion to black thought and to briefly point to the place of friendship in intel-
> lectual work coming from parts of Africa—intellectual work that has beau-
> tifully morphed into a network of friendships and affirmation in a world in
> which Africans are to be studied while taking the place of academic tour
> guides.
>
> —Neo Sinoxolo Musangi, "Homing with My Mother"

The first African feminist I ever met was Wambui Mwangi, my 1990 class-
mate at Smith College. It was the spring of 1988, at the Mwangi Cultural
Center, where all the heads of student of color organizations on campus
had gathered together to discuss and strategize our response to yet another
instance of institutional racism at Smith. That we were meeting at a center
with which she shared a name was not coincidental. In addition to founding the Smith African Students Association, in which capacity she attended
the meeting, Wambui was also renowned at the college for being N'gendo
Mwangi's daughter. Dr. Mwangi was the first African woman to attend
Smith, where she took a degree in biology in 1961, a fact commemorated a
decade later by the newly formed Black Students' Alliance when they named
the college's first cultural center in her honor in 1973 (Cole 2005). After
completing medical school in the United States, Dr. Mwangi had returned
to Kenya, where she was the first woman doctor in East Africa, a lifelong

MERIDIANS · feminism, race, transnationalism   17:2 November 2018
DOI: 10.1215/15366936-7176373 © 2018 Smith College

public health activist, and until her death in 1989 a trenchant critic of colonialism and authoritarianism in Kenya.

Despite several notable biographical, cultural, and temperamental differences between us, Wambui and I shared a fierce commitment to antiracist, anti-imperialist, critical feminism that predated our arrival at Smith. Consequently we became not only fast friends but self-declared sisters, kindred spirits who shared the experience of being raised by indomitable, courageous, and pathbreaking "single" mothers. Both women from what was then called the "Third World," our mothers defied dictators born of patriarchy, imperialism, and colonialism in our respective motherlands, and went on to complete their college educations in the United States at a time when few women did.

Inspired by our mothers and united by our politics, Wambui and I established Concerned Students of All Colors (CSAC) together with Pakistani, Korean, Indian, African American, Jewish, South African, WASP, poor white, and sundry other heritage Smith women. CSAC was an ad hoc radical multicultural group of students committed to addressing institutional racism and classism at Smith. Side by side across differences and divides, we organized meetings and protest rallies, held press conferences, provided radio interviews, and reported racist "incidents" at the college, which included incidents that targeted Wambui specifically, to the U.S. Department of Justice's Community Relations Divisions and the Massachusetts Commission against Discrimination. In sum, we insisted that the college live up to its founder's hope that Smith College would help to create a society in which "what are called [women's] 'wrongs' will be redressed, their wages adjusted, their weight of influence in reforming the evils of society will be greatly increased, as teachers, as writers, as mothers, as members of society, their power for good will be incalculably enlarged" (Smith College n.d.).

The work we did resulted in the *Smith Design for Institutional Diversity*, a historic college policy commitment that institutionalized programs to address the economic, educational, and sociocultural gaps that hampered the recruitment, retention and achievement of students, faculty, and staff of color, as well as low-income students at Smith; it also identified the "traditional norms" of elitism and white supremacy that would be challenged on campus by the time we graduated in 1990 (*Smith Design* 1988).[1] That particular aspect of the *Smith Design* drew national attention to the extent that the Harvard historian and Kennedy-era policy adviser Arthur

Schlesinger mentioned it by name in his 1991 anti-multiculturalism screed, *The Disuniting of America: Reflections on a Multicultural Society.* Just as Schlesinger and others feared, less than a decade after its articulation the *Smith Design* fomented transformations that allowed for *Meridians* to be imagined, conceptualized, and established at the college by the Women's Studies Program and, in turn, fostered epistemic, demographic, and paradigm shifts led by critical women of color in the U.S. academy.[2]

In the thirty years since then, Wambui and I both went on to earn PhDs in political science and sociology, respectively. Along the way, she worked for the Goree Institute in Senegal and I for the Ford Foundation's South Africa Program in New York; we each conducted research about and taught in the United States and Canada, as well as in our motherlands, Kenya and the Dominican Republic; and we shared the experience of transnationalism, internationalist multiple consciousness, and multilingual multicultural worlds. Ultimately, Wambui chose to return to Nairobi and like her mother devote herself to the uncompromising pursuit of justice, artistic creation, and scholarship.

Thus I admit that when Alicia and Gabeba approached *Meridians* about guest-editing a special issue on African feminisms, the possibility of obliquely honoring both Dr. Mwangis, N'gendo and Wambui, occurred to me. I was even more thrilled when I saw that Neo Sinoxolo Musangi's "Counterpoint" in this collection makes explicit not only Wambui's role in Kenyan feminist praxis but also in African feminism's expansive and generous branches. Like Musangi and Keguro, whom Neo quotes, I share their sense that "from Wambui Mwangi and Frantz Fanon I learn to begin from where I am standing. And this also means returning to where I started." So it is that, returning to where the possibility of *Meridians* at Smith was born, I dedicate this issue to Dr. N'gendo Mwangi (d. 1989), one of Africa's many original feminists who have nurtured and inspired their own and many others' daughters to create "network[s] of friendships and affirmation" that transform the known world into the beloved community of which we dream.

Notes
1   One of those programs, the Praxis internship program, still operates today, as does the Office of Institutional Diversity.
2   It was Mary Maples Dunn (1933–2017), Dr. Mwangi's dear friend, who began the process of developing and realizing the *Design's* vision during her tenure as president of the college from 1985 to 1995 (Slotnik 2017).

Works Cited

Cole, Kristen. 2005. "Thriving Mwangi Cultural Center Moves to Larger Home." News release. Smith College, January 12. https://www.webcitation.org /6fxEupNlS.

Schlesinger, Arthur. 1991. *The Disuniting of America: Reflections on a Multicultural Society.* New York: Norton.

Slotnik, Daniel. 2017. "Mary Maples Dunn, Advocate of Women's Colleges, Dies at 85." *New York Times*, March 22.

Smith College. N.d. "Sophia Smith." Accessed June 14, 2018. https://www.smith.edu /about-smith/smith-history/sophia-smith.

The Smith Design for Institutional Diversity: A Call to Action. 1988. Report prepared for the Smith College Board of Trustees, October 6. Mary Maples Dunn Papers, Smith College Archives, Smith College, Northampton, MA.

Alicia C. Decker and Gabeba Baderoon

African Feminisms
Cartographies for the Twenty-First Century

In 1981 Filomina Chioma Steady boldly proclaimed that black women, particularly those from the African continent, were the original feminists. In
her now classic anthology, *The Black Woman Cross-Culturally*, Steady argued
that "true feminism" stemmed from "an actual experience of oppression,
a lack of the socially prescribed means of ensuring one's wellbeing, and a
true lack of access to resources for survival" (36). In her mind, feminism
was simply a reaction to oppression, one that resulted in "the development
of greater resourcefulness for survival and greater self-reliance." Two years
later the budding Sierra Leonean anthropologist delivered a powerful key-
note address on African feminism at a research conference at Howard
University organized by the Association of Black Women Historians
(Terborg-Penn 1996, xix). This lecture provided the analytical scaffolding
that would frame intellectual discussions about feminism in Africa for
years to come. In the essay that grew out of this address, Steady (1996, 4)
noted:

> African feminism combines racial, sexual, class, and cultural dimensions
> of oppression to produce a more inclusive brand of feminism through
> which women are viewed first and foremost as *human*, rather than sexual,
> beings. It can be defined as that ideology which encompasses freedom
> from oppression based on the political, economic, social, and cultural
> manifestations of racial, cultural, sexual, and class biases. It is more
> inclusive than other forms of feminist ideologies and is largely a product

MERIDIANS · feminism, race, transnationalism   17:2 November 2018
DOI: 10.1215/15366936-7176384 © 2018 Smith College

of polarizations and conflicts that represent some of the worst and chronic forms of human suffering. . . . African feminism is, in short, humanistic feminism.

In the thirty years since this essay was originally published (i.e., 1987), scholarship on African feminisms has grown tremendously and is now being taught at universities across the world. In African countries such as Uganda, South Africa, Cameroon, Ghana, and Morocco, women's and gender studies courses, as well as departments and even schools, have become relatively commonplace. Both guest editors are products of this momentum, having earned graduate degrees from African universities that specialize in African feminist thought.[1] Both of us now teach in the Department of Women's, Gender, and Sexuality Studies at the Pennsylvania State University, and we are both deeply committed to the intellectual and activist work that Steady first described. As codirectors of the African Feminist Initiative, or AFI, we seek to promote the study of African feminist thought, as well as the history of African feminist activism, within the U.S. academy. In addition, we also strive to create equitable partnerships between scholars and practitioners of African feminism based in North America and Europe and those based on the African continent. This special issue of *Meridians* represents one such partnership.

Like the "true feminism" described by Steady in 1981, the African Feminist Initiative emerged out of struggle. It grew out of the recognition that African studies—at least within our university—was not a hospitable place to engage in feminist work, nor was women's, gender, and sexuality studies attentive enough to scholarly issues concerning women on the African continent. Instead of trying to work within the confines of an existing set of structures, the two of us decided to forge a different path, to create a new space where we could promote the type of scholarship that had been so critical to our own intellectual development. Because we had the good fortune of working at a university with no fewer than seven scholars who shared similar academic interests, we had the critical mass to make such an initiative successful. In April 2015, with generous start-up funding from the College of the Liberal Arts at Penn State, we launched the AFI.

The African Feminist Initiative is an intellectual collective of sorts. In addition to the two codirectors, it has an internal steering committee and an external advisory board. The former comprises Penn State faculty members with an interest in the field, while the latter consists of leading

African feminist scholars from around the world.[2] We also have a broad network of affiliates, both scholars and activists, who are involved in the work of the AFI and our mission. Membership is free and open to anyone with an interest in African feminist research, teaching, or activism. We hope that with the publication of this special issue, we will be able to expand our network even further.

Collaboration is central to everything that we do. During our launch event in October 2015, for instance, a number of students from Penn State worked closely with a group of students from the University of the Western Cape to stage a production of the award-winning play *Reclaiming the P Word*, which was created by students, faculty, and staff of the Gender Equity Unit at UWC to counter cultures of sexual violence. The director of the Gender Equity Unit, Professor Mary Hames, accompanied six of her students to the United States. Over the course of several days, the South African students met with their American counterparts, sharing stories and discussing how they would adapt the play for an American audience. The students ultimately staged two joint productions of the play before packed houses of more than four hundred people. They also gave a public presentation where they discussed the role of art in activism and how the play helped to foster transnational feminist solidarity.

One of the things that we wanted to do with the AFI was energize interest in African feminisms on campus. The play certainly helped to garner interest in the work that we intended to do, not just among faculty members and students but with members of the community as well. In an effort to highlight the rich diversity that is African feminisms, we have also sponsored a series of public lectures, panel discussions, and film screenings. These events nurture our local community and also provide African feminist scholars and activists with a venue in which they can share and get feedback on their work. Another way that we have tried to support our colleagues, especially those on the continent, is through our African Feminist Residency. This initiative offers visiting scholars and artists a quiet place to work on their own projects, away from the bustle of everyday life. Thus far we have hosted two feminists in residence and have at least two more lined up for next year. Some of our residents are self-funding, while others receive support from the AFI.

We have tried to increase awareness about African feminisms through the curriculum as well. Over the past few years, we have developed two graduate courses, African Feminisms and Gender and Islam, and as an undergraduate course, Women, Gender, and Feminisms in Africa. As the African Feminist Initiative continues to grow, we hope to increase the number of course offerings. At present, Penn State offers several dual-degree PhD programs, which allow doctoral students in fifteen disciplines to earn a second PhD in either women's studies or African studies. In the future, we hope to offer a dual-title PhD in women's studies *and* African studies, as well as a postdoctoral fellowship in African feminisms. Our ability to carry out these initiatives will depend on the administrative structure of our university in the coming years.

The recent passing of Winnie Madikizela-Mandela reminds us that we must never take for granted the contributions of our elders. In an effort to preserve the history of African feminisms, in terms of both intellectual production and activist endeavors, the AFI created an oral history project. Whenever guests of the African Feminist Initiative visit Penn State, we ask if we can interview them about their work and their relationship to feminism. Through these in-depth conversations, we have learned a great deal about the history of the field and the events that have inspired some of its most influential actors. In the near future we plan to post audio and/or video files of these interviews to our website so that they are widely accessible. Sharing this knowledge and disseminating this history is one of our major goals.

Another way that we share knowledge is through our listserv, which now has numerous subscribers in Africa and beyond. Members regularly post fascinating questions and comments about African feminist research, teaching, and activism, which often spark spirited exchanges. One such exchange began after one of us sent an email to the group with the standard feminist greeting, "Dear sisters, dear friends on the AFI list." In response, we received a most thought-provoking email from one of our earliest members: "Thank you my dear Gabeba and Alicia for adding me onto this list. However, it's interesting to see how feminist=woman=sister for many of us! I wonder how someone like me [who identifies as genderqueer] might survive and stay nourished in this space. I will remain hopeful 😊." The addition of that complex emoticon at the end of the sentence, that open-ended ending, provoked an important and necessary transnational conversation about solidarity terms and global "sisterhood." One of our board members, Margo Okazawa-Rey, offered to facilitate a discussion on this topic using Zoom software. We readily agreed, and several days later twelve participants spanning numerous time zones on both sides of the

Atlantic gathered in virtual space for our first African Feminist Dialogue. This technology allowed those of us with very different modes of communication and bandwidth to find one another—some of us by phone while commuting in city traffic, some of us from our offices in South Africa, Nigeria, and North America. It rendered our voices hearable across the different realities and long distances that often make this type of work challenging.

The conversation allowed us to reflect on the feelings of solidarity, community, comradeship, friendship, affection, and wordless connection that the word "sister" has held for many of us, despite existing debates about assumed meanings of the term. After an hour, the conversation showed no sign of ending. Another one of our board members, Charmaine Pereira, therefore proposed a new name that we could use in the interim to signal all of the meanings of our traditional greeting, but one that was not gendered in the old binary ways, namely, "AFIists" (i.e., members of the African Feminist Initiative). Many of us have begun to use that term as a new form of solidarity. Moreover, because the dialogue was such a vibrant intellectual mode of exchange, we decided to host one on a monthly basis. Both the listserv and the dialogue series have allowed us to expand the AFI far beyond our own university.

Hosting international conferences and workshops has also allowed us to foster greater collaboration among scholars and activists based in different parts of the world. Our first workshop took place in March 2016 and focused on human rights and subjectivity. In September 2016 we hosted a much larger conference on the state of the field of African feminisms. Then, in May 2017, we organized a smaller conference in Fez, Morocco, on African Muslim feminisms. At each of these gatherings, we invited participants from numerous African countries and at universities throughout North America and Europe. Non-African scholars have also been encouraged to participate, although we have consciously privileged African voices and experiences. We have also put great stock into mentoring graduate students and junior scholars, not only inviting them to our events but also helping them to revise their essays for publication. In this special issue, we are proud to feature some of their work alongside that of more established scholars and activists.

Despite these accomplishments, we have also been compelled to learn from our mistakes. One of the most painful lessons took place in August 2016, when three of our members participated in the Decolonizing

Feminisms conference at the University of the Witwatersrand. We initially envisioned this as an opportunity to launch the AFI on the African continent. We were excited about the work that we were doing and wanted to share it with the world. However, our panel faced serious criticism. Some aspects of the critique were merited, such as our not taking care to sufficiently ensure that our invitation to feminist scholars did not come across as a hunger to draw feminist students from the continent to North American universities, and appearing to think that we could "do" African feminism better than those on the continent. One feminist scholar from Latin America contested our not distinguishing our initiative from neoliberal interests in "inclusion" and "diversity" that view African scholars as raw material for a metric of inclusiveness. Although none of these criticisms reflected our actual goals or intentions, we were greatly disappointed and realized that we needed to talk about our work in a different way. Indeed we learned that we needed to think very carefully about the relationship between scholars based in Africa and those who form part of a significant new diaspora in northern universities, and how we might engage in productive and equitable partnerships. We have also come to realize that generational differences affect how we think about feminism and what our priorities should be. What is interesting to a midcareer scholar in the United States is not necessarily important to a college student in South Africa, so we have to find ways to engage in dialogue across multiple nodes of difference. This is the challenge, and the opportunity, for the African Feminist Initiative in the coming years.

o o o

Tsitsi Jaji is one of a formidable cohort of African feminist literary scholars who have earned acclaim in multiple genres, ranging across critical scholarship and creative writing. Jaji's poem "And They Didn't Die" is an homage to her mother. It draws its title from the famous novel of the same name by Lauretta Ngcobo, one of the great "ankestors," to use Jaji's resonant formulation from her collection *Beating the Graves* (2017), of African women's writing. Facing impending motherhood, the speaker contemplates her own transformation from daughter into "becoming Mother." The poem maps the borders between what "we cannot know" and "how it has always been," unshaken and yet without certainty.

Memoir has been one of the transformative avenues of feminist writing. In her personal reflection "Creating the Archive of African Women's

Writing: Reflecting on Feminism, Epistemology, and the Women Writing Africa Project," Abena P. A. Busia returns us to the genesis of one of the great achievements of the African feminist literary canon: the four volumes of *Women Writing Africa*, which Busia edited along with Tuzyline Jita Allan and Florence Howe. This massive task centering women's intellectual work in African epistemologies and archives took nearly two decades of devoted, complex, and challenging work, and Busia's memoir provides crucial insight into the making of a publication which has been central to teaching, knowledge making, and reading African women's writing since its publication.

The African Feminist Initiative would not be a success without the wisdom and generosity of our advisory board members. Charmaine Pereira has been actively involved in feminist politics on the continent for many years, coordinating the Initiative for Women's Studies in Nigeria, guest-editing special issues of *Feminist Africa*, and serving as an active member of the African Feminist Forum. She joined our board in 2017, after attending two of our conferences. Her thoughtful questions and insightful comments undoubtedly moved our deliberations to a much deeper level. In her essay "Beyond the Spectacular: Contextualizing Gender Relations in the Wake of the Boko Haram Insurgency," which she first presented at one of our conferences, Pereira examines some of the ways in which women and girls are made visible, or invisible, through various spectacles of violence. She argues, "While the forms that sexual and gender violence have taken during the insurgency are particularly egregious and thus distinct from those previously recognized, it is also the case that continuities in terms of gender and sexual violence *predating* the insurgency, in times of 'peace,' have been normalized." For this reason, she suggests, we must be attentive to the continuities and discontinuities that mark gender relations in contemporary Nigeria.

Fatima Sadiqi, a leading feminist scholar from Morocco, is another advisory board member who has contributed immensely to the AFI, participating in a panel discussion on African Muslim feminisms at Penn State in April 2016 and then helping us to organize a follow-up conference on the same theme in Fez. In her scholarship and activism, Sadiqi has worked hard to ensure that North Africa is part of African studies and not simply an extension of Europe or the Middle East. Her work bridges feminist networks in the North with those south of the Sahara and allows us to think critically about what African feminist solidarity really means.

In a fascinating interview, "Reflecting on Feminisms in Africa: A Conversation from Morocco," Aziza Ouguir, one of Sadiqi's first doctoral students, encourages her former mentor to reflect on feminisms in Africa today.

When several members of the AFI attended the Decolonizing Feminisms conference at Wits University in August 2016, we had the opportunity to hear a fascinating paper on African sex worker activism by Ntokozo Yingwana, a first-year South African PhD student. Her essay, "'We Fit in the Society by Force': Sex Work and Feminism in Africa," draws from compelling research she conducted with sex worker advocacy groups using body maps to explore what it means to be a sex worker and a feminist. Yingwana's embodied methodology allowed her participants to grapple with practices of exclusion and savior discourses that they encountered from other feminist groups. It also allowed them to theorize their own relationship to dominant feminisms and devise a definition of feminism in which sex workers' experiences of gender, labor, and sexuality were central and substantively engaged.

The third World Conference on Women, which took place in Nairobi in 1985, marked the end of the UN Decade for Women. While African women had been active participants in the previous Mexico City and Copenhagen conferences, this represented the largest gathering of women in the history of the United Nations. Many of the more than fifteen thousand women who participated in the conference, as well as the parallel NGO Forum, were African. It therefore served as a catalyst for women's mobilization throughout the continent. To give readers a sense of this historic conference, we have included excerpts from the International Women's Tribune Center compendium, *Decade for Women Information Resources #5: Images of Nairobi, Reflections and Follow-Up July 1986*, published one year after the conference.

Abosede George's contribution, "Saving Nigerian Girls: A Critical Reflection on Girl-Saving Campaigns in Colonial and Neoliberal Eras," examines how the media (and various concerned others) have framed certain categories of Nigerian girls as victims in need of saving. When she presented this paper at our first major conference in September 2016, the fate of the Chibok girls, abducted by Boko Haram in April 2014, was largely unknown. The hashtag #BringBackOurGirls, or #BBOG, was a powerful call to action, but it was not the first time that outsiders had taken an interest in the fate of Nigeria's most vulnerable. As George brilliantly illustrates, #BBOG was largely reminiscent of an antihawking campaign that targeted young female street vendors in the early twentieth century. Both campaigns "relied on a gendered notion of imperilment that centers the image of the youthful female body threatened by sexual violence from male aggressors in order to inspire salvationist impulses in their respective audiences." She suggests that in both cases, distant audiences were more receptive to the rhetoric than those who lived nearby. The latter were more likely to push back against the portrait of vulnerability that undergirded both campaigns.

From its inception, the AFI has aimed to be a hospitable space for activists, policymakers, practitioners, artists, teachers, and scholars. It is in this context that we welcome the work of Anne Moraa, a Kenyan activist and editor, who has developed materials for a girls' magazine about menstrual health. In her essay "Smoke Is Everywhere, But No One Is Running: A Kenyan Activist Speaks Out," Moraa shows that to address the challenges girls face on entering puberty takes serious political, artistic, intellectual, educational, and cultural labor. Statistics show that girls' encounter with menstruation often catapults them out of education. However, Moraa's approach goes beyond the technocratic solution of simply providing menstrual materials. To her, the challenge emerges when one talks to the girls themselves. She writes compellingly about what girls say about their bodies in a culture that often teaches them not to speak. Her essay provides an invaluable perspective from a literary activist.

In "Gender and (Militarized) Secessionist Movements in Africa: An African Feminist's Reflections," Jacqueline-Bethel Tchouta Mougoué proposes a new analytical framework to explain women's multifaceted participation in secessionist movements in Africa. Using historical and contemporary examples from across the continent, she convincingly demonstrates that African women have supported male-dominated secessionist movements in various ways in order to garner social and political power. Contrary to popular opinion, these women are not passive bystanders but important political actors in their own right. When Mougoué presented a preliminary version of this work at one of our conferences, her native country of Cameroon was embroiled in a fierce secessionist struggle. Through her careful analysis of the crisis, she helped us to understand why a feminist analysis of secessionist politics is so crucial at this historical moment.

Through her work as an editor of award-winning collections such as *Queer Africa: New and Collected Fiction*, Makhosazana Xaba has become one of the leading forces shaping literature, as well as gender and sexuality activism, in South Africa today. As a poet, she documents the intimate and bodily pursuit of liberation in a complex world where war has transmuted into more dispersed forms of violence. Interestingly it is in quiet retrospect after saying goodbye at the conclusion of their time together that the "three women" of her poem reflect on the "joys of sisterhood," a line recalling that great feminist novel *The Joys of Motherhood* by Buchi Emecheta. Afterward the women step into "freezing raindrops-filled winds" as "midnight approaches" but return in their reflections to what it means for women whose realities diverge and divide to grasp onto "the single holding thread: the warmth of sisterhood."

Selina Makana thoughtfully reflects upon the predicaments and promises of African feminist ethnography. Makana is a Kenyan scholar who researches women and war in Angola. In this compelling essay, which she initially presented at one of our conferences, she discusses what it is like to be both an insider and an outsider in the field. She describes this delicate balance as the "ebb and flow of the fieldwork process," something that she sees as akin to waves in the sea. Makana argues that African feminist researchers "must take questions of identity seriously in order to create nonhierarchical relationships with our research partners." Her essay pushes African feminist ethnographers to consider carefully the implications of doing fieldwork at "home."

Zimbabwe's long-serving president, Robert Mugabe, finally stepped down in November 2017 after the military seized power in a "non-coup." In "Finding Women in the Zimbabwean Transition," Chipo Dendere provides an African feminist reading of this highly anticipated political transition, as well as the early months of the new regime. As an activist scholar, she keeps her finger on the pulse of contemporary politics and reflects on life for women "in the trenches."

Since this issue is about the state of our field, many of the contributions pivot between questions of beginning and contemplating future paths. Toni Stuart, one of the most powerful of the younger generation of poet-teacher-performers in South Africa, writes in her poem "my mother's trousseau" about the delicate inheritances between mothers and daughters. In the poem, nothing in the speaker's and her mother's lives is easy or can be taken for granted, and therefore everything in the poem, though "fraught with frayed dreams," gains a sheen of tenderness. The speaker's description of her mother's trousseau is threaded with the words "not" and "no," defining this treasure chest against the expectations that it cannot fulfill. Despite what it does not have, the speaker gleans from her mother's trousseau some crucial lessons: "learning to leave," "unwrapping [fear] from my skin," and "how to breathe . . . on my own." This is an unforgettable poem about the inheritances and losses that pass between mothers and daughters.

Black feminist poetry and performance have become a vibrant space of artistic and activist expression around the African continent. Msia Kibona Clark's essay "Feminisms in African Hip Hop" extends a growing corpus of critical work on this powerful cultural form. The essay maps the complex relation of female artists to masculine dominance within hip hop and also to mainstream feminism, giving an original and vivid dimension to her analysis. The powerful resonance of hip hop lyrics and culture among both female and male fans, especially youthful ones, means that feminist emcees could potentially reshape gender conceptions on the continent, though Clark also notes the backlash the artists encounter for transgressing narrow codes of respectability. Clark's analysis draws on a broad archive of 324 songs, as well as vivid interviews with artists, and her immersion in hip hop culture in the United States gives a compelling comparative aspect to the essay. Themes such as heteronormativity, a focus on material realities, and patriarchal dynamics in the African hip hop scene make this an illuminating study of African culture.

In this compelling personal reflection about the logic of care at work in practices of language, love, and marriage among the older black women of their family, Neo Sinoxolo Musangi creates an African lexicon for belonging in which to be black and queer and feminist in Africa. The essay "Homing with My Mother / How Women in My Family Married Women" offers several lessons in method: conducting crucial historical work by "thinking with, and against, this archival record," while also turning firmly toward the contemporary and "what it might mean to be both African and queer, in the *here* and *now*." By pointing to the accommodations that the English language demands of African experience, the essay in turn insists on recognizing the intricate African epistemologies at work within practices of "woman-to-woman marriage" that Musangi proposes can "potentially enable us to rethink community formation beyond kinship and family ties." This erudite essay draws on a range of intertexts from across the continent and diaspora to theorize an embodied practice of relation that "does not take politely to 'direct translation.'"

Finally, Patricia McFadden draws on forty years of scholarship and activism to reimagine African feminist epistemologies and practice. In her manifesto "Contemporarity: Sufficiency in a Radical African Feminist Life," McFadden confronts the failures of neoliberalism not solely as political and economic policies but also as an impediment to the imagination. She therefore turns to "new sources of creative imaginaries" as a crucial feminist tool. Understanding her own life in Swaziland as such a source, she generates a radical theory and practice of sustaining the self "through ecological balance, a respectful interaction with nature, and nonmarket practices of sufficiency." McFadden reflects on ways of living that often elude theorizing because they are practiced far from urban centers and are unconnected to forms of consumption. Such lives are often by necessity attuned to living ecosystems from which they produce sustenance within a grounded community. From her experience of such a life, and her position within it as a radical intellectual, she crafts a feminist manifesto of "contemporarity."

As the essays in this special issue show, African feminisms are not only diverse in their various forms but are also in vibrant and sometimes tense relation to one another around topics such as sexuality, national policies, and transnational solidarity. Yet instead of being a disadvantage, such diversity actually spurs innovative and politically radical approaches in the field. The multiplicity of feminisms theorized in this issue allows us to challenge patriarchal ideologies and structures on myriad fronts, both on the African continent and beyond. From our inaugural conference on the state of the field of African feminisms in 2016 to the publication of this journal issue, we have been inspired and humbled by the writings of scholars, activists, artists, policymakers, and teachers who make up our community. As we continue to flourish and grow, we eagerly anticipate the conversations that are yet to come. We hope that you, our readers and AFI members, will join us in these discussions as we further map the rich terrain that is African feminisms today.

....

Alicia C. Decker is an associate professor of women's, gender, and sexuality studies and African studies at the Pennsylvania State University and codirector of the African Feminist Initiative. She is the author of *In Idi Amin's Shadow: Women, Gender, and Militarism in Uganda* (Ohio University Press, 2014) and coauthor with Andrea Arrington of *Africanizing Democracies: 1980 to the Present* (Oxford University Press, 2015).

Gabeba Baderoon is the author of *Regarding Muslims: From Slavery to Post-Apartheid* and the poetry collections *The Dream in the Next Body, A hundred silences,* and *The History of Intimacy.* With Alicia Decker, Baderoon codirects the African Feminist Initiative at the Pennsylvania State University, where she teaches women's, gender and sexuality studies and African studies.

Notes

1   Gabeba Baderoon was involved in discussions that led to the formation of the African Gender Institute (AGI) in 1996. During her years as a research fellow and PhD candidate, she played an active role in the AGI, including in their seminars and publications, such as the *AGI Newsletter* and *Feminist Africa.* In 2002 she was an associate of the AGI, where she worked on her doctoral project on representations of gender and Islam. Alicia Decker earned a master's degree at the School of Women and Gender Studies (SWGS) at Makerere University and a PhD in women's studies at Emory University. Both the AGI and the SWGS offer formidable models for bridging the gap between the academy and activists in effective ways. That said, both spaces have also faced the neoliberal turn in African universities, for instance, with the AGI's integration into a larger entity at the University of Cape Town, leading to questions about the future direction of women's studies and feminist training in African institutions. The African Feminist Initiative has drawn heavily from these continental models and has enjoyed a generous and receptive relationship with many stalwarts in these spaces.

2   For a complete list of current steering committee and advisory board members, as well as information on all of our initiatives, please visit the AFI website: http://afi.la.psu.edu/.

Works Cited

Steady, Filomina Chioma. 1981. "The Black Woman Cross-Culturally: An Overview." In *The Black Woman Cross-Culturally,* edited by Filomina Chioma Steady, 7–41. Rochester, VT: Schenkman Books.

Steady, Filomina Chioma. 1996. "African Feminism: A Worldwide Perspective." In *Women in Africa and the African Diaspora: A Reader,* 2nd edition, edited by Rosalyn Terborg-Penn and Andrea Benton Rushing, 3–21. Washington, DC: Howard University Press.

Terborg-Penn, Rosalyn. 1996. "Women in the African Diaspora: An Overview of an Interdisciplinary Research Conference." In *Women in Africa and the African Diaspora: A Reader,* 2nd edition, edited by Rosalyn Terborg-Penn and Andrea Benton Rushing, xvii–xxvi. Washington, DC: Howard University Press.

Tsitsi Jaji

. . . .

And They Didn't Die

for my mother, who has done all things well

> I bring a squall of quiet, my hectoring force, to shame
> the belated fog of orders and bandages into a fine mist.

> I am here to squelch reason's panic. Certainty
> is scrambled and we find only Vaseline, thick with scent,
> and too heavy to churn the waters. If they wept no tears
> they would not know I will not shed any.

> If there were no tremors they would not know me. Unshaken.

> I will outlive them. I will bury them in my question: What more?

> This is what we have done since before
> the border between wild and free was pinned

> like steel and plaster, animal and woman, birth
> and death. Only daughters are shouldered
> into becoming Mother, cold
> without children, colder still after birth.

> This is how it has always been.
> All we cannot know is when.

. . . .

Tsitsi Jaji teaches in the English Department at Duke University. She is the author of the award-winning *Africa in Stereo: Modernism, Music and Pan-African Solidarity* (2014) and two works of poetry, *Carnaval* (2014) and *Beating the Graves* (2017).

MERIDIANS · feminism, race, transnationalism   17:2 November 2018
DOI: 10.1215/15366936-7176395 © 2018 Smith College

Abena P. A. Busia

Creating the Archive
of African Women's Writing

Reflecting on Feminism, Epistemology,
and the Women Writing Africa Project

Abstract: This essay is a reflection of the monumental Women Writing Africa project by one of the project's three editors. Over the course of two decades, the project published four volumes documenting the history of literary expression by African women throughout the continent, including the stories of dispossession that mark the harrowing start of the slave routes. This intimate account engages with the context of feminist praxis on the continent and the politics of African feminist research and publishing. Women Writing Africa was a project of cultural renewal that restored African women's voices to the African canon and redrew the map of African literature. In their work, the editors and contributors confronted the intractable reductiveness around images of Africa—even within feminist circles—and addressed what it means to be "African" in the contemporary world. The editors' hope was to generate new readings of Africa's history by shedding light on women's writing and, in doing so, change assumptions of how knowledge is shaped.

Let me begin with my many beginnings. For the three codirectors and series editors of the four volumes of *Women Writing Africa*, the primary motivation for our two-decade project was our recognition that there was a story to be told that was not being told, but that the words were there to tell it. Such expression was for us both oral and written, ritual and quotidian, sacred and profane. We were as interested in dance songs and private

MERIDIANS · feminism, race, transnationalism   17:2 November 2018
DOI: 10.1215/15366936-7176406 © 2018 Smith College

letters as we were in legal depositions and public declamations. Our hope was to enable new readings of Africa's history by shedding light on the things that women do and say, for in doing this we sought to show where the fault lines of memory lie and so change assumptions of how knowledge is shaped.

The beginning of my thinking on this issue predates the start of the Woman Writing Africa (WWA) project and has multiple origins. In 1988, during a semester at Bryn Mawr College, I taught for the first time that wonderful novel by Mariama Bâ, *So Long a Letter* (1981). For the first class, I had assigned the opening chapters and prepared an introductory lecture about the significance of Bâ, the first winner of the Noma Prize for Publishing in Africa, and her work. I concentrated on the centrality of many of her themes to contemporary African thought. Then I talked about the representation of women in the novel and its importance for those of us in African and feminist studies. As we were about to explore the text itself, I was startled by a student who stopped me and said, "Look, before you continue, can you tell me what on earth is going on in the first pages? I thought you said it was a funeral."

I was struck by that moment, because I had made a classic error that I train other teachers never to make, and that is to take for granted the world in which the text was set because I was so accustomed to it. In particular, I had failed to explain the "performance" of the funeral rites, which were normative to me but would indeed seem completely alien to an American audience.[1] Performativity works only if everybody understands the languages, spoken and unspoken, of the rituals. This novel opened on a funeral, and the rites performed and described were so familiar to me that I forgot to introduce the ways of West African mourning. Speaking as an African woman who lives in the West, we have to bear in mind constantly how much of what we take as normative, our worldviews, our rituals, our aspects of daily living, are not recognizable and thus meaningfully legible in the context in which we live and work.[2]

Practically everywhere in the world, feminist studies has its roots in praxis. Particularly in Africa, there has always been a conscious linking of feminism to African realities. In a lecture titled "Creating and Sustaining Feminist Space in Africa," Bisi Adeleye-Fayemi (2000) asserts:

> First, feminism in Africa is located in the continent's historical realities
> of marginalisation, oppression, and domination brought about by

slavery, colonialism, racism, neo-colonialism, and globalisation. It also places the inter-connectedness of gender, women's oppression, race, ethnicity, poverty, and class at the centre of the discourse. It is therefore impractical to talk about a feminist theory in Africa without an under-standing of how these issues have shaped African women's lives and world view in historical terms. African feminist thought, by implication, is anti-imperialist, socialist-oriented, and keenly aware of the implica-tions of social injustices on society as a whole. It is also anti-racist because it challenges the institutional racism of global and regional structures, which exploit the continent and undermine its progress. This also enables African feminists to add their voices to the work of the other feminists from the global south who critique the Euro-centrism of white western feminists.

That is, African feminism is political at every level and is rooted in recognition of a deep need for transformational practices in every aspect, including our collaborations with northern allies.[3]

On the question of transformational practices, I am conscious of the fact that when I first started teaching in the United States nearly forty years ago, I found myself in the peculiar position of becoming overnight an "expert" in multicultural practices because I was born in Ghana, raised in England, and lived in the United States, teaching Americans about their own literature. This was particularly strange as African American litera-ture was the one area I had never formally studied. I realized quite quickly that this was true of many of my generation of teachers. However, arriving from the U.K. in 1980, I did not immediately appreciate how new the dis-cipline of African American studies was in the academy.

Nonetheless the dual process of working on multicultural education and the transformation of the curriculum around gender as well as race has made me conscious of a shift in the terms in which we speak—from the "multicultural" in the early 1980s to the "global" in the late 1990s to the "transnational" in the twenty-first century. This has happened in many sophisticated ways, but I see it as, in a sense, a shift from recognition of having to deal with the "barbarians at the gate" to having to work out strategies for being "at the gate of the barbarians." By this, I mean the shift from dealing with homegrown "foreigners" within one's borders to the adjustments of becoming the occupying armies in places like Vietnam, Grenada, and Baghdad. That, at least, is the American story.

I say that it is the American story because of course there are other, much older imperial stories, such as the ones captured by the slogan of black Britons in the late 1970s: "We are here because you were there." That is, the existence of certain debates and even disciplines in the academy has much to do with the presence and location of certain specific "barbarian" bodies. Those of us in English studies recognize that our discipline exists because intrepid imperialists of earlier generations in their various hearts of darkness needed to be equipped with the cultural rationale that could mask or justify military and economic needs. You cannot have a civilizing mission unless you can marshal the texts in place.[4] The relationship between the West and the Rest of Us has always been predicated on a struggle for power, and during the centuries that shape the lives we live today, that struggle has been an unequal one at every level.

The WWA project was a response to this inequality of power, yet it came with its own internal contradictions. WWA was conceived, directed, and enacted by African women, yet it is a project of the Feminist Press. Though we principally wanted to broadcast African women's voices throughout Africa and the rest of the world through the collection and publication of African women's written and oral texts, the reality remains that the publication was destined to be most readily available to North American and European audiences within the Feminist Press's distribution network. This was a serious matter for all of us, and the Feminist Press was assiduous in helping us redress this by finding, volume by volume, regional partners to publish and distribute the series within the continent.

The four published volumes include a compelling range of contemporary material, yet the texts illuminate a completely new perspective on the history of the continent through the voices of African women. The regional anthologies document the intangible heritage of African women, expressed in our literature and orature, through presenting songs, letters, journals, diaries, legal depositions, and other significant historical texts, as well as fiction, drama, and poetry. Each anthologized work is prefaced by a brief critical introduction or headnote, and each anthology is introduced by a broad-ranging essay that provides historical and social context. We made these decisions because we believe that it is wholly inadequate to present African women's literature without interrogating the political, economic, social, and cultural conditions in which that literature was and is still composed. We hope our readers agree that, in its entirety, *Women Writing Africa* not only allows us to reclaim individual pieces of expressive writing by African women but also provides the basis for a new reading of African historicity by bringing to a broad public the hitherto obscured history, culture, and thought of African women within our families, societies, and nations.

The working assumption of WWA was that the authority of African women scholars was primary in shaping the intellectual parameters of the project. We also aimed to promote egalitarian partnerships between African and non-African scholars and between scholars living on the continent and scholars based in North America, for we hoped to redress the imbalance of scholarly and literary production about Africa, and in particular, about African women. WWA was therefore a project, which in its very organizational structure, collection, preparation, and presentation of texts tried to take historical factors of inequality into account.

Our working structure comprised an international board of advisors and a U.S.-based executive committee of Africans and Americans, which were primarily consultative; a vast number of individual scholars in all fields (archivists, librarians, and cultural workers) sat on national boards and decided what to collect and what should represent their individual countries—theirs was the burden of finding the materials; and four regional boards comprising two or three representatives of each national committee who made collective decisions about the final selection of texts. These texts were then prepared for publication by the regional editors and project codirectors. The project editors and codirectors sat on all the committees except the national ones, though we were sometimes invited to these as observers.

This general outline was interpreted with great flexibility in every country and region. In the West African region, for example, we had to subdivide Nigeria into its three historic regions, whereas in Burkina Faso, a two-person committee effectively did everything. Furthermore, in Southern Africa, the regional board worked as an editorial board of the whole, while in West Africa we had two editors, an associate editor, and a board of consultant editors in various areas of specialization. However, we remained conscious of the fact that, by publishing works of the Global South in the Global North, we remained tied to those very conditions of inequality that the writing we were publishing was set against or interrogated. Those conditions affected and sometimes infected the very ways in which we did our work. The reality was that these aspirations often left the two of us African-born, U.S.-based codirectors caught in the crossfire of competing social realities, despite consensual ideological and pedagogical agendas.

Women Writing Africa had three codirectors: Tuzyline Jita Allan, a Sierra Leonean professor of English at Baruch College in New York, who originally thought up the project; Florence Howe, the director (now emerita) of the Feminist Press, a lifelong second wave U.S. feminist and civil rights activist; and myself, a Ghanaian-born professor of literatures in English and women's studies at Rutgers University, who joined a few months after the project's inception at the invitation of Tuzyline and the colleagues she initially consulted. For each of us, the road to the project was very different. Howe built up the Feminist Press over thirty-eight years as a project of radical feminist knowledge-making and publishing. In light of this, however, within the WWA project, she constantly reminded us that the mission of the press was to promote and educate about women's works primarily *to an American audience*. However, for Tuzyline and me, African women born on the continent but living in the diaspora among other immigrants in the academies of the West, this project had a different, particular resonance.

The lack of respect for the places we were from in the places where we lived and worked was my original intellectual pursuit. I started my academic career at Oxford University by writing a dissertation on images of Africa in British postwar popular fiction. Over the course of two decades of working on WWA, this pursuit changed. My concern with images of Africa in the West gave way to other dreams, hopes, and aspirations. The earlier impetus did not leave, but the latter gave me a different hope. Working with colleagues based on the continent inspired me to see the legacies of our histories, including the legacies of the Atlantic Crossroads, which have so obsessed me, from a different perspective than the one learned in Europe or the United States. I learned, for instance, that for those left behind, knowledge cannot begin as it does in the U.S. academy, from the searing memory of a Middle Passage scarcely survived. It begins with the trauma of a sudden disappearance at the end of an unexpected road. That is, our memories of the same history are differently marked.

Over the years I grew increasingly aware of the fact that part of the role of WWA was to give voice to peoples left behind, symbolized in Western discourse by the marked absences of Equiano's mother or Caliban's mother. We were tracing the legacy of her long memory; we were also recalling the stories of those left behind. These ancestors resorted to rituals of resistance and remembrance, and sometimes of sacrifice. Their communities kept their legacies in such places as the registry of names, and the choruses of songs. For us in this collective project, which involved approximately two hundred women in nearly two dozen countries on two continents, tracing this work was very challenging, for this legacy existed hidden in secret, and hidden in plain view, through every historical period. What rendered this task even more complex was the diversity of the world's second largest continent.

One of our first struggles was claiming our definition of Africa by refusing the colonial division between North and sub-Saharan Africa. Yet, in addition to a hard-won internal debate, civil war deprived us of Algerian scholars at North African regional meetings; U.S. State Department bans prevented us from assembling in Alexandria after September 11; and our hopes for a fifth volume were shelved not only for financial reasons but also because the countries that would have been brought together in a Central Africa volume were engulfed in strife and civil war. Nonetheless we had more than enough to work with in the countries to which we did have access.

Even before we began, I had the profound sense that there was a story to be told that was not being told and that the words were already there to tell it. What we needed to do was put it together, anthologize it, give it a more self-evident shape. And in marshaling those words anew there was another story that we were *untelling*, the imperial story that denied the wealth of our agency. Those two gestures I recognized. I also recognized that in that telling and untelling lay the danger of betraying other stories that were not even recognized, specifically, the story of the participation of women in these debates. However, it seems to me that the profound betrayal, for want of another word, lay not so much in the absence of women's stories as in the failure to see that they existed—that women had a separate story to be told. The inability to be conscious of women's stories seemed to me an even greater betrayal than the absence of the texts themselves.

As editors, we were faced with the responsibility of redress, yet also the difficulty of finding a way through a prehistory not of our making that skewed the way we did our work. How, then, did we weigh the story we wished to tell against addressing the issues raised by other people's stories? As my account of teaching *So Long a Letter* illustrates, I wanted to get to one point and found myself having to begin with other things first, which changed the nature of what I said. To what extent must we always first accommodate such explanatory stories in order to get to the story we want?

As a community of African feminist scholars, we had to contend with the influence of dominant ideas of Africa and its impact on us as an international, interracial, transcontinental working group. To an extent greater than we expected, these forces sometimes also manifested themselves among us. What concerned me and many of my sisters on the continent is how and in what context our voices are heard. The shift from the global theoretical must always come down to the case of actual Africans, and hence the issue of the "intractable nature" of the "idea of Africa" and the authority and agency of African women has to be addressed. To create *Women Writing Africa*, African women claimed the authority to determine how we are portrayed. We could not do that until we faced what it means to be African in the first place.

For those of us working on the project and despite our best efforts, the various legacies of structural inequality confronted us with a range of challenges, for instance, the radical difference in infrastructural capabilities between West Africa and Southern Africa, where communications systems are far more efficient. Within the Southern Africa region, we also had to contend with the legacy of British colonialism and apartheid, which has left South African institutions generally, and historically white ones in particular, much better endowed. This has had several effects, from being able to pick up a telephone that works internally and internationally, to having access to computers, email facilities, graduate assistants, and well-stocked libraries, to having none of the above.

We had to contend internally with the implications of this for the ability to deliver the necessary work according to a timetable dictated by the needs of a press in New York. From the Global South, it may have looked like a press with the resources to pursue its own programs, yet within the Global North it was a small independent press with a radical agenda and publishing policies struggling against a rising corporate tide for its very survival. In this market-driven economy and amid stubbornly exotic or bizarre images of Africa, African self-definition was difficult to assert.[5] I can give a range of personal examples, from not being given voice-over film work because my voice did not sound "African" enough—as if there were only one way for Africans to sound—to a debate in the West Africa/Sahel committee of WWA concerning whether or not I could be included in the volume as a Ghanaian writer. This is a fine-grained, though painful example of a circumstance in which even among fellow workers, my ability to self-define was thwarted. In that volume, where the inclusion of a diaspora woman such as the eighteenth-century slave Madlena von Poppos, stolen from what is now Benin and writing from St. Thomas, now part of the U.S. Virgin Islands, met with little controversy, the question of which displaced people could be regarded as African was less easily resolvable in the case of contemporary writers. Was a Caribbean-born woman married to a West African, living and working in West Africa, an African woman writer or not? Did the definition depend on her, the place of her birth, or her community, however defined? If it depended on us, what were the criteria for our rules? My own case of exclusion perhaps dramatizes the dilemma.

We tried as much as possible to ensure that the choice of texts selected from any given country rested with the national editors and the regional boards. The Ghanaian committee put forward for consideration a selection of my poetry and auto-ethnographic pieces. Yet the fact that I had been educated in Europe and taught in the United States was held against me by the press, where, for funding purposes, among other reasons, I was considered an American. There was real resistance to my being included as a Ghanaian or African writer. The Ghanaian committee considered this decree untenable and wished to fight it. In any event, we decided not to include the original works of any of the editors or editorial consultants. I decided it was more important for me to be an editor than to be included as a writer. I asked for the matter to be dropped. However, I am profoundly conscious of a sense of compromise; the Ghanaian committee was right to wish to fight.

This was an enterprise in which the majority of the people involved, and the majority of the people making what we thought were the final editorial decisions, were African-born women. It was also a project in which I was a codirector, coeditor, and associate editor of the particular volume in question, yet my statement about my own self-definition could not be heard. And in calling a truce for the sake of peace and expediency before the issue was settled, I left unresolved the question of the authority of my own self-definition, and the question of the authority of the Ghanaian committee to accept me as a Ghanaian writer. Sidestepping the issue did not resolve the problem; it merely buried it.

I am raising precisely the question of the limits of our authority as African women, even in relatively safe spaces. There are so many occasions, from the politics of citation to the politics of publishing itself, where our authority over our own lives and work is questioned. There are times when our work on our own communities is rejected because we do not cite the

Euro-American scholars regarded as authorities in the fields of our lives. In comparison to such experts, neither our experiential nor our academic credentials are considered authority enough.[6]

We are proud of the way we worked together to bring WWA to fruition. The four published volumes are the result of the most active years of my life as a scholar, and I am both humbled and enriched by the experience. They are superb anthologies that contain literary and historical gems that reveal the depth and variety of our responses to our dynamic and changing histories and social circumstances, and they have re-created the African canon. These are moving testimonies to the quality of our responses to the quotidian, dramatic, and sacred moments of our lives. For the most part, we worked on the volumes collaboratively and well, as equals. Yet it would be untrue to pretend there were no tensions in trying to hold true to our noble intentions.

Women's knowledge is often hidden, and African ways of knowing are habitually discredited. African women's ways of negotiating the world are thus frequently invisible and assumed to lack significance. "Achimota: From the Story My Mother Told Me," one of the poems from my collection *Testimonies of Exile* (1990), addresses a central point of the WWA project, the question of our enduring memories, and the many ways we find, as Toni Morrison says, "to keep our memories alive." My mother told me the story, passing on its legacy, and I passed on her words to another generation through that poem. The title is critical. The place name Achimota is a Ga phrase meaning, quite literally, "you don't call out for somebody here," which conveys the sedimented histories encoded in a familiar term for a place.

For me, the journey of WWA had many beginnings. One was the invitation from Tuzyline Jita Allen to join her and a group of colleagues to discuss a project on research and publishing a range of African women's voices. However, by the time that meeting took place, I had already had the conversation with my mother and written "Achimota" about a part of Accra's unrecorded, or differently recorded, history. So the question of the traces of our legacies was already strong in my mind. In addition, shortly after I arrived in Ghana to set up the Ghana committee of WWA, I heard a friend, the scholar and poet Kwodwo Opoku-Agyeman, ask, "Whatever happened to Equiano's mother?"[7] I have never forgotten that question. Over the years I have grown increasingly aware that an important part of the WWA project is to help us find answers to that question. Whatever did happen to Equiano's mother, what and where are the traces of her grief? Where do we find the legacy of her memory? In speaking of the long memory, we also recall the stories of those left behind.

At the time Kwodwo posed the question, he and I were team-teaching a course on African American literature at the University of Cape Coast. One of its most moving moments came during the students' oral presentations on slave narratives, when they made a profound observation. They acknowledged the ways in which the slave narratives, returning to us from the other shores of the Atlantic, helped them face this history. It was as if, finally, they suggested, you have some sense of the children's return and could begin to speak of and process the loss. Something survived. Some remained to speak their name to their waiting siblings and the world, like an answer to prayer, like a response to an unheard call.

The WWA project succeeded in ways we scarcely dreamed, winning several awards, including the Choice outstanding academic title award in 2006 for volume 2, *West Africa and Sahel*. The project inspired many to continue the work through national volumes, such as *Women Writing Botswana*, edited by Margot Lederer, due to be published in 2018. However, the evidence of the success I value at least as much has been largely private, oral and anecdotal, through which colleagues have conveyed their sense of the project's momentous achievement.

Abena P. A. Busia received a D.Phil. from Oxford University in 1984. She is currently Ghana's ambassador to Brazil. Prior to this, she served as chair of the Department of Women's and Gender Studies at Rutgers University, where she is a professor of English and comparative literature. Busia is an internationally known author and poet.

Notes

1   In Ghana, for example, the signs of ritual mourning are encoded in the colors people wear and in the nature of the dances they perform, among other things.

2   The debate about meaning making in avowedly multicultural and/or gendered contexts is a rich one beyond the scope of this paper. As Simon Gikandi points out, "In order for these fictions to become global, they have to be involved in a fascinating and sometimes disturbing act of cultural translation because their audiences are no longer located in their sites of referent" (quoted in Jefferess 2006). Yet my student's question raises the issue of cultural translatability, and perhaps resistances to such translation. Linguistically I was teaching the

English translation of a French text in which the people described in the opening scenes were likely speaking Wolof. An ethical reading requires acknowledgment of many competing histories.

3   Working on *Women Writing Africa* showed us the extent to which the strategic interventions of African women can be found as much in subversive lullabies and work songs as in academic treatises and legal depositions. This is not to ignore the complexity of the relationship between theory and activism and the often fraught debates about theorizing in African contexts. Obioma Nnaemeka's (2003) "Nego-Feminism: Theorizing, Practicing, and Pruning Africa's Way" offers a bold intervention. "In other words," she writes, "seeing feminist theorizing through the eyes of the 'other' from the 'other' place, through the 'other' worldview has the capacity to defamiliarize feminist theory as we know it and assist it not only in interrogating, understanding, and explaining the unfamiliar but also in defamiliarizing and refamiliarizing the familiar in more productive and enriching ways" (381).

4   The literature on the development of a canon of English literature as integral to the imperialist project is extensive, though I would single out the opening of Edward Said's (1993) *Culture and Imperialism* as a comprehensive place to begin.

5   African self-definition is a subject about which many people have written extensively. For my own responses to these issues, see Busia 1986, 1989–90, 1998, 2003.

6   For a collection of important, provocative essays on the authority of African women and the troubled relationship between African women and the Western feminist academy, see Oyewumi 2003. See also Boyce Davies and Ogundipe-Leslie 1995.

7   The epistemic and hermeneutic ground from which this question is posed is a "Black Atlantic" world away from grappling with whatever happened to Caliban's mother. That is, a desire to know Equiano's mother's story stems from a fundamental recognition of her humanity and an inclusionary ethics that recognizes she too has a story, even if seemingly unrecorded.

Works Cited

Adeleye-Fayemi, Bisi. 2000. "Creating and Sustaining Feminist Space in Africa: Local-Global Challenges in the 21st Century." Dame Nita Barrow Distinguished Visitor Lecture, Ontario Institute for Studies in Education, University of Toronto, November 30, 2000.

Bâ, Mariama. 1981. *So Long a Letter*. Oxford: Heinemann.

Boyce Davies, Carole, and Molara Ogundipe-Leslie, eds. 1995. *Moving beyond Boundaries (Vol. 1): International Dimensions of Black Women's Writing*. New York: NYU Press.

Busia, Abena. 1986. "Miscegenation as Metonymy: Sexuality and Power in the Colonial Novel." *Journal of Ethnic and Racial Studies* 9, no. 3: 360–72.

Busia, Abena. 1989–90. "Silencing Sycorax: On African Colonial Discourse and the Unvoiced Female." *Cultural Critique* 14 (Winter): 81–104.

Busia, Abena. 1990. *Testimonies of Exile*. Trenton, NJ: Africa World Press.

Busia, Abena. 1998. "Re: Locations—Rethinking Britain from Accra, New York and the Map Room of the British Museum." In *Multicultural States: Rethinking Difference and Identity*, edited by David Bennett, 267–81. London: Routledge.

Busia, Abena. 2003. "In Search of Chains without Iron: On Sisterhood, History, and the Politics of Location." In *African Women and Feminism: Reflecting on the Politics of Sisterhood*, edited by Oyeronke Oyewumi, 257–68. Trenton, NJ: Africa World Press.

Jefferess, David. 2006. "Postcolonialism's Ethical (Re)Turn: An Interview with Simon Gikandi." *Postcolonial Text* 2, no. 1. http://postcolonial.org/index.php/pct/article/view/464/845.

Nnaemeka, Obioma. 2003. "Nego-Feminism: Theorizing, Practicing, and Pruning Africa's Way." *Signs: Journal of Women in Culture and Society*, 29, no. 2: 357–85.

Oyewumi, Oyeronke, ed. 2003. *African Women and Feminism: Reflecting on the Politics of Sisterhood*. Trenton, NJ: Africa World Press.

Said, Edward. 1993. *Culture and Imperialism*. London: Chatto & Windus.

Charmaine Pereira

....

Beyond the Spectacular
Contextualizing Gender Relations in the
Wake of the Boko Haram Insurgency

Abstract: The aim of this essay is to interrogate gender relations in the wake of the Boko Haram insurgency in a way that recognizes continuities as well as discontinuities across multiple dimensions of social relations. The essay begins by outlining the changing trajectory of the Boko Haram insurgency and scholarly efforts to understand it as a social phenomenon. The second section discusses how research and media recognition of Boko Haram's violence in relation to women led to a focus on spectacular events, such as mass abductions and suicide bombings. It is critical to recognize the politics of visibility and nonvisibility regarding women in the gendered dynamics set in motion by Boko Haram's spectacles of violence. Finally, the essay points to ways in which feminist analyses of conflict and militarism throw light on the more suppressed yet critical dimensions of gender relations that surface in the wake of the Boko Haram insurgency.

In this essay, I focus on the Boko Haram insurgency in North East Nigeria, interrogating which aspects of gender relations are placed in the foreground and which recede into the background, with a particular focus on how women are positioned by the group's activities.[1] I am a feminist scholar-activist of Indian descent who has lived in Nigeria for over two decades, with interests in sexual politics, including those manifested in the practice of sharia law in Northern Nigeria (Pereira 2005, 2010). Disentangling the connections and disconnections between violence in times of conflict and in so-called times of peace is the space from which I write. In

MERIDIANS · feminism, race, transnationalism   17:2 November 2018
DOI: 10.1215/15366936-7176417 © 2018 Smith College

doing so, I draw on my engagement in the first year of the Bring Back Our Girls campaign and my activist interest in combating violence against women, whether or not conflict is recognized.

Contemporary Nigeria is marked by a range of conflicts and is significantly militarized as a polity. The Boko Haram insurgency in the North East is one of the more violent and intransigent of these, a phenomenon that defies straightforward explanation given the "constant evolution of the sect and its frequent reincarnation in different, even contradictory guises" (Mustapha 2014, 166). Some analysts have addressed the gender dynamics of Boko Haram in terms of violence (e.g., Omego 2015). While this approach is important, it does not address the broader political and economic contexts within which much of this conflict is situated.

My aim in this essay is to conduct a critical gender analysis of the continuities as well as discontinuities across multiple dimensions of social relations in the wake of the Boko Haram insurgency. I begin by outlining the changing trajectory of the conflict and scholarly efforts to understand it as a social phenomenon. The second section discusses how research and media recognition of Boko Haram's violence in relation to women lead to a focus on spectacular events, such as mass abductions and suicide bombings. Finally, I point to ways in which feminist analyses of conflict and militarism throw light on the more hidden yet critical dimensions of gender that surface in the wake of the Boko Haram insurgency.

How Do We Understand Boko Haram?

Abdul Raufu Mustapha's (2014, 187) painstaking analysis of the available evidence on Boko Haram and its campaign of violence points to a "twin process of doctrinal fragmentation and radicalisation *within* the Muslim community that provided the initial propulsion toward social disorder." Locating these twin processes in historical and political context is a useful prelude to understanding the Boko Haram insurgency.

Doctrinal differences and disputes within Islam in Northern Nigeria have been a recurring feature since the Sokoto Jihad of 1804. Two rival Sufi brotherhoods, Qadiriyya and Tijaniyya, contain the majority of Muslims in Northern Nigeria. By the 1970s the rise of Salafist and Shi'a doctrinal tendencies had begun a process of intensification of sectarianism. The reformist Salafist group Jama'atu Izalatil Bid'a wa iqamat al-Sunna (Society for the Eradication of Innovation and the Reinstatement of Tradition), established in 1978 and popularly known as Izala, was bitterly opposed to

Sufism, as well as the Shi'a group that had emerged in Northern Nigeria around the same time. Further fragmentation in the contemporary period has given rise to myriad competing sects and groups, including some idiosyncratic sects that are oriented toward violent politics. "This process of the fragmentation of Muslim identities has resulted in the individualisation of religious affiliation and heightened competition for followership in a 'prayer economy' led by the *'ulama'* " (Mustapha and Bunza 2014, 54–55). The "prayer economy" is particularly significant in its intertwining of concerns that are simultaneously pious and material, given the context of generalized poverty across the North. There are material benefits to the cultivation of a mass followership since not only do members give donations for the leader's upkeep, but also greater numbers entail increased influence and prestige for the leader.

The backdrop to all this, from the mid-1960s onward, was Nigeria's corrupt military state. Nigeria is a federal state that was organized into three regions after independence in 1960. The Northern Region's population is greater than the combined population of the other two, effectively translated into political power for the North. The southern regions developed further in economic and educational terms, and thus controlled the economy and the bureaucracy. With the first military takeover in 1966 and the rise of oil rents from 1970, regional autonomy eroded. Northern political and military elites had privileged access to the federal center, which led to the abandonment and impoverishment of their home region (see NBS 2012). Wider economic and political developments have also compounded the failure of political leadership in the North. In the 1980s and 1990s, structural adjustment led to rapid de-industrialization, impoverishing the North even further. The privatization policies introduced since 1999 resulted in control of key sectors of the economy being retained by the South. The end of military rule in 1999, and the transition to civilian administration, also marked a political swing away from the North. Politics since this time has become increasingly authoritarian and manipulative, and even more corrupt. The consequences are rising inequality and growing economic crises (Mustapha 2014).

Salafi doctrinal disagreements with Sufis gave rise to a number of Salafi scholars leaving Izala to form separate organizations. The leader of the youth wing of the breakaway group Ahl al-sunna (People of the Sunna), set up by Shaikh Ja'afar, was Mohammed Yusuf, a former student of Ja'afar's from Maiduguri. Between 1998 and 2003 Yusuf used Shaikh Ja'afar's support to build up a following at the Indimi Mosque in Maiduguri as well as in neighboring countries (Mustapha 2014). Although Ja'afar and Yusuf were initially very close, ultimately ideological differences led to a split between them. While Ja'afar's Ahl al-sunna pushed for increased Islamization of the country's political institutions, Yusuf's group advocated "the necessity of a radical withdrawal from anything related to the Nigerian state, including working for the police, participating in the government, working in the administration of Sharia within the framework of the state, and studying in formal educational institutions" (Brigaglia 2012, 22). Yusuf's deepening radicalization led to his espousing doctrines that ran counter to Shaikh Ja'afar's, resulting in his ban from preaching at the Indimi Mosque (Mustapha 2014).

The Yusufiyya movement that Yusuf formed later transmuted into Jama'atu Ahlul Sunna li Da'awati wal Jihad (People Committed to the Propagation of the Prophet's Teachings and Jihad), otherwise known as Boko Haram (Mustapha 2014). Yusuf used the term *boko* in the way it was commonly understood in Hausa, meaning "modern secular education brought to Nigeria by the colonial administration" (Anon 2012, 124). For Yusuf, it was haram for Muslims to learn or accept any aspects of such education that contradicted the Qur'an and Sunna. The Nigerian educational system was also haram because men and women were not supposed to occupy the same space in classrooms (Anon 2012).

Yusuf's rejection of the authority of the Nigerian state due to its reliance on government based on *kufr*, or unbelief, was unyielding. His "absolutist arguments are clear indications of the will to power that led him to violent confrontations with Nigerian security forces" (Anon 2012, 127). In turn, the security forces' repressive and heavy-handed responses were critical in shaping Boko Haram. Mustapha (2014, 147) explains:

> Between [2003] and 2014, the group metamorphosed from a group of angry Islamist young men wielding sticks on the streets of Maiduguri to an entrenched insurgency capable of deploying Armoured Personnel Carriers (APCs) and Somalia-type mounted machine guns or "technicals," and engaged in ruthless bombing campaigns across numerous Nigerian cities. It is a testament to the poor management of the situation by political and military authorities at all levels of the Nigerian federation that this transformation . . . was able to take place unchecked.

Kyari Mohammed (2014) identifies three phases in the formation of

Boko Haram. The first (2003–4) was an insurrectionary phase of disengagement from the secular state by about two hundred young men,
including Yusuf's followers. The group carried out a series of grave attacks
on police stations, government buildings, and prisons between December
2003 and October 2004. Heavy clashes with the military ultimately flushed
the group out of their rural enclave. The state blamed Yusuf for the upris-
ing, and he fled to Saudi Arabia, while surviving members returned to
Maiduguri to regroup.

Boko Haram's second phase (2005–9) is known as the radical proselyti-
zation phase, or the *dawah*. In 2005 Yusuf returned to Nigeria in an arrange-
ment brokered by Borno State Deputy Governor Adamu Shettima Dibal
and Shaikh Ja'afar. Although Yusuf had assured the shaikh that he would
not participate in violent jihadi ideology, the *dawah* phase was nevertheless
marked by doctrinal extremism, recruitment, indoctrination, and the radicalization of its members. Yusuf built a base for his sect on land given to
him by his father-in-law in Maiduguri (Mohammed 2014). At the heart of
this base was the Markaz, a place for continuing education and networking, named after Ibn Taymiyya, the thirteenth-century Islamic scholar
who was one of the founders of Salafism. In his sermons Yusuf elaborated
upon his own doctrines while also expressing trenchant criticism of the
corruption characterizing the governor's administration of Borno State.[2]
Although arrested several times for his fiery sermons, Yusuf returned
unscathed each time, strengthening his reputation among followers as
someone capable of standing up to the authorities and defending his followers' interests (Mohammed 2014).

The armed insurrection phase of Boko Haram, its third phase, began in
June 2009 when clashes broke out between police and sect members who
were holding a motorcycle procession in Maiduguri. Fourteen sect members were shot and wounded. Following this event, Yusuf swore vengeance
against the state. The following month, Boko Haram retaliated against the
police in Borno, Bauchi, Yobe, Gombe, Kano, and Katsina states. In Borno
State, for instance, eight hundred people were killed, including twenty-
two police officers. They also burned over twenty churches and destroyed
two hundred houses and police stations. In retaliation, the army razed the
Markaz to the ground and arrested hundreds of Boko Haram members,
including Yusuf, whom they summarily executed on July 30, 2009. Alhaji
Buji Foi, former commissioner of religious affairs and a financier of Boko
Haram, and Alhaji Baba Fugu Mohammed, Yusuf's seventy-two-year-old

father-in-law, were also arrested and extrajudicially killed. Boko Haram then went underground for a short period.

The radical Islam of Boko Haram was propelled by the conviction that "it is the duty of Muslims to revolt against and change apostate rulers and governments in order to help re-establish a proper Islamic state" (Mohammed 2014, 21). After resurfacing in 2010 with a new leader, Abubakar Shekau, Boko Haram devastated the North with targeted assassinations, drive-by shootings, suicide bombings, and the planting of improvised explosive devices. They targeted individuals with whom they disagreed on doctrinal and political grounds. They also attacked schools, churches, mosques belonging to perceived opponents, the police, the military, traditional authorities, political leaders, and symbolic targets, such as the police headquarters in Abuja (June 2011) and the UN building in Abuja (August 2011) (Mustapha 2014).

From 2010 to 2013 Boko Haram also expanded their links with international terrorist organizations, amplified by the crisis in Mali, the training they received from other Islamist groups in West Africa, and the relatively free flow of arms from post-Gaddafi Libya. The Nigerian state enhanced "security" measures in the region, which prompted Boko Haram to even greater violence, including forcibly recruiting young men or inducing them to join as informants or combatants. Insurgents roamed rural areas in Borno State, extorting money and provisions from inhabitants and sacking villages perceived as hostile. They were also involved in kidnapping for ransom, sometimes in neighboring countries. By early 2014, killing, bombing, and looting had become daily events in the three North East states (Mustapha 2014). One year later, on March 8, 2015, Boko Haram pledged allegiance to the so-called Islamic State. It is worth noting that Boko Haram is not a homogeneous group. Differences in emphasis over tactics have led to the formation of splinter groups, such as Ansaru, whose main direction is the targeting of foreigners and foreign interests (Mohammed 2014).

Since 2002 the Boko Haram insurgency has claimed an estimated 29,000 lives (Bloom and Matfess 2016). Over two million have fled their homes (International Organization for Migration 2016). Some 200,000 are now refugees in Cameroon, Chad, and Niger Republic (Regional Protection Working Group 2017). Sadly, the already disastrous humanitarian situation is far from abating. Although the government has recovered significant territory since the election of President Muhammadu Buhari in 2015, many trouble spots remain. Northern Adamawa remains very turbulent. Since 2016 Madagali has seen an increase in suicide bombs as military operations have taken place around Sambisa Forest (ACAPS 2017). While relatively safe in earlier years, the University of Maiduguri has recently come under serious attack for the first time since 2009 (SBM Intelligence 2017).

Boko Haram, Women, and Spectacles of Violence

In her review of the role of women in violent jihadi groups in Somalia, Kenya, Nigeria, Yemen, Pakistan, Afghanistan, Syria, and Iraq, Sarah Ladbury (2015, 1) points out that most research focuses on women and girls as victims of jihadi violence and as suicide bombers. Boko Haram's mass abduction of girls and women from a school in Chibok, and their use of girls and women as suicide bombers, fits this assessment. Both tactics constitute theaters for Boko Haram's treatment of women in *spectacles* of violence, thus symbolizing the brutality of the insurgency. My interest is in the ways both research as well as media attention to these spectacles of violence shape perspectives on gender. Diana Taylor's work on the Argentine junta's actions of "disappearing" those whom they characterized as enemies of the state in the "dirty war" is useful in this regard. Taylor (1997, xi) draws on performance theory to argue, "Understanding spectacle . . . is dependent on a complex scene of interface: understanding *both* the local cultural specifics of national dramas *and* the way that national and international spectacles interface and produce each other." In the rest of this section, I examine Boko Haram's mass abductions of girls and women, as well as their use as suicide bombers, before addressing the question of what is achieved by the enactment of spectacular events.

The first indication that Boko Haram might engage in the abduction of women was in January 2012, when Abubakar Shekau released a video message threatening to kidnap the wives of government officials in response to the government's imprisonment of the wives of Boko Haram members. The video stated the following: "We attacked the securities base because they were arresting our members and torturing our wives and children. They should know they have families too, we can abduct them. We have what it takes to do anything we want."[3] They released a more forceful message later that year, in September 2012:

Now they have continued capturing our women, this week about seven women were captured and we don't even know where they are, but they are being held by infidel enemies of Allah. In fact, they are even having sex with one of them. Allah, Allah, see us and what we are going through. . . . Since you are now holding our women, just wait and see what will happen to your own women. Just wait and see what will happen to your own wives according to Shariah law, just wait and see if it is sweet and convenient for you.[4]

On May 7, 2013, Boko Haram carried out coordinated attacks on the police station, military barracks, and government buildings in Bama, Borno State. The insurgents engaged in a fierce battle with security forces and captured twelve women and children. They also freed 105 prisoners in the predawn raid. Altogether they killed fifty-five people (BBC News 2013). Shekau claimed the abductions in the name of Boko Haram and threatened to make the hostages his "servants" unless the government released Boko Haram members and their wives from prison (Zenn and Pearson 2014). The Bama abductions were a response to the government's arrests in 2012 of more than one hundred people—the wives and children of several Boko Haram leaders, including Shekau's own wives. Among those arrested were the wife and children of the Kano commander; the pregnant wife of the Sokoto commander, who gave birth in prison; and the wife of the suicide bomber who attacked This Day media house in Abuja in 2012. Arresting a suspect's family and friends is a common policing practice in Nigeria (Zenn and Pearson 2014).

On the night of April 14, 2014, 276 schoolgirls from the Federal Government Girls Secondary School in Chibok were abducted en masse, over a period of four hours, by Boko Haram members dressed in military fatigues. The students were due to sit their final year exam. The insurgents not only abducted the girls in a convoy of Hilux trucks and motorbikes, but also burned buildings and ransacked the town. Prior to the abduction, Shekau had warned in a video that girls should stay at home since Western education was sinful. He went further to declare, "In Islam, it is permissible to abduct infidel women. Next, we will start abducting women and selling [them] in the marketplace" (El-Affendi and Gumel 2015, 135). In a video broadcast on May 5, 2014, Shekau claimed responsibility for the abduction and reiterated his promise to sell the schoolgirls as slaves (Bakejal 2015). Over the coming months, Boko Haram kidnapped hundreds of other women and girls (Amnesty International 2015). The most recent incident of mass abduction was on February 19, 2018, when 111 schoolgirls were captured from Government Girls Science and Technology College in the town of Dapchi, Yobe State. One month later, 105 of the schoolgirls were returned (Marama 2018).

Boko Haram also frequently used women as suicide bombers. Between April 2011 and May 2017, for instance, women and girls carried out most of the suicide bombings in the Lake Chad region—174 out of 216. They often attacked civilian targets, such as markets, bus stations, and educational establishments, while men tended to attack state institutions, such as police and military installations (Warner and Matfess cited in Nagarajan 2017). Given increased state surveillance, Boko Haram's use of women and girls as suicide bombers seemed to be an adaptation of their operational tactics, designed to get maximum media attention. According to Jennie Stone and Katherine Patillo (2011, 165):

> Almost all of the strategic benefits derived from female suicide bombers are fed by and dependent on media attention. . . . Historically, female suicide bombers have attracted more media attention than their male counterparts. Women are traditionally viewed as nurturers and the life-blood of the family. Thus, when they come to take part in suicide operations, the juxtaposition of a nurturer taking life elicits a great deal of shock and media attention.

We should therefore read these acts of violence not simply as physical horrors but also as gendered strategies of communication.

So what is achieved through these spectacular enactments of violence? In her discussion of the "performative deployment of power," Desiree Lewis (2011, 212) writes, "Many repressive and coercive mechanisms are manifested in spectacles. . . . Visual images, acts of display and spectatorship, and representations of human bodies have all had tremendous impact within these spectacles."[5] Moreover, she argues that "graphic demonstrations of humiliation and degradation enact particular groups' control over and naming of the bodies of projected outsiders," pointing to the sense in which such acts "centralize gendered and sexualised meanings in ways that often encode complex patterns of authority and contestation" (Lewis 2009, 1).

Although Lewis was primarily addressing the "performative deployment of power" by politicians, her insights are also relevant to Boko Haram in their spectacles of violence. Both the mass abduction in Chibok and the use of girls and women as suicide bombers illustrate the power of control over women's bodies. Abductions constitute a literal instance of "woman grabbing," a form of action in Boko Haram's repertoire that adds to the capture of territory. The Chibok abductions involved sabotage, apparent retribution for the capture of the wives of Boko Haram members, and mockery of the government. By capturing schoolgirls from a government institution, Boko Haram aims to erase their presence from the educational institutions so vilified by the sect. Hilary Matfess (2017, 87) points to "the effectiveness of female abductees (particularly the Chibok girls) as a symbol for cultivating fear." Beyond this, the mass abduction gave the insurgents an international profile and greater bargaining power in relation to the state.

Boko Haram's use of girls and women as bombers entails the power to decide whether or not a woman's body becomes an instrument of death, which suicide bombing encodes in both physical and symbolic senses. Such acts taunt the state by displaying Boko Haram's continued capacity to outdo the security services in inflicting brutality and repression while eluding their own capture. Each "bases their sense of supremacy on subjugation of [the other]" (Taylor 1997, 32). Boko Haram's use of girls and women in suicide bombings constitutes yet another graphic display of power over the men who are leaders in the women's communities, the father figures in the women's families, and society in general, regarding the insurgents' continued power to disrupt everyday life, even in the face of territorial loss.

The hypermasculinity of Boko Haram combatants appears to have specific resonance with a section of men in the North East, more specifically, disenfranchised, unemployed, and angry young men (Zenn and Pearson 2014). By flaunting the power to transgress, Boko Haram's spectacles of violence constitute an assertion of the masculinity of its members over and above the masculinities of the men in authority in the state and society. As Taylor (1997, 34) explains:

> The struggle, as each group tried to humble, humiliate and feminise the other, was about gender. It was about claiming the position of power associated with maleness and forcing the other into the female position of surrender. Gender, then, was not simply the regulatory social system through which each sex assumed and incorporated the attributes assigned to it; it was also performative in that gender roles could be assumed or imposed, either unconsciously and apparently "naturally," or through open or coercive acts of violence.

Boko Haram's gendered spectacles thus aid in the construction of ascendant manhood in a gendered "caliphate" in deliberate efforts to *feminize* their opponents through violence. The power of the gendered constructions resulting from these efforts is that they operate at a level below consciousness. It is feminist analysis that brings them to the surface.

In the Shadow of the Spectacular

Taylor's (1997, 27) discussion of political spectacle is fueled by the goal of "mak[ing] visible again, not the invisible or the imagined, but that which is clearly *there* but not allowed to be seen." Drawing on this impetus, I argue that it is critical to recognize the politics of visibility and nonvisibility in the dynamics set in force by a focus on the spectacular. I begin by considering what lies hidden, "there *and* not there," from the focus on Boko Haram's spectacles of violence involving women.

Boko Haram's mass abduction of the Chibok schoolgirls is widely known and has generated considerable media as well as research attention (e.g., Maiangwa and Amao 2015; Oriola 2017). The less visible reality is that abductions of women and girls by Boko Haram have taken place daily, prior to 2014. Between 2011 and 2014, for instance, Boko Haram abducted three thousand women and girls from seven local government authorities in Borno State (Ladbury 2015). Such abductions have generally taken place in less dramatic form than the mass abduction of the Chibok girls, typically in smaller groups, but the cumulative human loss is greater.

Men and boys have also been abducted. On February 25, 2014, Boko Haram invaded Buni Yadi, the only coeducational school in Yobe State. After setting fire to the hall where students carried out their variety and leisure activities, they attacked Niger House, a boys' hostel, going "from bed to bed, methodically killing sleeping, male students" (Odinkalu 2017). Over a period of several hours, the insurgents demolished the school with explosives and assault weapons. Some of the boys from Niger House managed to escape alive and raised an alarm with students in the other hostels. In the chaos that followed, students tried to escape but did not initially know which way to flee. From the boys' hostels, Boko Haram moved to that of the girls. Insurgents instructed the girls to "leave the premises, forget going to school and go and get married" (Odinkalu 2017). As they left, their hostel was set alight and all twenty-four buildings in the college destroyed. The massacre left fifty-nine students dead (Hemba 2014). This atrocity highlights the brutality of Boko Haram's gendered treatment of adolescent boys and girls. While the insurgents continued to slaughter boys and men over the years, the hands-off treatment of girls was limited to the early days of the group's evolution.

Boko Haram are not the only perpetrators of sexual violence in the North East. Women and girls in camps and informal settlements, as well as in host communities, face sexual violence while collecting firewood, fetching water, and using toilets and showers (Nagarajan 2017). Members of the military, community self-help militias, and community members have raped women and girls, and engaged in other forms of sexual violence (CIVIC 2015).

Elsewhere government agents too have carried out abductions of women. Since 2011, armed soldiers and police officers have preyed upon women found on the streets of Abuja, dragging them onto buses and sexually assaulting them, accusing them of being prostitutes. The women come from all walks of life—they are students, employees, shoppers, married women—and are told to pay N5,000 to secure their freedom. Those who cannot pay are tortured, brought before a mobile court, and then sent to a "rehabilitation camp" for sex workers (Isine and Akurega 2014). In 2014 Dorothy Njemanze, an actor and activist, and three other women who had been assaulted by state agents took the government to the Regional Court of the Economic Community of West African States. On October 12, 2017, in a landmark ruling, the court found the federal government of Nigeria guilty of multiple violations of the women's human rights (*Premium Times* 2017). It was the first time that an international court ruled on violations of the Maputo Protocol.

Moving beyond the Spectacular

The end of military rule in 1999 did not coincide with withdrawal of the military from the public sphere. Since 2014 the military have been deployed in thirty-two of the federation's thirty-six states (Alli 2014; Oyedele 2017). The lack of police capacity to address rising criminality in the form of kidnapping, murder, armed banditry, communal clashes, and theft has been dealt with by sending in troops to beleaguered communities. Yet the military have not been trained to deal with traditional policing duties and their responses have been typically heavy-handed, if not brutal (Ibrahim 2013). Not only has the military presence and occupation within the country now become the new "normal," but the militarization of society more generally has proceeded at an astonishing rate. The existence of a civilian government does not in itself change the character of the military or of governance, or even of the political culture. This dynamic has also played out in other political contexts, such as Uganda (Decker 2014).

Prevailing analyses suppress recognition of the gendered dimensions of the state, governance, and politics. Little, if any, attention is paid to the pervasiveness of hypermasculinity in the workings of the state under militarism. Legacies of prolonged military rule are marked by the normative construction of political leadership as masculine, while simultaneously resting on the expectation that men should be married to be considered "responsible" (Mama 1998). At the same time, the gendered construction of women as needing "protection" by military men is embedded in the normalization of military rule (Enloe 1993). Hypermasculinity was a critical feature shaping the brutality of a military despot such as Idi Amin, and strategic reiterations of violence were central to his displays and consolidation of military power (Decker 2014).

The aftermath of violent conflict and military rule is an all-too-common pattern of widespread sexual violence, not only in the communities most directly affected by the conflict but in society at large, as the legacies of war in Sierra Leone and Liberia make clear (Mama and Okazawa-Rey 2012). One perspective on the generalized lack of security in the North East of Nigeria posits, "The missing link in the construction of a sustainable security architecture for the region is intelligence-gathering, surveillance, community security and policing—all of which are outside the traditional remit of the military" (SBM Intelligence 2017). Even though *security* is understood here as placing community (and not the regime's) needs at its heart, the question of *whose needs* in the community will be prioritized and whose might be rendered of less significance is not addressed. Matfess (2017, 45) makes the important point that "insurgent abuse against women is ultimately an extension of the patterns of neglect and abuse that women have suffered for decades."

Feminist efforts to construct more robust notions of "security" emphasize instead the need to transcend gendered dichotomies—men as warriors, women as peacemakers—that support militarism and war (Tickner 2004). Reconceptualizing security means no longer treating it primarily as referring to the state but instead taking people's well-being and interests seriously (Clarke 2008). Ultimately this would mean women and men living as equals in a world that valorizes freedom from violence.

When we focus primarily on Boko Haram's spectacles of violence the diverse categories of women are rendered less visible. Selective recognition of women as victims obscures understanding of the ways in which gendered relations and processes are embedded in complex social relations. Normative social expectations among the poor in Northern Nigeria, justified by recourse to particular interpretations of Islam, include the belief that girls should get married at the onset of puberty. Impoverished parents tend to view girls' education as an expensive luxury relative to the material benefits that marriage is believed to confer. At the same time, the belief that men should be providers for the family is strong. Polygyny is widespread, often justified by men as their entitlement according to Islam. In differing ways, these normative expectations are woven into the themes addressed below.

Women within Boko Haram

There are no neat binaries of association with Boko Haram (i.e., voluntary or forced), but rather a spectrum that spans abduction, coercion, pressure, and the desire to belong. Young women are more likely to join through the forced rather than the voluntary end of the spectrum (Mercy Corps 2016). Women's participation is conditioned by roles played by the men in their lives and shaped by societal and cultural expectations that they should be dependent on men for their livelihoods. Once their husbands or fathers become active members of the insurgency, women have few options other than to join Boko Haram (Usman et al. 2014). Not all wives are powerless, however. In some instances, women who engaged in dialogue with their husbands were persuaded to join, due to ideological or personal motivations, or else they persuaded their husbands to join (Mercy Corps 2016).

Matfess (2017, 64) points out that "the dominant narrative of women being coerced, conscripted and abducted into [Boko Haram] is an incomplete one." Positive trajectories for young women's association with Boko Haram include attraction to the special opportunities provided for women by Boko Haram, especially that of acquiring religious knowledge that would otherwise be denied to them by patriarchal norms outside the group, and opportunities for higher status by carrying out tasks for the group (Mercy Corps 2016). Boko Haram is also popular with many young women because Mohammed Yusuf encouraged marriage within the sect through inexpensive, quick weddings. Yusuf also ordered the dower to be paid to the bride, not her family (International Crisis Group 2016). Not only does marriage into Boko Haram provide a means for women to develop their own identities but the appeal of the sect is magnified in comparison to the narrow opportunities for women that they would otherwise face (Matfess 2017).

Women and girls within Boko Haram have carried out a range of activities, indirectly and directly linked to the use of violence. Women have been engaged in logistics, conveying money and weapons to terrorist cells, and as recruiters, seeking new members and sifting through grassroots volunteers, usually by working through family ties or other personal relationships (Usman et al. 2014). Women have persuaded family members to join, been responsible for recruiting members outside their families, and taught new girls and women what was expected of them. Women are also recruited into the organization as informants, cashiers, and those responsible for domestic chores, such as cooking and fetching firewood and water. Their more direct association with violence takes the form of engagement in bomb making, participating in attacks on villages and towns, and serving as suicide bombers (Nagarajan 2017).

Community Acceptance

Several women and girls abducted by Boko Haram have become pregnant and given birth to children as a consequence of their "marriages" to insurgents and/or sexual slavery. When the women and girls return to their communities, they and their children are viewed with great suspicion, many fearing that they have been indoctrinated and radicalized by Boko Haram. This fear has been fed by Boko Haram's use of girls and women as suicide bombers, reinforcing the belief that whether they joined the group or were coerced, their return to the community is ultimately adding to insecurity in the region.

Husbands' and fathers' feelings range from complete rejection and fear to acceptance. Husbands who had been married for more than five years and who had had children with their wives before abduction tended to welcome their wives on return. Fathers were concerned about their daughters' future. Community leaders, as well as religious and traditional leaders, held a broad range of views, some of which were negative and extreme. This included blaming the women for the abuse they experienced at the hands of Boko Haram, believing they had joined the group voluntarily (International Alert/UNICEF Nigeria 2016).

Because of these experiences of violence, returnees suffer varied degrees of trauma. In the absence of services, women spoke of having to support their traumatized husbands. Women suffered high levels of trauma themselves, many facing severe psychological distress after witnessing the killing of their husbands and children, being raped by sons who are members of Boko Haram, or being abducted and forced into sexual slavery (Nagarajan 2017).

Gendered Challenges in De-radicalization

Considerable heterogeneity exists in women's conditions of life under Boko Haram. Aisha, one of the wives of Mamman Nur, a leading Boko Haram commander, described how she enjoyed "respect, influence and standing" within Boko Haram, with abducted women as her slaves. They did everything for her—washed, cooked, and babysat—during the three years she spent in a Boko Haram base in Sambisa Forest. Although she was initially kidnapped, Aisha was not forced to marry her husband, the suspected strategist behind the 2011 suicide attack on the UN headquarters in Abuja. She was courted for months and received numerous gifts; when Aisha asked Nur to divorce his second wife because Aisha did not like her, he did so right away. Another wife, Halima, also enjoyed an easy life in the forest. They had regular supplies of food and clothes, a hospital staffed with doctors and nurses, and Halima had her own room in the house she shared with her husband (Nwaubani 2017b).

Both women were among a group of seventy, including children, who had been moved from Sambisa by the military to a safe house in Maiduguri. They were undergoing a de-radicalization program, designed to "challenge the teachings they received and beliefs they adopted while under the control of Boko Haram" (Nwaubani 2017b). De-radicalization is a fuzzy concept whose lack of conceptual clarity is mirrored in the broad range of activities covered across countries and programs (Schmid 2013). The Neem Foundation, which carries out the de-radicalization program in the North East, employs psychologists who treat trauma and provide counseling. Islamic teachers discuss religious and ideological beliefs, including challenges to interpretations of the Qu'ran. The director of the program, Fatima Akilu, reports large shifts in the women's beliefs over its nine-month duration, with most of the women now believing that their former husbands' actions were wrong (Nwaubani 2017b). Yet the very stigma associated with Boko Haram itself creates incentives for returnees to present their experiences as ones of coercion and abduction, even when this has not been the case (Matfess 2017, 95). Not all women who have been part of Boko Haram, therefore, are likely to admit this.

Once a de-radicalization program ends, women married to Boko Haram militants no longer have the freedom and autonomy they experienced in Sambisa. "These were women who for the most part had never worked, had no power, no voice in the communities, and all of a sudden they were in charge of between 30 to 100 women who were now completely under their control and at their beck and call," said Akilu. "It is difficult to know what to replace it with when you return to society because most of the women are returning to societies where they are not going to be able to wield that kind of power" (Nwaubani 2017a).

Akilu points out that not all women captured by Boko Haram received the same treatment: "Those who were treated better were the ones who willingly married Boko Haram members or who joined the group voluntarily and that's not the majority" (Nwaubani 2017a). Apart from a lack of power, other factors also cause women to return to Boko Haram even after participating in de-radicalization. These include (1) a lack of support in sustaining livelihoods in tough economic conditions, (2) stigma and rejection from their communities due to their association with the insurgents, and (3) the desire to be reunited with their husbands (Nwaubani 2017a).

Livelihoods

Violent conflict has led to increased poverty for women due to years of missed harvests, loss of equipment and business sites, difficulty finding buyers for goods since income levels have been severely reduced, and depletion of capital due to displacement or hosting friends and families who have been displaced. Farmers, many of whom are women, have been unable to farm due to Boko Haram terrorizing rural areas; famine looms on the horizon. Men, who were previously breadwinners, are in many cases no longer there. Even when men are present, they are generally unable to provide for their families. This forces women to find new ways of earning income, including survival sex. Where humanitarian assistance is given to families via men, sometimes men favor one wife over others or sell goods received instead of passing them on to their family. Men may keep this money or use it to marry another wife. As a result, many agencies distribute food and other items to women, which affects gender dynamics within the household (Nagarajan 2017).

Sexual Exploitation

The majority of displaced women in the North East experience the intimate relations among gender, class, and sexual politics viscerally. Those who were already poor prior to the conflict, particularly women, feel most keenly the generalized lack of resources available to displaced persons. Gender and class inequalities combine to render women susceptible to sexual exploitation, particularly in displacement camps. Given the lack of recognition of women's independent needs for livelihood generation, women have few options for survival. One of the most egregious dimensions is corruption in the implementation of humanitarian aid. Supplies for displaced persons have been siphoned off and sold by state officials (Malik 2015). A report by Refugees International states, "The nexus between food insecurity and sexual exploitation in this setting is irrefutable" (Vigaud-Walsh 2016, 12). The situation is so bad that some women cross camp barriers at night in order to engage in sex for food. Within camps, different categories of men also prey upon women for sex (CIVIC 2015).

Women's access to sexual and reproductive health services, particularly abortion, is limited. This is problematic, given high levels of sexual violence and exploitation, the lack of sex and relationship education, difficulties in negotiating safe sex, the stigma surrounding pregnancy outside of marriage, and the lack of formal adoption services. While the law prohibits abortion except when the mother's life is at risk, those with money can get medical abortions; the poor or those without connections must rely on dangerous methods or local herbs. In response to the large number of abducted women and girls and the problems they have faced on return, the Federation of Muslim Women's Associations in Nigeria issued an advisory in 2014. In it they pointed out that Islam provides for abortion for a certain period of pregnancy and does not allow stigmatization of women who had been abducted and raped or of any children born to them (Nagarajan 2017).

Concluding Thoughts

I began this essay by focusing on the importance of context for understanding the broad spectrum of gender relations in the wake of the Boko Haram insurgency. These gendered dynamics are marked by the *coexistence of discontinuity as well as continuity*, with implications for selective visibility. A key problem arising from a focus on the spectacular, in the form of the extreme violence of Boko Haram, is that discontinuities are more readily recognized than the continuities. While the forms that sexual and gender violence have taken during the insurgency are particularly egregious and thus distinct from those previously recognized, it is also the case that continuities in terms of gender and sexual violence *predating* the insurgency, in times of "peace," have been normalized. This dynamic is not particular to the Boko Haram conflict but is instead a more general feature of violent conflicts (see Mama and Okazawa-Rey 2012).

What is required is a recognition of the gender politics of visibility and nonvisibility regarding diverse categories of women, given the dynamics set in force by a focus on spectacular acts of violence. The state, by unleashing brutality against citizens in general, and Boko Haram in particular, has contributed to the insecurity in the North East and beyond the boundaries of recognized conflict. Recognizing the multiplicity of sites and domains for gendered negotiations and contestations can change our comprehension of the conflict itself.

The complexity of processes surrounding how local gender relations are being reconfigured in the wake of the Boko Haram insurgency demands greater understanding, if the multiple forms of destruction and violence unleashed are to be addressed. The challenges of understanding why some angry young men in North East Nigeria would turn to violent conflict are intricately tied to those of understanding why some women who have been captured by Boko Haram are willing to return. Neither can be addressed without changing the conditions that render their new lives more attractive or, at the very least, less unattractive. Feminist thought and practice have enabled the connections between these erstwhile separate spheres to be traced. To unravel the violent legacies of neoliberal, militarized "development," feminist thought and action in pursuit of more just and egalitarian societies are required now more than ever.

....

Charmaine Pereira is a feminist scholar-activist based in Abuja, Nigeria. She edited special issue 22 of the journal *Feminist Africa*, on the theme "Feminists Organising—Strategy, Voice, Power" (2017), and *Changing Narratives of Sexuality: Contestations, Compliance and Women's Empowerment* (Zed Press, 2014). Pereira is the author of *Gender in the Making of the Nigerian University System* (James Currey/PHEA, 2007).

Notes

1   Deep thanks go to the editors of this issue for their encouragement in completing this essay and their helpful comments on a preliminary draft, to Alicia Decker for her invaluable help in gaining access to necessary journal articles, to Amina Mama for her critical support, and to the anonymous reviewers for their comments. All responsibility for the final essay remains mine.

2   During the 2003 elections, the sect collaborated with the governor, but they subsequently fell out of political favor. The conspicuous opulence of the wider Western-educated elite amid the grinding poverty of most of the population was also the target of Yusuf's criticism.

3   Transcript of Shekau's video message, Reuters, January 27, 2012, cited in Usman et al. 2014.

4   Transcript of Shekau's video message.

5   The term *performative* refers here to the performance of power, as distinct from the performativity of actions functioning as speech acts.

Works Cited

ACAPS. 2017. "Crisis Profile 2017. Northeast Nigeria: Adamawa State Crisis Profile." https://reliefweb.int/report/nigeria/acaps-crisis-profile-northeast-nigeria -adamawa-state-crisis-profile-2017.

Alli, Y. 2014. "We've Deployed Troops in 32 States, says NSA Dasuki." *The Nation*, February 25. http://thenationonlineng.net/weve-deployed-troops-in-32-states-says -nsa-dasuki/.

Amnesty International. 2015. "'Our Job Is to Shoot, Slaughter and Kill': Boko Haram's Reign of Terror in North-East Nigeria." Report. London: Amnesty International.

Anon. 2012. "The Popular Discourses of Salafi Radicalism and Salafi Counter-radicalism in Northern Nigeria." *Journal of Religion in Africa* 42: 118–144.

Bakejal, N. 2015. "Inside the Search for the Chibok Schoolgirls Abducted by Boko Haram." *Time*, April 23. https://www.google.com.ng/amp/amp.timeinc.net/time /3833024/chibok-boko-haram/%3fsource=dam.

BBC News. 2013. "Nigeria: 'Many Dead in Boko Haram Raid' in Borno State." May 8. www.bbc.com/news/world-africa-22444417.

Bloom, M., and H. Matfess. 2016. "Women as Symbols and Swords in Boko Haram's Terror." *Peace* 6, no. 1: 105–21.

Brigaglia, A. 2012. "A Contribution to the History of the Wahhabi *Da'wa* in West Africa: The Career and the Murder of Shaykh Ja'afar Mahmoud Adam (Daura ca. 1961/1962–Kano 2007)." *Islamic Africa* 3, no. 1: 1–23.

CIVIC. 2015. "'When We Can't See the Enemy, Civilians Become the Enemy': Living through Nigeria's Six-Year Insurgency." Report. Centre for Civilians in Conflict, USA.

Clarke, Y. 2008. "Security Sector Reform in Africa: A Lost Opportunity to Deconstruct Militarised Masculinities?" *Feminist Africa* 10: 49–66.

Decker, A. 2014. *In Idi Amin's Shadow: Women, Gender and Militarism in Uganda*. Athens: Ohio University Press.

El-Affendi, A., and S. Gumel. 2015. "Abducting Modernity: Boko Haram, Gender Violence and the Marketplace of Bigotry." *Journal of Women of the Middle East and the Islamic World* 13: 127–40.

Enloe, C. 1993. *The Morning After: Sexual Politics at the End of the Cold War*. Berkeley: University of California Press.

Hemba, J. 2014. "Nigerian Islamists Kill 59 Pupils in Boarding School Attack." Reuters, February 26. https://www.reuters.com/article/us-nigeria-violence/nigerian-islamists-kill-59-pupils-in-boarding-school-attack-idUSBREA1P10M20140226.

Ibrahim, J. 2013. "The Norms for Civil-Military Relations in Nigeria." *Premium Times*, October 28. https://www.premiumtimesng.com/opinion/147394-norms-civil-military-relations-nigeria-jibrin-ibrahim.html.

International Alert/UNICEF Nigeria. 2016. "'Bad Blood': Perceptions of Children Born Out of Conflict-Related Sexual Violence and Women and Girls Associated with Boko Haram in Northeast Nigeria." Research Summary. February. https://www.unicef.org/nigeria/Nigeria_BadBlood_EN_2016.pdf.

International Crisis Group. 2016. "Nigeria: Women and the Boko Haram Insurgency." *Africa Report* 242, no. 5. https://www.crisisgroup.org/africa/west-africa/nigeria/nigeria-women-and-boko-haram-insurgency.

Isine, I., and M. Akurega. 2014. "Investigation: How Abuja NGO, AEPB, Arrest Innocent Women, Label Them Prostitutes." *Premium Times*, February 10. https://www.premiumtimesng.com/news/154446-how-abuja-ngo-aepb-arrest-innocent-women-label-them-prostitutes.html.

Ladbury, S. 2015. "Women and Extremism: The Association of Women and Girls with Jihadi Groups and Implications for Programming." Independent paper prepared for the Department of International Development and the Foreign and Commonwealth Office, United Kingdom. January 23.

Lewis, D. 2009. "Gendered Spectacle: New Terrains of Struggle in South Africa." In *Body Politics and Women Citizens—African Experiences*, edited by A. Schlyter, 127–37. Sida Studies No. 24. Stockholm: SIDA.

Lewis, D. 2011. "Representing African Sexualities." In *African Sexualities: A Reader*, edited by S. Tamale, 199–216. Oxford: Pambazuka Press.

Maiangwa, B., and O. B. Amao. 2015. "'Daughters, Brides and Supporters of the Jihad': Revisiting the Gender-Based Atrocities of Boko Haram in Nigeria." *African Renaissance* 12, no. 2: 117–44.

Malik, S. 2015. "Displaced Persons Face Hunger as Relief Materials Disappear in IDP Camps." International Centre for Investigative Reporting, September 21. https://www.icirnigeria.org/displaced-persons-face-hunger-as-relief-materials-disappear-in-idp-camps/.

Mama, A. 1998. "Khaki in the Family: Gender Discourses and Militarism in Nigeria." *African Studies Review* 41, no. 2: 1–17.

Mama, A., and M. Okazawa-Rey. 2012. "Militarism, Conflict and Women's Activism in the Global Era: Challenges and Prospects for Women in Three West African Contexts." *Feminist Review* 101: 97–123.

Marama, N. 2018. "Breaking: Dapchi Girls Have Been Brought Back—Parents." *Vanguard*, March 21. https://www.vanguardngr.com/2018/03/dapchi-girls-brought-back-parents/.

Matfess, H. 2017. *Women and the War on Boko Haram: Wives, Weapons, Witnesses*. London: Zed Press.

Mercy Corps. 2016. "'Motivations and Empty Promises': Voices of Former Boko Haram Combatants and Nigerian Youth." April. https://www.mercycorps.org /sites/default/files/Motivations%20and%20Empty%20Promises_Mercy% 20Corps_Full%20Report.pdf.

Mohammed, K. 2014. "The Message and Methods of Boko Haram." In *Boko Haram: Islamism, Politics, Security and the State in Nigeria*, edited by M. Perouse de Montclos, 9–32. Ibadan, Nigeria: African Studies Centre.

Mustapha, A. R. 2014. "Understanding Boko Haram." In *Sects and Social Disorder: Muslim Identities and Conflict in Northern Nigeria*, edited by A. R. Mustapha, 147–98. London: James Currey.

Mustapha, A. R., and M. Bunza. 2014. "Contemporary Islamic Sects and Groups in Northern Nigeria." In *Sects and Social Disorder: Muslim Identities and Conflict in Northern Nigeria*, edited by A. R. Mustapha, 54–97. London: James Currey.

Nagarajan, C. 2017. "Gender Assessment of Northeast Nigeria." Managing Conflict in North East Nigeria. https://chitrasudhanagarajan.files.wordpress.com/2018 /03/gender-assessment-of-northeast-nigeria.pdf.

NBS. 2012. "Nigeria Poverty Profile 2010." Report. Abuja: National Bureau of Statistics.

"Nigeria Emergency Operations." Situation Report. April 2016. https://nigeria.iom .int/sites/default/files/dtm/Nigeria%20Situation%20Report%20-%20April% 202016.pdf.

Nwaubani, A. T. 2017a. "Letter from Africa: Freed Boko Haram 'Wives' Return to Captors." *BBC News*, July 26. http://www.bbc.com/news/world-africa-40704569.

Nwaubani, A. T. 2017b. "Power, Sex and Slaves: Nigeria Battles Beliefs of Boko Haram Brides." Reuters, February 8. http://news.trust.org/item/20170208060545 -tibww/.

Odinkalu, C. 2017. "In Memory of the Children Massacred in FGC Buni-Yadi on 25 February 2014." *Premium Times*, February 25. https://opinion.premiumtimesng .com/2017/02/25/177120/.

Omego, C. 2015. "The Role of the Mass Media in the Fight against Terrorism and the Instrumental Use of Women in Boko Haram Insurgence in Nigeria." *LALIGENS: An International Journal of Language, Literature and Gender Studies* 4, no. 2: 78–96.

Oriola, T. 2017. "'Unwilling Cocoons': Boko Haram's War against Women." *Studies in Conflict and Terrorism* 40, no. 2: 99–121.

Oyedele, D. 2017. "Army Currently Deployed in 32 States, Says Burutai." *ThisDay*, February 15. https://www.thisdaylive.com/index.php/2017/02/15/army-currently -deployed-in-32-states-says-buratai/.

Pereira, C. 2005. "Zina and Transgressive Heterosexuality in Northern Nigeria." *Feminist Africa* 5: 52–79.

Pereira, C. 2010. "Reflections of a Feminist Scholar-Activist in Nigeria." In *African Feminist Politics of Knowledge: Tensions, Challenges, Possibilities*, edited by A. Adomako Ampofo and S. Arnfred, 83–110. Uppsala: Nordiska Afrikainstitutet.

Premium Times. 2017. "Press Release: ECOWAS Court Orders Nigerian Govt to Pay N18 Million to Women Maltreated for Allegedly Being Prostitutes." October 12. https:

//www.premiumtimesng.com/news/top-news/245936-ecowas-court-orders
-nigerian-govt-pay-n18-million-women-maltreated-allegedly-prostitutes.html.

Regional Protection Working Group. 2017. "Regional Protection Strategic Framework: Responding to the Protection Crisis in the Lake Chad Basin." Dakar:
United Nations High Commission for Refugees, Regional Representation for
West Africa. https://reliefweb.int/sites/reliefweb.int/files/resources/lcb_
protection_strategy.pdf.

SBM Intelligence. 2017. "Analysis: Scrutinizing the Boko Haram Resurgence." https:
//reliefweb.int/report/nigeria/analysis-scrutinising-boko-haram-resurgence.

Schmid, A. 2013. "Radicalisation, De-Radicalisation, Counter-Radicalisation: A Conceptual Discussion and Literature Review." ICCT Research Paper. March. The
Hague: International Centre for Counter-Terrorism.

Stone, J., and K. Pattillo. 2011. "Al-Qaeda's Use of Female Suicide Bombers in Iraq:
A Case Study." In *Women, Gender and Terrorism*, edited by L. Sjoberg and C. Gentry,
159–75. Athens: University of Georgia Press.

Taylor, D. 1997. *Disappearing Acts: Spectacles of Gender and Nationalism in Argentina's Dirty
War*. Durham: Duke University Press.

Tickner, J. A. 2004. "Feminist Responses to International Security Studies." *Peace
Review: A Journal of Social Justice* 16, no. 1: 43–48.

Usman, Z., S. El-Taraboulsi, and K. Gambo Hawaja. 2014. "Gender Norms and
Female Participation in Radical Movements in Northern Nigeria." Unpublished
manuscript.

Vigaud-Walsh, F. 2016. "Nigeria's Displaced Women and Girls: Humanitarian
Community at Odds, Boko Haram's Survivors Forsaken." Field Report.
Washington, DC: Refugees International.

Zenn, J., and E. Pearson. 2014. "Women, Gender and the Evolving Tactics of Boko
Haram." *Journal of Terrorism Research* 5, no. 1: 46–57.

Fatima Sadiqi and Aziza Ouguir

....

Reflecting on Feminisms in Africa
A Conversation from Morocco

Abstract: Aziza Ouguir talks with Professor Fatima Sadiqi, one of Africa's most prolific and well-respected feminist scholars, about African feminisms north and south of the Sahara.

Ouguir: *Feminism* is a heavily contested word in many parts of the world, so I am curious, do you define yourself as a feminist?

Sadiqi: I grappled with the terms *feminist* and *feminism* for a long time as the two do not have clear counterparts in my mother tongues: Berber and Moroccan Arabic. I was introduced to the terms through French and English while a student at Mohamed V University (Rabat, Morocco) and was immediately attracted by the semantics of the concepts that the terms carried (that is, ways of improving girls' and women's lot in society and individually). I was attracted to these meanings because very early in my life I noticed that being a girl meant a lot of behavioral restrictions at home, at school, and especially on the street. I first felt this way around the age of ten or so, when I wanted to play with my brother and his male friends but was told to go home. I went home with tears in my eyes: I could not understand because I loved my brother, who was only eighteen months younger than me. I then sought to outsmart him by working harder at school. Later on, and as I was becoming a scholar, different and sometimes contradictory discourses guided my subject positioning as a woman. In retrospect, the fact that I often changed locations as I was growing up (my father was

MERIDIANS · feminism, race, transnationalism   17:2 November 2018
DOI: 10.1215/15366936-7176428 © 2018 Smith College

in the military and we had to move from town to town) constantly shaped and reshaped my identity and made it fluid. This allowed me to constantly carve new spaces in the constant movement, explore possibilities of pursuing knowledge, and hold them open for the future. All of this shaped my feminist identity.

AO: Right, you have said that you outsmarted your brother by working harder at school. This means that education is an empowering tool for girls and women. What do you think of girls' education in Morocco?

FS: An absolute necessity. It builds self-confidence in them and in that way helps them navigate the ups and downs of life. I am a staunch believer in the human mind not only as a source of creativity and wisdom, but also as a protection in difficult times.

AO: Certainly I agree with you, and I myself benefited personally from education. So who were your feminist role models?

FS: First, I would say my father, who had eight sisters and no brothers and who genuinely believed in women's power. This gave me tremendous self-confidence. Then I would say Fatima Mernissi, who was teaching at the university when I was a student. I used to follow her public statements and writings and the controversy she often occasioned. My father's attitude I readily accepted, because he was the one who took me to school and believed in me, and Mernissi (the person and her lectures and writings), because she talked about things that were meaningful to me. For example, she talked about the role of the male elite, especially the *fiqh* (legal interpreters of the Qur'an and *hadith*, Prophet Muhammad's sayings and deeds), in marginalizing women at home and in the public sphere. Her arguments made sense to me. To my knowledge, Mernissi was the first Moroccan scholar to attribute women's oppression to the legal interpretations of the sacred texts.

AO: You have said that Mernissi played an important role in building a feminist vision and identity. Do you feel that the two of you have a lot in common?

FS: Difficult to say. Maybe intellectually. Fatima Mernissi belonged to a wealthy family and was what I may term an "urban" feminist, whereas

I see myself as starting from zero socially speaking. I have a rural background, and I could access education only because my father had to move to the city because of his military profession. But when I met Fatima Mernissi for the first time, in the 1990s, I immediately sensed the strong appeal of her mind; we became friends and we stayed so until her death. When I started my fellowship at Harvard, I was told that only one North African woman preceded me there and that was her! Margot Badran, Raja Rhouni, and I are editing a book in her memory. The three of us belong to three generations, all of which were heavily impacted by Mernissi.

AO: You also mentioned that Mernissi was the first scholar who problematized *fiqh* as a patriarchal interpretation of Islam and the core of Muslim women's oppression and marginalization. Could you explain that?

FS: Mernissi spent years discussing *fiqh* with Ahmed Khamlichi, an enlightened Moroccan scholar of *fiqh*, and came to the conclusion that this discipline was "man-made "in the sense that it transformed the Qur'an and hadith into law that basically served men over women.

AO: In Mernissi's writings, she advocates *ijtihād* (independent reasoning) to promote women's rights and gender equality. In your opinion, what are the conditions for the achievement of *ijtihād* to introduce Islamic laws that respect gender equality, social justice, and democracy?

FS: We do have a few Moroccan women who embarked on *ijtihād*, like Farida Bennani and Asma Lamrabet, but I still think that the road is long for women's *ijtihād* to have the authority of men's simply because women lack this authority in the family and in society. What I mean by authority here is power that is accepted by society.

AO: Authority is what we as women feminists seek to achieve. Can you tell us about some of your major contributions to the feminist movement? More specifically, you are the founder of the gender program at our university. What have been the visible impacts of gender studies on your students and their personal lives? Could you give us some examples of these positive impacts?

FS: I think I brought in my Berber identity, my rural background, and my love of languages. I did that through positioning myself in the Moroccan feminist discourses as a Berber feminist linguist. I think I have come a long way from the time I used to hide my Berber identity—and was even summoned by the police when I wrote *Grammaire du Berbère*—to today where Berber feminist NGOs [nongovernmental organizations] have emerged as strong and novel voices in Morocco and the region. These NGOs address, among other matters, language, identity, and "ruralness," issues that were sidelined by the mainstream Moroccan feminist movement. They use *Tifinagh*, the Berber alphabet, in addition to Arabic or French, and they position their work within human rights, diversity, freedom of expression, and development frameworks. I am also thrilled that I founded and directed the first gender studies graduate program in Morocco and that you [Ouguir] are among the first Ph.D. holders of this program. Many of my former students told me that this program changed their lives personally and professionally. Several of my former students are now colleagues and researchers like yourself, and some of them have created their own gender studies programs. This is a source of pride for me.

AO: This means that activism and scholarship are very important tools in promoting women's rights.

FS: When I researched feminist and gender theories in the West, I learned a lot. But when I started thinking about Moroccan and African women, I realized how important the context is. In our part of the world, theory is imbricated with activism, and both need to be rooted in our societies without of course losing sight of the bigger contexts.

AO: I totally agree with you. Here is another question: What advice would you give to younger women (and men) who are just starting their careers and want to "make a difference"?

FS: To let their voices be heard and use whatever medium to make this happen, include men in their struggle, and continue to network locally, regionally, and globally. They need to use the new spaces to create more spaces.

AO: Recently I have spoken to a number of men and women friends about their views on feminism. By and large they tell me they want to distance themselves from it. This surprised me a bit because they are all very knowledgeable, well-educated, and independent. Some of them told me feminism has become so ideological that they cannot identify with it. Others told me that feminism is a waste of time. Do you see this same thing in young women?

FS: I don't think it is a waste of time, and I don't think one can force people to identify with the term. Feminism is a perspective on life and how men and women could lead a comfortable life together. The word itself scares many people because it involves power relations and, of course, men and privileged women are often reluctant to lose power. I also think that beyond terminology the concept of feminism as a search for a just life is generally appealing to people of both sexes.

AO: One of the important issues you discussed during your different academic meetings is the concept of equality; you argued that the theory of change should evolve around the idea of social justice. How would you describe your theory of change? And do you think change happens through transnational relations and meaningful connections with other people?

FS: Equality is certainly part and parcel of social justice, and positive change from this perspective comes through awareness, itself an outcome of many factors, prominent amongst which is education. For the change to be sustainable, it needs cross-cultural interfeeding, which comes through networking and transnational relations. For example, much headway in North African feminisms came about through comparisons with sub-Saharan African feminisms, and it looks like this will be developed more in the future as part of the exciting relations that are being built between the countries of Africa.

AO: A good point. It is true that African feminism has had some significant victories. In your opinion, what have been some of these victories for African feminists over the years?

FS: I think the main constituent of pioneer African feminisms was fighting oppression and other types of victimization such as class and religion. They understood that oppression generated its antithesis, which is power, and boldly confronted this oppression by attacking their two major challenges: misogyny and patriarchy. They wanted to reappropriate their voices and excelled in doing so through political struggle, social struggle, and scholarship or writing. They wanted to include their voices and histories as herstory and succeeded in establishing what many of us refer to as a countermemory by subverting the canon. I witnessed this firsthand during my twelve-year involvement in editing one of the anthologies of *Women Writing Africa*. Another victory is the ability of these feminists to resist male hegemonic political and social discourses and become agents in their homes, communities, and beyond. They created genuine social movements, which basically fought for authority in a space-based patriarchy and scored significant educational, social, political, and legal gains along the years. They even became strong players on the political scene and were initiators of the culture of street demonstrations.

AO: I have read *Women Writing Africa: The Northern Region*. It is an interesting volume. Its different chapters studied different historical Maghrebian and African women who played a role in history. As you said, these historical women are the pioneers of African feminism. They deserve to be highlighted as role models. In your opinion, how do we make these historical women relevant to women today? How do we bridge that gap which separates the past and the present?

FS: We do that by keeping the conversation going. As you know, women's rights have been highly contested and hyperpoliticized, and they have served all sorts of agendas, from the colonialist and neo-imperialist to the anticolonialist and postcolonialist to the religious extremist. This sustained institutional instrumentalization of women's rights has been first problematized, then contested by generations of African feminists and gender experts of both sexes, writing and speaking from positions within civil society, politics, and academia. Now things are changing. While the institutional instrumentalization of women's rights in Africa has not undergone any substantial change, the strategies and practices of contestation have dramatically changed, and this, in turn, is transforming feminisms and gender from inside and in interesting ways because both the older and the younger generations are involved in the change.

AO: Last week I watched a TV program about the sexual abuse of very young girls in African countries, and what is worse is that there is not adequate punishment or justice for these crimes. Can you explain why this is? What can we do to change this?

FS: Social change is slow, and changing mentalities takes time. This is where feminism and advocating women's rights are an absolute necessity.

AO: Exactly. Like any feminist movement, African feminists have some challenges. Could you tell us about these key challenges?

FS: The major challenge is patriarchy and the glass ceiling.

AO: Right, global networks remain a crucial strategy for African feminists to get together and stay together across distances like geography, language, and culture. They empower women to achieve more. They give women an opportunity to discuss and share stories that connect them and create different strategies to fight oppressions and patriarchy. Throughout my research, I can articulate feminism as a big umbrella that gives shelter to a number of feminists who disagree on different policy issues, but there is a common thread: feminists believe that women are human beings and deserve to be treated with the same dignity and respect. What do you think?

FS: Today African feminists understand that the self is not singular, but multiple. They understand that, for example, it is not enough to say "African women" or "Muslim women" because these expressions hide myriad other parameters, which include the location of the self and the perspective of the voice. Unlike the former generations of African feminists, the new generation does not focus on the discourse of oppression but rather on the multifarious combinations of difference that might or might not include oppression. For example, a Berber woman could be privileged by her role in her community but oppressed by her rural background; an Islamist woman could be privileged in certain spaces because of her ideology but oppressed because of her gender. Everything has become "relational" for the younger generation of African women because of the multiplicity of the self and because gender is sometimes included and sometimes excluded from other axes of identity. The inclusion/exclusion depends on various variables, like the point of reference or the available conditions. Young female feminists in today's Africa confront sexual harassment, taboo, and so on, and maneuver what is generally referred to as "geographies of identity," or intersectionality, according to their point of reference or conditions. Unlike the previous generation, today's rising generation of feminists move the political to the micropolitical and hence use new strategies and practices. This does not mean that they have discarded gender and feminism; on the contrary, gender and feminism continue to influence the younger generation's views and practices. They use the accumulated feminist knowledge of their predecessors to re-create new ways of protesting and resisting, and have a new language to do so. For example, the use of aesthetic graffiti and creative poetic expressions to confront the state and establish a novel relation with politics is remarkable. Further, the new generation is aware of the importance of combining the local and the global (what is referred to as the *glocal*) in their strategies. I see this in their organizational skills and strategies of resistance, such as those used in combating sexual harassment, lobbying, and coming up with action plans geared toward securing the agency and authority they have. I think the power of the new generation of African feminists is that they do not seek power; they defy it.

AO: In your opinion, how is feminism in North Africa (or Morocco specifically) similar to or different from feminisms in sub-Saharan Africa? Do you think it is possible to create a global feminism where North African, sub-Saharan African, and Western feminisms can meet?

FS: I was faced with this very question during my twelve years working as an editor of *Women Writing Africa: The Northern Region*. I think African women, regardless of geographical origin, face the same problems and experience more or less the same challenges in their strategies of resistance. The ebb and flow of women's lives and experiences is certainly different as women are divided by class, level of education, choice, and opportunities, but the open space and the possibility of creating new ones are common to all African women in this time and age. They face the same "precarity," to use Judith Butler's term, and seek to transform their lives. I think it is possible to create layers of "global" feminist discourses where North African, sub-Saharan African, and Western feminisms can meet. This can be done by adopting a perspective that highlights heterogeneity and diversity, in addition to gender, to combat masculinization and militarization, which result in a gendered grammar of violence where violations of men's bodies are considered political and those of women's bodies are considered cultural, meaning acceptable. Academia is crucial in these endeavors.

AO: That is true, Professor, but let me add something. I just want to say that "being a feminist" needs other important actions. Throughout my research on Moroccan female religious agents and their perception by Moroccan feminists, I noticed that feminism does not mean only liberation of women; it also means addressing the needs of the most vulnerable. Being a feminist also means being persistent and a part of a global movement. Connecting people and working together empowers women belonging to different cultural environments. This collective work fights patriarchal discourses and achieves rights not only at the national level but also at the global one. Moroccan or African and Western collective organizing for change endows feminists and women with power and authority. Feminists in academia and activism are trying to make the world peaceful. In your opinion, how can feminists advocate and contribute to the achievement of a peaceful world?

FS: They are already: the UN approved Resolution 1325, according to which women need to be at the table of peace negotiations, a landmark in the history of mankind. The lobbyists were of course feminists from all nations. I had the honor to be one of them. In Forward Global Women, Women Crossing Borders for Peace, we focus on this issue. I think more such networks are needed.

AO: Coming back to our original topic: What does it mean to be a feminist in Morocco or Africa today?

FS: To be a feminist in today's Morocco is to be aware of women as human beings with specific concerns and to be aware that women and their concerns deserve respect. In the past, it meant endeavors to search for these concerns and express them. Moroccan feminism democratized civil society and the public sphere and opened fresh vistas of research. A new generation of female feminist voices with unexpected potential is emerging and re-creating African feminisms from the inside. It is true that this is happening within a context wrought with ambiguities, but it is happening; for example, taboo topics are being addressed, and young men are expressing views on gender equality.

AO: What is your vision for the future? Are you optimistic about the current state of humanity?

FS: I am by nature optimistic. I think that bridging the generational gap among feminists will help bridge a larger gap within Africa between those who support the voices of young feminists and those who fear what is happening in Libya, Somalia, and Nigeria, for example, and want to glorify "traditional" gender norms in a nostalgic way. Hope springs from the cracks of both sides, as gender—visible or invisible—will continue to lead change.

AO: Well, I just want to thank you for doing this interview and for all your longtime support of feminism. As you know, you have always been an inspiration to me as well as to other young feminists, so thank you again for this thoughtful and interesting conversation.

....

Fatima Sadiqi is a professor of linguistics and gender studies at the University of Fez. Her work focuses on women's issues in modern North Africa, the Middle East, and the Mediterranean world. She is the author and editor of numerous books, including *Women, Gender and Language* (Brill, 2003), *Moroccan Feminist Discourses* (Palgrave Macmillan, 2014), *Women's Movements in the Post–"Arab Spring" North Africa* (Palgrave MacMillan, 2016), and *Daesh Ideology and Women's Legal Rights* (Cambridge University Press, 2017). She is also a public speaker and a member of many national and international scholarly and policymaking boards. She served as director general of the Fez Festival of Sacred Music and an administrative board member of the Royal Institute of the Amazigh Language and Culture. Professor Sadiqi has received prestigious awards and fellowships from institutions such as Harvard University, the Wilson Center, the Rockefeller Foundation, and Fulbright. She currently serves on the editorial board of the *Oxford Encyclopedia of African Women's History*.

Aziza Ouguir earned her Ph.D. from the University of Amsterdam in 2013 and is currently working as a researcher in Morocco. Her work focuses on Islamic feminism, feminine Sufism, and gender issues. She is a research member of IARG, the International Association of Religion and Gender.

Ntokozo Yingwana

....

"We Fit in the Society by Force"
Sex Work and Feminism in Africa

Abstract: What does it mean to be an African sex worker feminist? In answering this question this essay draws from two qualitative studies with two African sex worker groups in 2014 and 2015—the South African movement of sex workers called Sisonke, and the African Sex Worker Alliance (ASWA). Although participants were initially reluctant to give a precise definition, many pointed to elements that could constitute such an identity. Based on their embodied lived experiences, each participant illustrated and described what it meant for them to be an African, a sex worker, and a feminist, and then collectively discussed these in relation to each other and the social dimensions they occupy. Even though these three identities may seem incongruent, in certain embodiments they actually inform each other. The aim of this work is for all feminists to recognize each other as comrades in the struggle for gender and sexual liberation, thus strengthening solidarity across social justice movements.

In 2013 a group of twelve sex workers in Cape Town, both cis and transgender women, established AWAKE! Women of Africa. All members identified as feminists and were part of the larger movement of South African sex workers called Sisonke (meaning "We are together" in isiZulu). These women were particularly concerned with sexual and gender-based violence. As a group, they regularly took part in international campaigns, such as One Billion Rising/V-DAY and the 16 Days of Activism for No Violence against Women and Children. However, despite their active engagement in women's rights campaigns, other feminists were not always

MERIDIANS · feminism, race, transnationalism   17:2 November 2018
DOI: 10.1215/15366936-7176439 © 2018 Smith College

accepting of them, assuming that they needed to be rescued from sex work rather than recognized as feminists and comrades in the struggle for gender and sexual liberation. Indeed the reluctance by some feminists to believe that anyone would consent to selling sex results in the "active exclusion of sex workers and their positive experiences of sex work from feminist spaces" (Ditmore et al. 2010, 38). Consequently members often left feminist dialogues feeling disempowered and disillusioned by the genuine lack of feminist solidarity.

I recall a particularly unpleasant incident involving one of the group's members at a feminist discussion held in Cape Town sometime in 2013, attended by members of civil society, governmental officials, and academics.[1] During this particular meeting, Leigh, one of the trans-women members of AWAKE!, asked to use the toilet and was dismissively pointed toward the men's lavatory.[2] This lack of feminist recognition left us angry and wounded. I remember us discussing the incident on our taxi ride back to the office. There could not have been any confusion; at the meeting she had explicitly introduced herself with the pronoun *she* and clearly presented as a woman. The only conclusion we could arrive at is that the meeting organizer had chosen to be blatantly insensitive to our colleague's gender identity. This, we felt, was completely unfeminist. It made us realize that there is a significant disconnect between our understanding of what feminism is, compared to that of mainstream feminists. Dudu, one of the founding members of the group, recounted the unfriendly reception she often received in feminist spaces: "What confused me is that when everyone introduced themselves as feminist and we introduced ourselves as sex workers . . . they were not happy; not like, you know when people are happy they would be like, 'Oh wow! Sex workers are feminists.' And then the topic continues. But it was like ignorance. And at that time I hadn't learned how to stand up for myself and say, 'Yes, we are [feminists].'" Because of the aforementioned incident and continuous alienation by other feminists, the group decided to take a step back to re-evaluate what it means to be a sex worker who also self-identifies as a feminist within an African context. This was done not only to gain the feminist language and confidence needed to articulate a specific political identity but primarily to dismantle and redefine (African) feminist understandings of sex work altogether in order to be able to assert one's agency in volatile feminist spaces. Because at the time I was working as the advocacy officer at the Sex Workers Education and Advocacy Taskforce (SWEAT), AWAKE! allowed me to join them on their journey of self-discovery. This was the genesis of the first study in 2014. One of the crucial insights to come out of this study was that being an African and a sex worker did not exclude one from feminism.

It is from this premise that in 2015 I embarked on a follow-up study with members of the African Sex Worker Alliance (ASWA) who also self-identify as feminists. ASWA is a network of sex worker movements across Africa, of which Sisonke is a member. It advocates for the recognition of the profession to ensure that "the health and human rights of all sex workers living and working in Africa are protected" (ASWA n.d.). The alliance was established during the first African Sex Worker Conference, held in Johannesburg in 2009 (NSWP n.d.). Currently ASWA comprises just over seventy-five member organizations from twenty-three countries across the continent.

Sisonke and ASWA welcomed the prospect of collaborating on these studies, as the findings would help them to strategize and strengthen solidarity building with feminists who might still be reluctant to support sex workers' rights. As Chi Mgbako and Laura Smith (2011, 8) assert, "The establishment of African sex worker collectives and women's rights organizations that view themselves as partners and supporters of sex workers will provide African sex workers with the tools, skills, knowledge, and confidence necessary to advocate for their rights in different forums." Mgbako and Smith emphasize the need for sex worker rights-based feminist transformation within the African continent. Unfortunately "there have been very few studies of prostitution as a distinct occupational category in African societies" (Oyewùmi 2003, 37). This research therefore serves as an important corrective.

Based on those qualitative studies, this essay asks the following question: What does it mean to be an African sex worker feminist? Although participants were initially reluctant to give an actual definition, fearing that they lacked the "proper" academic language, they ultimately pointed to elements that could constitute such an identity. Drawing from their embodied lived experiences, each participant described what it meant for them to be an *African*, a *sex worker*, and a *feminist*, and then collectively discussed these in relation to each other. This essay follows a similar structure, culminating in an analysis of what these intersectionalities mean for African sex worker feminists. I conclude that even though these three identities may seem incongruent, in certain embodiments they actually inform each other. My aim with this work is for all feminists to recognize each other as comrades in the struggle for gender and sexual liberation, thus strengthening solidarity across social justice movements.

African Feminist Theorizing on Sex Work

Although exploring the various strands of feminisms is beyond the scope of this essay, a brief discussion of the salient principles that feminists generally agree upon and orient their positionalities around would be useful. bell hooks (2000, 1) explains that generally speaking, feminism is a "movement to end sexism, sexist exploitation, and oppression." In addition, Chimamanda Ngozi Adichie (2013) succinctly defines a feminist as "a person who believes in the social, political, and economic equality of the sexes." These definitions suggest that feminism and feminists concern themselves with fighting sexism, while promoting gender and sexual equality. I also draw from Desiree Lewis's (2001, 5) definition of African feminism, which she describes as "a shared intellectual commitment to critiquing gender and imperialism coupled with a collective focus on a continental identity shaped by particular relations of subordination in the world economy and global social and cultural practices." It is also important to remember that an "ongoing process of self-definition and re-definition" characterizes African feminist movements (Akin-Aina 2011, 66). Hence this essay contributes toward the project of self-redefining (African) feminisms, in particular, by introducing the concept of an African sex worker feminist.

Carol Leigh (1997, 230) (aka Scarlot Harlot), who is credited with coining the term *sex work*, attributes much of her political development to third-wave feminism. She maintains that sex work is the only "word for this work which is not a euphemism." Traditionally known as prostitution, sex work refers to the exchange of sex for money or a reward of pecuniary value (Richter 2012, 63). I employ the term *sex work* as it is devoid of much of the stigma attached to the word *prostitution* (Krüger 2004, 138). Most important, my decision to use *sex work* in this study is informed by the participants' preference in self-identifying as sex workers instead of prostitutes.

Feminist scholarship on sex work primarily falls into two opposing schools of thought: the sexual exploitation approach and the sex work model (MacKinnon 2011, 272). The sexual exploitation approach views sex work as the "oldest oppression," an institutionalized form of sex inequality that is intrinsically exploitative. In contrast, the sex work model considers selling sex as a form of employment like any other, as well as the "oldest profession"

(Nagle 1997; Alexander 1997; Jeffreys 2011). However, the research that informs this essay goes beyond this polarized (predominantly Global North) feminist debate, which presents sex workers as either vulnerable victims or active agents. Kamala Kempadoo (2001, 37) cautions against the "reduction of prostitution to masculine violence and sexual slavery" as this is inadequate when trying to capture the varied lived experiences of women of color who sell sex. Such framings limit the debate to questions of choice and consent rather than locating sex work within the broader context of livelihoods, relationships, and everyday lives. This approach is particularly unhelpful when trying to understand the realities of African sex workers. Instead Mgbako and Smith (2011) call for a more nuanced approach; one that transcends the victim/agent dichotomy while acknowledging the complexities of sex workers' lives.

Unfortunately there is little African feminist theory on sex work (Krüger 2004, 142). However, theories produced by African feminist scholars such as Chi Mgbako (2016) and Sylvia Tamale (2008, 2011) provide useful starting points. For instance, Tamale's (2011, 147) study of sex work and sexuality in contemporary Uganda reveals some of the hidden complexities regarding sex workers' "erotic sexuality, gender power imbalances and control of women's bodies." According to Tamale, the femininity that Ugandan sex workers perform is "one of defiance and agency; one mostly driven by economic survival but which subverts and parodies patriarchy" (157). As her research demonstrates, the very nature of sex work flouts hegemonic notions of women's sexual pleasure and penetrative sex. This speaks directly to women's bodily autonomy and sexual agency. Tamale goes on to assert that because sex work offers possibilities for economic and sexual liberation, African feminists should use the gender and sexuality analysis of sex work to draft a progressive continental agenda. Furthermore, she proposes that the campaign for the decriminalization of sex work be launched within feminist movements as a subversive force against heteropatriarchal control and oppression over women's bodies.

How African Sex Workers Identify with Feminism

In both studies I employed a Feminist Participatory Action Research (FPAR) approach. I joined AWAKE!'s weekly meetings to discuss literature on various strands of feminism and their social implications, specifically in relation to African sex workers' lives. Group members received diaries to reflect on these ideas. We also robustly engaged in contemporary feminist debates, such as the omission of Maya Angelou's sex work past in her obituary, and hooks's reference to Beyoncé Knowles as an "anti-feminist—that is a terrorist" to young Black women's minds (Diaz 2014). As AWAKE! grew confident in its self-identification as a feminist group, members started attending public lectures and privately meeting with visiting postcolonial feminist scholars, such as Nivedita Menon and Chandra Mohanty. Through this collective learning, members came to the realization that being an African and a sex worker did not exclude them from feminism, and that actually in certain embodiments these identities intersected to inform each other.

The seventeen feminists in the follow-up study later affirmed these initial findings. These ASWA members represented sex worker movements and/or organizations from seven African countries: Ethiopia (Nikat), Kenya (Kenya Sex Workers Alliance, and the Bar Hostess Empowerment and Support Programme), Mozambique (Tiyane Vavasate), Nigeria (Precious Jewels), South Africa (Sisonke), Tanzania (Warembo Forum), and Uganda (Wonetha and Lady Mermaid Bureau). All members presented as Black Africans and strongly self-identified as feminists. They were male, female, or gender nonconforming. The FPAR methodology for this second study involved an arts-based workshop, which included body mapping and a continuum/positionality exercise, followed by a focus group discussion and semistructured interviews. Participant observation and daily audio diaries also provided insights, which guided my analysis of the body maps and transcripts.

Although participants in both studies were initially reluctant to give a precise definition of what it means to be an African sex worker feminist, many pointed to elements that could constitute such an identity. The following discussion examines what it means to be an *African*, a *sex worker*, and a *feminist*. The essay culminates with an intersectional analysis of what it means to be an African sex worker feminist.

To Be an African

In both studies most of the participants reported that many African cultures and religions deem sex work and feminism as either socially unacceptable or spiritually immoral. Please note that *African culture* is not used here with the blanket assumption that all cultures on the continent are homogeneous but rather to "highlight those aspects of cultural ideology that are widely shared among Africans," such as the ethos of *ubuntu* and the legacies of imperialism and colonialism (Tamale 2008, 49). When asked how they reconciled culture, sex work, and feminism, Cynthia, one of the AWAKE! members, replied, "Okay, in our feminist group . . . it also goes into our culture, in our Black people culture, because most Black men believe in patriarchy. That you have to be at home, I have to go out and work, and come back and bring back the money. And you just stay in the house—you know?" Some of the participants were perplexed as to why sex work was culturally unacceptable. According to them, sex has always held some form of monetary value in many African cultures. Frieda, a member of AWAKE!, recounts the ritual of virginity testing in Xhosa culture to illustrate this point: "I remember when I was a virgin we used to go fetch water from the river. And if you were a maiden at that time you walked around bare-breasted and just wore a cloth here at the bottom. But if it so happened that you broke the law and had sex with a boy, you would walk around naked with a spear. . . . And then the mothers would go and ask for damages money, their rights from the boy's house. So what money is it that they were asking for?" The ritual of virginity testing is practiced to discourage girls from having sex before marriage. When asked to clarify the connection she implied between the "damages money" and sex work, Frieda went on to explain, "That is what I'm saying—that the way I see it, we have been selling [sex] for a long time. It is just that they were not aware of it at the time that they were doing sex work. Because if your daughter is damaged, you wouldn't just let them walk around bare-breasted to demand at the boy's house. And the girl at that time becomes embarrassed, because now the whole village knows that you are no longer a virgin." The girl's atonement for losing her virginity is to walk naked in public, while the women in her village march her to the boy's home for "damages money." Frieda equates this "damages money" to payment for sex. The girl is also made to feel ashamed for having had sex. What is interesting is how this sense of bodily shame has become ingrained in social understandings of sex through such culturally sanctioned practices.

Some of the ASWA participants colored their body maps black in complexion in order to illustrate being Black Africans, while a few female-bodied participants also exaggerated the sketches of their buttocks on the body maps to accentuate the voluptuous figure often associated with an African woman's body. During the FPAR workshop I first asked them, "How does being an African manifest on your body?" One participant described her body map as such: "Uhm, this is breasts. This is big ass.

I don't know if you [can see but] . . . I tried to push it out." Larger buttocks, or steatopygia, are often perceived as the "physical manifestation of [B]lack women's hypersexuality" (Oyewùmi 2003, 37). Perhaps it was this notion of hypersexuality that the participants hinted at with these illustrations.

Some of the male-bodied ASWA feminists took issue with how African masculine ideals often clashed with their self-identification as sex worker feminists. Daniel explained his body map as follows: "The fact that as an African man—quote, unquote—the definition of an African man is a strong, muscled, dark [man]. . . . So you have to be tall, dark, handsome, and a provider, hence the big muscles, the fish and the machete thing. So that's the image of what an African man—that you should be that." He lamented the assumption that as a male sex worker he is often presumed to be either gay, transgender, or at least effeminate (that is, have long hair, wear miniskirts, and be covered in makeup). Although he occasionally indulged in such acts of beautification (as part of his sex work), Daniel stressed that this should not be misread as emasculating. He argued that instead, his disruption of African hegemonic ideals of manhood was a feminist political act. According to him, "The fact that sex workers are sex working is feminist enough. The fact that they have taken, you know—they have decided to be sex workers in sex work, given that the whole 'sex work, oh, it's un-African, blah, blah, blah, it's wrong, it's immoral' [is a feminist act]."

Another participant, Haadiyah, added that being a feminist was also considered by some religions to be a sin, just like being a sex worker. "I come from a Muslim family," she explained. "When it comes to [being] religious, it's a sin to be a sex worker, and again it is something very bad—like a sin—to be a feminist, because if I'm a woman I'm supposed to be married to a man. As a Muslim, as someone coming from a Muslim family." Many of the participants expressed a sense of emancipation for having gone against sociocultural norms and religious beliefs by being both sex workers and feminists. They pointed to social expectations that they refused to adhere to, such as being submissive to their husbands, as demonstrations of their feminism. Jolly, for instance, questioned why in certain African cultures wives are expected to kneel in front of their husbands and beg for things they need, even though they are supposed to be equal partners in marriage:

> I looked at the women who did what the society wanted and they were not
> in good condition. Being beaten up by their husbands. In our culture

here [in Kenya] you have to kneel down when asking [for] money to make your hair. You have to kneel down when you don't have money for soap. You know, you want salt [then] you all have to crawl down in front of a man to get just a few shillings to buy salt. I was like, no, no, no, no—it can't be like this. Why do I have to kneel down to beg? Yeah, when you are married to someone you have to be equals. You have to respect each other. The fact that he is the one who works and brings food on the table doesn't give him the powers, you know, that you have to kneel down and crawl over him, you know, for him to provide something.

At the age of seventeen, Jolly was asked to marry a man who had raped her. When she refused, her sister kicked her out of her home. She then left to work as a bar hostess but later turned to sex work because it generated a better income. For her to defy the cultural expectation of marrying the man who had raped and impregnated her, and then selling sex to support her baby, was empowering and liberating for her as an African sex worker feminist. Patricia McFadden (2003, 5) asserts that feminist choice needs to be (re)imagined as having the "courage to step out of the cages of cultural practices and values that not only oppress us, but also presume the terms of our 'freedom.'"

To Be a Sex Worker

For all participants, sex work is primarily a source of livelihood, as it affords them the opportunity to be self-employed. On their body maps, many of the ASWA feminists circled and labeled their genitals as banks to illustrate this point. Penelope noted, "It [her vagina] is a bank: an ATM. You see? So when I do business that's my bank. Because all the men that got to be attracted it's because they wanted to have sex. So I charge for them. I don't do it for free. I always tell my fellow sex workers that I get paid to come. I don't just come for free. I'm very expensive [laughs]." Her response also alludes to her own sexual pleasure derived from selling sex and evokes notions of Audre Lorde's (1982) "erotic as power." Sex-positive feminists such as Andrea Cornwall assert that promoting women's sexual agency actually builds on the feminist principle of erotic justice (Cornwall et al., 2013, 21). They suggest that "sexual pleasure as a feminist choice can be part of reclaiming women's agency" (3). However, Kempadoo (2001, 42) cautions that for transnational or postcolonial feminists to speak about sex work as also involving "women of color's sexual agency, needs, and desires is indeed tricky ground, for it is constantly in danger of sliding into, and reinforcing, the sexualisation of women of color." With that said, it is important to note that most of the participants described deriving some form of empowerment from doing sex work. "Because if I negotiate with a man, I tell a man I want a hundred dollars, and he gives me my money," claimed Jolly. She explained, "I decide what style of sex, how, the time, [and] I decide the place. How do you tell me that that kind of work is not empowering?"

A certain degree of courage is necessary to ask a client to pay for sexual services. Lisa Glazer (1997) recalls that in Lusaka (Zambia) in the 1970s, there was not much of this contemporary Western-style impersonal form of sex work. She notes that shantytown beer brewers sometimes had sex workers in their premises in order to attract male customers. "However, some of these 'prostitutes' who wanted money in exchange for sex were sometimes too shy to demand it" (151). Such conservative attitudes toward sex are common in most African communities, with more contemporary sex workers challenging them. Dudu, a member of AWAKE!, observes that society tends to place an exaggerated significance on sex when in essence it is merely a natural bodily function. According to her, this inflated notion of sex contributes to society's misconception of sex work:

> The other thing is that psychologically people tell themselves that sex is a *huuuuge* thing, just because we've said "sex work." I could say, "I'm finishing my supper, I'm going to go do my sex work with my husband." We are going to work—of course. We are going to do sex and I'm going to work. I mean, I'm going to do sex work with my husband. But because people's minds are like, "Ah—you are a woman," they think I can't stand on the road and say no to a man, that I can't choose who I want to have sex with.

Menon (2012, 180) affirms this observation and further argues, "We need to demystify 'sex'—it is only the mystification of sex by both patriarchal discourses and feminists that makes sex work appear to be 'a fate worse than death.'" Nonetheless one of the ASWA feminists indicated on her body map that having multiple sexual partners "bring[s] negative health impact[s]." There is plenty of evidence that STIs and HIV/AIDS are prevalent among sex workers, and even more so among sex workers in Africa. According to the Joint United Nations Programme on HIV/AIDS study of sixteen countries in sub-Saharan Africa in 2012, more than 37 percent of the surveyed sex workers (across genders) were living with HIV (UNAIDS 2014). Inasmuch as selling sex can be economically viable, sexually liberating, and empowering, it can also have negative and even fatal implications for one's sexual health.

To Be a Feminist

Participants acknowledged that defining feminism or what it means to be a feminist—let alone an African sex worker feminist—was difficult because current understandings of feminism are largely informed by Global North scholarship. Hence many objected to a single scholarly definition of feminism, which they felt was removed from their realities as African sex worker feminists. Daniel, for instance, explained, "The definition of feminism, because already in the larger African context, the larger discussion about feminism is that it has been largely guided by . . . a white model of feminism—an American-European, that kind of feminism." He asked, "Do we even have a word for 'feminism' in any African language?" However, he does not believe that feminism did not exist in Africa prior to colonization. Indeed many AWAKE! and ASWA feminists attested to having been feminists long before reading any book or attending any workshop about feminism. For them, feminism was not so much a foreign concept as a foreign term. In addition, participants strongly felt that they should be allowed to theorize for themselves a form of feminism that resonated with their lived realities. Hence they vehemently rejected the notion of a universal textbook definition of feminism. Jolly maintained, "We should not all have the same definition of feminism. No, no, no, no, no. The way they understand feminism it is their own. Let them change or let them not change, we don't care. But let them allow us to think, you know, and understand feminism the way we want. Or the way we know it should be. It's not about the definition that is in the books, because I never went to school to study feminism, but I understand what feminism is."

Many of the participants were able to draw correlations between sex work and feminism. Rose even argued that being a sex worker intrinsically made her a feminist: "For me I'd say feminism is sex work. . . . If a person knows who a sex worker is, a sex worker is a best definition of feminism. Because . . . like [another participant] was saying, our society tells you what a woman should do, what a woman should wear. You're supposed to get married and have one husband, you know, have children. A sex worker is the opposite of that. We fit in the society by force." The participants all agreed that feminism was not merely an identity but also something one does and lives by. Therefore advocating and lobbying for sex workers' rights was highlighted as a demonstration of one's activism and, by extension, evidence of one's feminism. According to Amina Mama (2007), early African feminisms were informed by activism, and political action was essentially combined with intellectual work. She explains, however, that the connection between feminist activism and feminist scholarship in African contexts has been compromised by the development of the "Western-style separation between thought and action" (154). For the participants, however, the two can never be divorced from each other, as ASWA member Anita explained: "I consider myself as a feminist. . . . Yeah, because I fight for the rights of others. And I myself, I'm an activist in the women's movement. So I consider myself as a feminist."

During the continuum exercise, many of the ASWA feminists positioned themselves in strong agreement with the statement "Feminism impacts on my sex work." When asked to explain her positionality, Amaka of ASWA explained how being a feminist emboldened her to be assertive in her sex work when clients tried to demand services she was not willing to offer: "Why I strongly agree is because as a sex worker in Africa I will be able to tell a man, 'Although you are paying me, I don't want this' or 'Because you are paying me it shouldn't make me do whatever you want. I do what I want. If you know you cannot cope with it you can go.'" Even though "most of them [clients] they get very very angry" when she refuses them certain services, Amaka claims she never relents. That is how feminism informs her sex work; she would rather lose clients and their money than compromise herself. However, even though most participants affirmed that feminism informs their sex work, some expressed that the two could at times be antagonistic. One participant, Onko, positioned himself in the *neutral* middle of the continuum. When asked why, he replied:

> Uhmm . . . because . . . sometimes because of circumstances and different situations and yeah—at work *neh* [right]? You're a sex worker and you're at work, and for some reasons your feminism standards, your feminism understanding at that particular time will not work for you. I'm not saying it's right, right? But I'm saying you've been here at a hotspot for the whole night, it's a winter cold, very winter cold. And you know, you've not seen one client, and then one client comes, but you're, you know? That situation—I must pay rent, I must do this-this, so you end up doing something. . . . Yeah.

He acknowledged the challenges of realistically living up to feminist ideals when doing sex work. This demonstrates the constant (re)negotiation with both patriarchy and feminism that African sex worker feminists often have to engage and contend. With that said, it is important to note that no one stood on the *strongly disagree* end of the continuum.

To Be an African Sex Worker Feminist

All in all I was interested in learning how the participants reconciled the intersectionalities of being an *African*, a *sex worker*, and a *feminist* within the same embodiment and varying social dimensions. One of the participants, Daughtie, explained:

> But for me, feminism is not like a different element of the person who you are. . . . And for me, I'm always just aware that whenever I take particular positions and people might think, "This is just an angry bitter woman," I'm not. I'm just, uhm, being very political because everything about being a young, Black, African woman who is a sex worker living with HIV, single parent, is political. All those definitions of me are political, and that's why I make a conscious awareness decision to actually affirm myself as a feminist.

For her, being an African sex worker feminist does not mean ascribing to one particular type of identity but rather simultaneously embodying and occupying multiple intersecting political spaces. Unfortunately, as mentioned earlier, these nuances and complexities are often missed when trying to understand sex work within the African context. Daughtie continued:

> And so, I just—I feel as if, uhm, right-wing feminists have decided to take the extreme. And I don't. Our world is not a world of extremes. There are so many gray and pink lines in between and we cross them more often than ever. . . . There is so much in between here, and there is so much of our struggle in between addressing violence on sex workers, addressing, uhm, stigma and discrimination of sex workers from and in many multiple levels. We're talking from the self, to the individual, to the family, community, societal—before we even get talking at the national level.

This is the dilemma faced by African sex worker feminists who are often forced to reside either in the pro– or anti–sex work camp, even when their lived experiences speak to both sides. The participants made repeated appeals for fellow feminists to start engaging more concretely with their realities. And as Onko reminds us, we live in a racially defined and class-based society: "The hustle that we Black African sex workers would face on the road or on the street is different to what my fellow white sister who is a sex worker faces in an escort house where she is given a medical aid and everything else that she needs. And where she has a madam who understands that she needs to be taken care of in order for her business to continue, right? But we at times as Black African sex workers, we are on the streets, and we're trying to hustle." Mama (2007, 152) argues that the major contribution to feminist epistemology of those based in the Global South is the "insistence on being constantly alert to the politics of location and diversities of class, race, culture, sexuality and so on." African sex worker feminists have much to teach us about this.

Conclusion

This essay has demonstrated that being an African, a sex worker, and a feminist may not be as incongruent as is often assumed. In fact in certain embodiments, the three identities can inform each other. For the participants in both studies, being an African means embodying a particular type of physique, most likely a dark-skinned complexion or a curvaceous figure (if one is a woman). It means sharing a colonial history of white oppression and a struggle for liberation. It means ascribing to ideologies of social cohesion and togetherness, such as *ubuntu*, while defying those sociocultural norms that dehumanize. All participants agreed that selling sex was a viable livelihood strategy for them, as it provided some degree of economic survival and independence. The work comes with the need to beautify oneself in order to be able to attract clients. It is about having the courage to ask for money in exchange for sex. It is also about getting paid to be sexually aroused. However, sex work also comes with its own dangers, such as the high risk of contracting STIs, namely HIV/AIDS. Being a feminist means being empowered and having agency to make informed choices. As feminists, the participants fight against heteropatriarchy and other forms of social injustice, and they also engage in activism and movement building. However, living up to feminist ideals all the time (and in every given situation) is not always feasible; considering the varied lived realities, and constraining and oppressive social contexts.

So what does it mean to be an African sex worker feminist? It means embodying a political identity that intersects with multiple social dimensions. It is about constantly (re)negotiating with both patriarchy and feminism. It is about having to manage the tensions of pro– and anti–sex work extremists who claim to know what is best. It is also about finding a language of feminism that speaks most honestly to the nuances of selling sex in Africa. It is therefore important for other feminists (especially those who are pro– and anti–sex work) to be aware of the intersectionalities (and contradictions) that African sex worker feminists embody, as this will allow for engagements that are far more constructive.

African sex worker feminists demonstrate that feminist scholarship has to be informed by our lived experiences, complex realities, and political agendas, and in so doing result in collective solidarity and activism. They encourage us to challenge and destabilize heteropatriarchy by brazenly flouting gender and sexual expectations. They dare us to explore our sexualities and unashamedly use our bodies to support our livelihoods. These are some of the lessons that African sex workers can teach us about feminism. In return, African sex worker feminists can gain the confidence that comes with self-identifying as feminists, which instills assertiveness in sex work and when engaging in volatile feminist spaces. I trust this essay will enable us to start learning from one another and strengthen the solidarity between sex worker feminists and other feminists.

. . . .

Ntokozo Yingwana is a researcher and Ph.D. candidate with the African Centre for Migration and Society at the University of Witwatersrand. Yingwana identifies as an African feminist scholar-activist; focusing on gender, sexuality, and sex worker rights' activism on the continent. She serves on the board of the Sex Workers Education and Advocacy Taskforce.

Notes

1   AWAKE! strategically engaged in such feminist spaces as a means of lobbying for sex workers' human rights across various social justice movements. However, most feminists and women's groups on the African continent fail to take into consideration sex workers' struggles for human rights in their own activism and organizing (Mgbako 2016).

2   In this essay, I use the participants' first names or pseudonyms to protect their identities.

Works Cited

Adichie, Chimamanda Ngozi. 2013. "We Should All Be Feminists." YouTube, April 12. https://www.youtube.com/watch?v=hg3umXU_qWc&feature=youtu.be.

Akin-Aina, Sinmi. 2011. "Beyond an Epistemology of Bread, Butter, Culture and Power: Mapping the African Feminist Movement." *Nokoko* 2: 65–89.

Alexander, Priscilla. 1997. "Feminism, Sex Workers and Human Rights." In *Whores and Other Feminists*, edited by Jill Nagle, 83–97. New York: Routledge.

ASWA. N.d. "What Is ASWA: Vision." Accessed December 7, 2017. http://aswaalliance.org/about2/.

Cornwall, Andrea, Kate Hawkins, and Susie Jolly, eds. 2013. *Women, Sexuality, and the Political Power of Pleasure.* London: Zed Books.

Diaz, Evelyn. 2014. "Bell Hooks Calls Beyoncé a 'Terrorist.'" BET, May 7. http://www.bet.com/news/celebrities/2014/05/07/bell-hooks-calls-beyonce-a-terrorist.html.

Ditmore, Melissa, Antonia Levy, and Alys Willman. 2010. *Sex Work Matters: Exploring Money, Power and Intimacy in the Sex Industry.* London: Zed Books.

Glazer, Lisa M. 1997. "Alcohol and Politics in Urban Zambia: The Intersection of Gender and Class." In *African Feminism: The Politics of Survival in Sub-Saharan Africa*, edited by Gwendolyn Mikell, 142–58. Philadelphia: University of Pennsylvania Press.

hooks, bell. 2000. *Feminism Is for Everybody: Passionate Politics.* Cambridge, MA: South End Press.

Jeffreys, Elena. 2011. "Why Feminists Should Listen to Sex Workers." *The Scavenger*, June 10. http://www.thescavenger.net/feminism-a-pop-culture-sp-9560/feminism-a-pop-culture/732-why-feminists-should-listen-to-sex-workers.html.

Kempadoo, Kamala. 2001. "Women of Color and the Global Sex Trade: Transnational Feminist Perspectives." *Meridians: Feminism, Race, Transnationalism* 1, no. 2: 28–51.

Krüger, Rosaan. 2004. "Sex Work from a Feminist Perspective: A Visit to the Jordan Case." *South African Journal of Human Rights* 22, no. 1: 138–50.

Leigh, Carol (aka Scarlot Harlot). 1997. "Inventing Sex Work." In *Whores and Other Feminists*, edited by Jill Nagle, 223–32. New York: Routledge.

Lewis, Desiree. 2001. "African Feminisms." *Agenda* 50: 4–10.

Lorde, Audre. 1982. "Uses of the Erotic: The Erotic as Power." In *Sister Outsider: Essays and Speeches*, 53–59. New York: Crossing Press.

MacKinnon, Catharine. 2011. "Trafficking, Prostitution, and Inequality." *Harvard Civil Rights–Civil Liberties Law Review* 46, no. 2: 271–309.

Mama, Amina. 2007. "Critical Connections: Feminist Studies in African Contexts." In *Feminisms in Development: Contradictions, Contestations and Challenges*, edited by Andrea Cornwall, Elizabeth Harrison, and Ann Whitehead, 150–60. New York: Zed Books.

McFadden, Patricia. 2003. "Sexual Pleasure as Feminist Choice." *Feminist Africa* 2: 1–8.

Menon, Nivedita. 2012. *Seeing Like a Feminist.* New Delhi: Penguin Books.

Mgbako, Chi A. 2016. *To Live Freely in This World: Sex Worker Activism in Africa.* New York: NYU Press.

Mgbako, Chi A., and Laura A. Smith. 2011. "Sex Work and Human Rights in Africa." *Fordham International Law Journal* 33, no. 4: 1178–220.

Nagle, Jill. 1997. Introduction to *Whores and Other Feminists*, edited by Jill Nagle, 13–33. New York: Routledge.

Ndlovu, Hlengiwe. 2017. "Womxn's Bodies Reclaiming the Picket Line: The 'Nude' Protest During #FeesMustFall." *Agenda* 31, nos. 3–4: 68–77.

NSWP. N.d. "African Sex Worker Conference and Formation of ASWA." Accessed December 7, 2017. http://www.nswp.org/timeline/event/african-sex-worker -conference-and-formation-aswa.

Oyewùmi, Oyèrònké. 2003. "The White Woman's Burden: African Women in Western Feminist Discourse." In *African Women and Feminism: Reflecting on the Politics of Sister-hood*, edited by Oyèrònké Oyewùmi, 25–43. Trenton, NJ: Africa World Press.

Richter, Marlise. 2012. "Sex Work as a Test Case for African Feminism." *BUWA! A Journal on African Women's Experiences* 2, no. 1: 62–69.

Tamale, Sylvia. 2008. "The Right to Culture and the Culture of Rights: A Critical Perspective on Women's Sexual Rights in Africa." *Feminist Legal Studies* 16, no. 1: 47–69.

Tamale, Sylvia. 2011. "Paradoxes of Sex Work and Sexuality in Modern-Day Uganda." In *African Sexualities: A Reader*, edited by Sylvia Tamale, 145–73. Cape Town: Pamba-zuka Press.

UNAIDS. 2014. *The Gap Report*. Geneva: UNAIDS. July 16. http://www.unaids.org/en /resources/documents/2014/20140716_UNAIDS_gap_report.

Callan Swaim-Fox

....

Decade for Women Information Resources #5
Images of Nairobi, Reflections and Follow-Up,
International Women's Tribune Center

After originally declaring 1975 "International Women's Year," concerns over the strategic global challenges facing women led the United Nations to expand the period, creating the "United Nations Decade for Women" from 1975 to 1985. Throughout this time, sundry organizations, communities, and nations joined forces with the UN to organize, direct energy and resources toward women's struggles, and unite in global conferences in Mexico City and Copenhagen (United Nations 1985, 3). From the beginning, nongovernmental organizations (NGOs) were instrumental in this work and after the first International Conference of Women in 1975, global NGOs sought to stay connected in their individual efforts (Walker 2004, 91–92). Thus, a group of women founded the International Women's Tribune Center (IWTC) to provide resources, toolkits, and methods of connecting networks of global activists (Walker 2004, 91–92). By 1985, the IWTC partnered with the UN to provide resources for the third and culminating International Women's Conference and NGO Forum, which took place in Nairobi, Kenya (Walker 2004, 93).

The Conference and Forum of July 1985 brought women from around the world to discuss, theorize, present, and reimagine solutions to women's issues. Though the original plan was to reflect upon the actions taken toward the goals set for the previous decade, the conference and forum brought up many new ideas and methods for reaching solutions, notably

MERIDIANS · feminism, race, transnationalism   17:2 November 2018
DOI: 10.1215/15366936-7176450 © 2018 Smith College

new uses of technology and media (Okello-Orlale 2006, 49–50). The various discussions led the participants to create a concrete list of further actions to enact in their communities called the "Forward Looking Strategies for the Advancement of Women Towards the Year 2000" (Walker 2004, 95–96). Furthermore, the conference brought issues that had previously been underrepresented or ignored in the women's movement to the forefront; for the first time in a UN meeting, the concerns of lesbian women were discussed.

Another underrepresented issue addressed in the conference were challenges specific to African women. The location of the conference in 1985 not only allowed African women to play a key role in organizing the conference, forum, and activities surrounding it, but the accessibility of the location enabled women from many African nations to attend the conference and lead activities and workshops (NGO Committee 1985, 2). Through this, African feminists were able to express their concerns to the wider community and connect with both national and international activists and groups. These connections led to organization-building after the conference and challenged other attendees' often stereotypical, colonial, and/or racist conceptions of African women and their experiences.

The following excerpts come from a document created by the IWTC a year after the 1985 Conference and Forum. They present the main ideas and discussions of the Nairobi conference to the global network fighting for women's rights. The IWTC deliberately used images and drawings for accessibility, promoting the main takeaways of the conference to a wider audience (Walker 2004, 93). Beyond illustrating the core ideas, the pamphlet also provides a view of contemporaneous reactions to the meeting. Together, these excerpts of the document allow us to ponder the effects of the conference on both African and global feminisms. They also challenge individuals to consider the gains achieved and struggles remaining since the meeting in 1985. All images are from the Decade for Women Information Resources #5: Images of Nairobi, July 1986, International Women's Tribune Centre. From the International Women's Tribune Centre Records, Sophia Smith Collection, Smith College (Northampton, Massachusetts).

Callan Swaim-Fox is an undergraduate student studying History, Women and Gender Studies, and Archival Studies at Smith College. She is originally from Cleveland Heights, Ohio, and aspires to illuminate the stories of marginalized people throughout history in her future career.

Works Cited

NGO Committee. 1985. "From Mexico to Nairobi." *NGO News*. Smith College Special Collections, International Women's Tribune Centre Records, 1970–2000, MS 373.

Okello-Orlale, Rosemary. 2006. "Looking Back and Ahead: The Media and the Struggle for Gender Equality after the Nairobi UN Women's Conference." *Agenda: Empowering Women for Gender Equity* 69: 48–56. http://www.jstor.org/stable /4066812.

United Nations Commission on the Status of Women. 1985. "The State of the World's Women, 1985: World Conference to Review and Appraise the Achievements of the United Nations Decade for Women: Equality, Development and Peace, Nairobi, Kenya, July 15–26, 1985." Plymouth, England: New International Publications.

Walker, Anne S. 2004. "The International Women's Tribune Centre: Expanding the Struggle for Women's Rights at the UN." In *Developing Power: How Women Transformed International Development*, edited by Arvonne S. Fraser and Irene Tinker, 90–102. New York: Feminist Press.

DECADE FOR WOMEN
INFORMATION RESOURCES

#5

IMAGES of NAIROBI

Reflections & FOLLOW-UP

JULY 1986

PREPARED BY THE INTERNATIONAL WOMEN'S TRIBUNE CENTRE,
777 UNITED NATIONS PLAZA, NEW YORK, NY 10017, USA.

IMAGES OF NAIROBI

In July, 1985, more than 17,000 women converged at Nairobi, Kenya, to participate in the culminating conferences of the United Nations Decade for Women (1976-1985).

It was the third and final gathering to celebrate what began as a year for women, (U.N. International Women's Year, 1975), and developed into the U.N. Decade for Women.

3

...We came singly and in groups. We were women of all ages, all colours and callings. We were women from different economic, social and political systems and we came from world capitals as well as small villages...

nairobi facts
in a nutshell...

WORLD CONFERENCE:

* Kenyatta Conference Centre, July 15-26, 1985
  157 Member States represented, also representatives of UN agencies, inter-governmental organizations, NGOs and national liberation movements.
* 75% of delegates were women..
* Women headed 85 of the 157 delegations.

FORUM '85:

* University of Nairobi, July 10-19, 1985
  15,000 women representing 150 countries
  60% from Third World countries
* Open to all
* Organized by NGO Planning Committee representing more than 60 International NGOs, with committees in New York, Geneva, Vienna and Nairobi.

6

The bulletin board adjacent to the information desk at the main campus of the University of Nairobi listed each day's scheduled workshops. More than 1200 workshops were held during the 10 days of the FORUM. 315 on Development; 215 on Equality; 147 on Peace; 139 on Health; 90 on Employment; 73 on Education. Other workshops focused on a diversity of issues including media, young women and girls, older women, disabled women, refugees and migrants, networking, science and technology, energy and environment, and many more. Special events were organized around specific themes, including women and peace (Peace Tent), appropriate technology for women (Tech and Tools), films and videos by, for and about women (Film Forum), women and religion (Karibu), and a kaleidoscope of cultural activities .

The official NGO Planning Committee report on FORUM '85 is available from: IWTC, 777 United Nations Plaza, New York, NY 10017.

7

THE PEACE TENT

The 3 striped tents that formed the centrally located complex known as The Peace Tent, were an important feature of FORUM '85. They were a safety valve and focal point for some of the more hotly contested and difficult global issues under discussion in Nairobi, and for many, became symbols of the spirit of the FORUM itself. The grassy area around the tents also served as a place for groups to gather, and the oversized patchwork globe at the entrance to the main tent set the tone with its declaration: "As a woman I have no country. My country is the whole world."

For more information on The Peace Tent and any future actions planned, contact:

Feminists International for Peace and Food (FIPF)
c/o F. Farenthold
2100 Travis Street
Suite 1203
Houston, TX 77002, USA

Women in Europe who were involved with The Peace Tent in Nairobi, are planning to hold "Peace Tents" in different countries in Europe during the summer of 1986. Other women are involved in organizing The Great Peace Journey, a campaign to challenge governments on their commitment to peace. After a successful effort in Europe in 1985, the Peace Journey will focus, during 1986, on Africa, Asia, Australia, North and South and Central America. To become involved in your area, contact: The Great Peace Journey, International Secretariat, P.O. Box 228, S-75104 Uppsala, Sweden

Information sources include: Forum '85 Final Report: Nairobi, Kenya (NGO Planning Committee); Decade Postdate (IWTC); FIPF; The Great Peace Journey poster.

8

RACISM

Problems of racism are a constant topic of discussion and dialogue within the women's movement globally. Targets of racism vary from country to country, but effects are amazingly similar. Take for instance the area of income. In the U.S., blacks are more than twice as likely to have incomes below the poverty line than whites; in Australia, aboriginal households receive 60% of the income of white households; in the U.K., 16% of blacks compared with 9% of whites live in poverty; and in New Zealand, Maoris are four times as likely to be unemployed as non-Maoris. (From New Internationalist, October 1983)

For women, throughout the Decade, combatting racism in society as well as within the women's movement has been an issue of primary concern. During the Decade we came to understand that although we may share a bond in being oppressed first as women, we need also to examine the ways in which we all have accepted and used racist biases and assumptions to the detriment of other women. The recognition of differences - between women of color and white women, and among women of color - is the key. All women, and white women in particular, need to explore these differences, not deny them. Indeed, it is the denial - ignorance and ignoring of differences - which is racist. (ISIS, #21)

The Women's Coalition for Nairobi, a diverse, multi-racial coalition of women from women's, labor, peace, civic, religious and political organizations in the United States, was one group that came to Forum '85 to raise and discuss issues of racism with women from around the world. They presented important perspectives on the situation of black women in the United States. For instance:

AND THEY SHALL BEAT THEIR POTS AND PANS INTO PRINTING PRESSES

AND WEAVE THEIR CLOTH INTO PROTEST BANNERS

Women Unite!

NATIONS OF WOMEN SHALL LIFT UP THEIR VOICES WITH NATIONS OF OTHER WOMEN

NEITHER SHALL THEY ACCEPT DISCRIMINATION ANY MORE.
— MARY CHAGNON

IWTC poster, 1985

43

RACISM

In America, while the number of single female households has grown in the population at large, the number is most pronounced among blacks. By 1980, nearly one-half of all black families were headed by women, and the proportion is climbing. With infrequent exceptions, this situation is equated with poverty and reflects the dual burden of race and gender discrimination. More than half of those families live below the poverty line.

In workshops and interviews, the Women's Coalition for Nairobi presented the view that "women who fight against oppression and for equality must fight racism, classism, fascism and join in solidarity with oppressed people worldwide."

Other initiatives by women, working in coalition to combat racism, are surfacing in different regions. One example is the coalition of indigenous women, including Native Americans and Aboriginals who are working together on both analysis of and action against the effects of racism on the economic, social and political involvement of indigenous women. Latin American women are taking up issues of the effects of racism on black and Indian women in countries throughout the region. As one discussion at the 2nd Latin American and Caribbean Feminist meeting (Peru, 1983) pointed out: Racial discrimination goes together with economic exploitation and social and political subjugation. To be a woman from a group encountering racial discrimination is to be triply exploited.

From each country and culture that women confront racism, the important perspective they bring is that racism cannot be considered separately from other inequities--classism, sexism, imperialism, etc.--and that recognizing and working through our differences might be the first step toward building forceful coalitions to work for change.

Information from: "Upfront;" "Forum '85;" "Women for Racial and Economic Equality (WREE);" "VIVA;" "The Effects of Racism and Militarization on Women's Equality," The Women's Coalition for Nairobi.

WRITE:

UPFRONT - A Black Woman's Newspaper
P.O. Box 2293
Washington, D.C. 20013 USA

International Resource Network of Women of African Descent
159-00 Riverside Drive
Suite 905A
New York, NY 10032 USA

Indigenous Women's Rights
World Council of Indigenous People
555 King Edward Ave.
Ottawa, Ontario, Canada

African Association of Women
for Research and Development (AAWORD)
Boite Postal 3304
Dakar, Senegal

Pax Romana
c/o Linda Wirth
PO Box 85
1211 Geneva 20 Switzerland

READ:

THE EFFECTS OF RACISM AND MILITARIZATION ON WOMEN'S EQUALITY. Available from: The Women's Coalition for Nairobi, 130 E. 16th St., New York, NY 10003 USA.

44

SEXUALITY

One of the challenges of the UN Decade for Women has been for women to claim their right to sexuality and sexual freedom. There are a broad range of concerns related to sexuality that women are addressing, ranging from concerns about reproduction and control over our own bodies, to the rights of lesbians. These issues were addressed frankly and openly in numerous workshops during the 10 days of Forum '85.

For many African women, the issue of female circumcision and their determination to define and respond to the complexity of the problem, has been of primary concern. At Forum '85, women from the Sudan, Zambia, Benin, Nigeria, Liberia, Burkina Faso, Mali, Togo, Ghana, Senegal and Egypt described the current realities related to female circumcision in their countries and explained why many women still want to be circumcised. They pointed out that in societies where a woman's survival depends upon being married, it is not possible to take the risk of not being circumcised, since uncircumcised women may have a more difficult time finding a husband.

Women at Forum '85 speaking out on female circumcision, many of whom were part of the Inter-African Committee, emphasized that a great deal of public education needs to be carried out in the countries in which female circumcision is practised and that "Men and women can understand that the practice should be stopped if they can learn that it can lead to women becoming sick and infertile, and that this pain does not have to be accepted as part of 'being a woman'".

In addressing family planning and reproductive policies, women have begun to separate the question of sexual freedom and reproduction, posing the issue clearly as one of control over our own bodies. That effort now has to address new technologies such as invitro fertilization, genetic engineering and sex determinism. In the Asian Women's Research and Action Network report, the Malaysian representative wrote, "An · example of the state dictating women's (reproductive) role is the 70 million population policy announced by the Prime Minister whereby women are urged to conceive 5 children each to meet the projected population in 115 years' time. The official rationale is that Malaysia must adopt a heavy industrialization policy to compete with Korea and Japan...A major criticism against this policy deals with the derogatory and utilitarian manner in which women are treated - women are not given control over their bodies. The patriarchal state has emphasized the reproductive role of women, therefore reinforcing their subordination."

The World Council of Churches sponsored a two-year study project, the results of which were presented at Forum '85, comparing the teachings of different religions about women's sexuality and bodily functions such as menarche, menstruation, contraception, pregnancy, birthing, lactation and menopause. "The study was conceived on the basis of a common conviction among some women from different religious traditions that religious views, teachings and practices--related to women--play a significant part in determining their status and role in

51

SEXUALITY

society," said Maria Assad.

The events that took place in July 1985 at both the governmental and non-governmental meetings were notable on many fronts, not the least of which were some of the progressive statements made by governmental delegates to the United Nations conference. In relation to sexuality, the statement made by the head of the Netherlands delegation, Ms. A. Kappeyne van de Coppello, which included reference to the rights of lesbians marked the first time such a statement was made at a United Nations meeting. She said, "Among the many different groups of women who are attending this Conference, lesbian women are in a special position...(and) suffer twice as much in many parts of the world. Repression goes so far that it appears that as a group they do not exist at all. We can regard the fact that lesbian women are beginning to be visible and are articulating their claims to equal treatment as a hopeful sign in the struggle for equal rights and opportunities in which lesbian women share."

Charlotte Bunch, of the International Feminist Networking Coordination Project, has pointed out that, "Lesbians everywhere in the world work on every issue," and the lesbian workshops in Nairobi represented the breadth of their concerns. Lesbians have helped to define violence against women as a male attempt at ownership of women, not a product of human nature or sexual passion. Likewise, lesbians have led the way in challenging domestic violence programmes that define their goal as keeping families together, arguing that this approach may not be in the best interests of women victims of abuse. A priority for lesbians working internationally has been to connect lesbianism with other issues.

Information from: WIN News; "Connexions"; "New World Outlook"; "Listen Real Loud"; "Women's Global Network on Reproductive Rights."

WRITE:

Feminist International Network of Resistance to Reproductive and Genetic Engineering
Box 571,
Winchester, MA 01890 USA

or

Box 583, London NW3 1RQ, England

International Lesbian Information Service, Centre Femmes
5 Bd St., Georges
1205 Geneva, Switzerland

World Council of Churches
Sub-Unit on Women in Church and Society
150 route de Ferney
CH1211 Geneva 20, Switzerland

Inter-African Committee
Babiker Badri Foundation
Ahfad University College for Women
Omdurman, Sudan

Women's Global Network on Reproductive Rights, Postbus 4098
1009 AB Amsterdam, Netherlands

READ:

GLOBAL LESBIANISM I AND II, special issues of Connexions magazine. Available from: People's Translation Service, 4228 Telegraph Av., Oakland, California 94690, USA.

52

The Daily Nation, Nairobi, Kenya, July 24, 1985.   Adapted by IWTC

"Oh! I almost forgot to mention dear. Today at the Forum, we agreed to replace all you men in government positions with women. Hope you don't mind..."

The Sunday Nation, Nairobi, Kenya, July 14, 1985.   Adapted by IWTC

"My God! They know! What'll we do now?"

60

Abosede George

. . . .

Saving Nigerian Girls
A Critical Reflection on Girl-Saving Campaigns in the Colonial and Neoliberal Eras

Abstract: This essay discusses girl-saving campaigns in Nigerian history, focusing on the two that have been most extensively documented: the girl hawker project of the early twentieth century, which climaxed with the 1943 passage of the first hawking ban in Nigeria, and the #BringBackOurGirls campaign, which started in 2014 and is still ongoing. Though separated by time and space, in order to inspire salvationist impulses in their respective audiences both campaigns have relied on a gendered notion of imperilment that centers the image of the youthful female body threatened by sexual violence from male aggressors. Yet through its reliance on certain restrictions, gendered and otherwise, the portrait of the vulnerable girl that campaigners outline inadvertently prompts disidentifications as well.

Driving across Lagos's Third Mainland Bridge with some friends in the middle of January 2017, I found myself involved in a debate of sorts. Three of us believed that one thousand days earlier, the insurgent group Boko Haram had abducted 276 adolescent girls from the northeastern Nigerian town of Chibok, and we wanted to discuss matters extending from that basic starting point. Vee, the fourth passenger in our car, insisted that no such event had ever taken place.[1] In her view, the high level of ethnic suspicion in the country, the incredible persistence of the Chibok story three years after it came to global attention, and the apparent silence of the few girls who had been released from Boko Haram strongholds, all supported a conspiracy theory that the abduction had never actually happened. The

MERIDIANS · feminism, race, transnationalism   17:2 November 2018
DOI: 10.1215/15366936-7176461 © 2018 Smith College

event, she insisted, had to be a piece of propaganda that was created to serve the interests of unknown political actors. It was all, as Vee put it, "just politics."

What did it mean to say that the abduction of 276 schoolgirls, on which a global salvationist campaign to #BringBackOurGirls had been built, was "just politics"? Was her statement a brand of denialism? The central denial story in the case of the missing Chibok girls concerned President Goodluck Jonathan, who infamously dragged his feet on launching a rescue mission in the belief that the abduction had been orchestrated by his regime's political enemies. Certainly Vee's perspective reflected a widely shared culture of deep political suspicion that obtains in contemporary Nigeria. As our arguments intensified, it became clearer that Vee was also articulating a critique of the distinction between the Chibok girls and other missing persons in Nigeria, victims of Boko Haram or otherwise, who had not received anywhere near the same levels of domestic or international attention. Hers was a critique of a hierarchy of suffering that the girl-saving campaign fundamentally relied on. It is a critique that raises certain questions about girl-saving campaigns: Do girl-saving campaigns privilege particular forms of sexualized suffering? At what risks politically, and to what effect on girls? I would argue that girl-saving projects tend to reify a model of girlhood that constrains the full complexity and humanity of girls. By selecting out girls as targets of sexualized harm, they can have the effect of diminishing other forms of harm that girls may suffer or the harm experiences of those who are not girls.

This essay discusses girl-saving campaigns in Nigerian history, focusing on the two that have been most extensively documented. The earlier campaign, what I have referred to elsewhere as the girl hawker project, unfolded from the late 1920s through the 1940s, reaching a climax in 1943 with the passage of the first street-trading ban in Nigeria (George 2014). The current campaign, widely known as #BringBackOurGirls, was started in 2014 and three years later is still ongoing. Although these two girl-saving campaigns are separated by more than half a century and differ from each other in many ways, they share the commonality of occurring or having occurred in globalized contexts that required campaigners to simultaneously address proximate and distant audiences. The globalized context of the girl hawker project was early twentieth-century Lagos during a time of entrenched British colonial rule, while the twenty-first-century #BringBackOurGirls campaign took form on the internet during a time of globalized neoliberalism and Islamophobia.

Girls faced real and pressing dangers in both contexts. These dangers included but were not limited to being subjected to kidnapping, rape, sexual slavery, social marginalization, and the psychological trauma that accompanies all of these. These dangers compounded and complicated various forms of structural inequality based on gender, age, class, caste, citizenship, and other factors that would precede and outlast acute traumas. Antihawking activists, however, who sought to save working-class girl hawkers from danger in the city of Lagos, translated complex local realities into frameworks that would be legible and compelling to culturally distant and paternalist British colonial officials. The simplification that translating the antihawking message required provoked challenges to antihawking activists from culturally proximate yet critical neighbors. Similarly, contemporary campaign organizers who sought to compel a rescue mission fronted by the Nigerian national government also had to toggle between distant yet formidable international online publics and proximate and more critical yet disempowered neighbors.

Though separated by time and space, in order to inspire salvationist impulses in their respective audiences both campaigns relied on a gendered notion of imperilment that centers the image of the youthful female body threatened by sexual violence from male aggressors. The effects of this strategy on distant and proximate audiences were similar in both campaigns, with the more distant audiences being more receptive and the more proximate audiences being less so. But the similarities do not stop there. In both campaigns, proximate audiences ultimately pushed against the portrait of vulnerability that the campaigns relied on and the particularization of the figure of the girl as a peculiarly imperiled subject.

The details of the story of the Chibok girls are that on April 14, 2014, an insurgent group called Boko Haram abducted 276 secondary school girls who were preparing to take their West African senior school certificate exam in the town of Chibok in northeastern Nigeria. April 2014 was not the first time that Boko Haram had launched a mass raid. Two months earlier they had attacked a school, murdered the schoolboys they found there, and taken about fifty girls to their hideaways. There had been other raids besides these featuring attacks on and abductions of girls, boys, and adults. To the people of northeastern Nigeria, Boko Haram was a well-known threat. For days and then weeks after the abduction of the Chibok girls, there appeared to be no serious government response. Some parents of the kidnapped girls resorted to setting up their own search parties and tried to go after the insurgents and rescue their daughters themselves.

Their efforts were in vain. Days passed one after the other, until a couple of weeks had passed, and there was still no news of the girls and no official plan to go after them.

By the end of April, Nigerian women activists, using the power of social media, had dramatically amplified the cry of the Chibok parents. In their frustration with the official silence surrounding the abduction, Oby Ezek-wesili, a cofounder of Transparency International, and Hadiza Bala Usman, a pro-democracy activist, began tweeting the phrase BringBack-OurGirls to draw the internet's attention to what was happening in north-eastern Nigeria. These women were affiliated with the Nigerian human and civil rights organization Women for Peace and Justice, which has been one of the groups at the helm of the #BBOG campaign. Within a week of the first tweets, the phrase had been retweeted one million times. Nigerian activists, ordinary Nigerians online, Africans online, those in the diaspora, celebrity entertainers, world leaders, millions of people from all over the continent and around the world, all demanded that the Nigerian government Bring Back OUR Girls. Depending on who was tweeting or retweeting, there was in that four-word phrase a powerful statement of nationalism or universalism. For a moment, the abducted schoolgirls seemed to be claimed as everyone's girls.

When the Bring Back Our Girls hashtag was first launched in April 2014, the image that initially accompanied the slogan dramatized the theme of vulnerability in girlhood. The image was a strategically edited version of a photo that had been taken three years earlier in Guinea Bissau by Ami Vitale. Vitale stated that in her Guinea Bissau photographs, she sought to "tell a different story from the two narratives we (meaning non-Africans) so often hear from Africa, that of the horrors or that of the exotic."[2] Vitale's original photo is a full-color portrait of a girl looking out of a window frame. Her extensions are growing out and she wears bangles on both arms—a sure sign of care or leisure or conspicuous consumption that would be recognized by young girls around the world. Another girl stands nearby, behind her to the right. Farther in the background we can make out two or three more figures, all of whom appear to be bareheaded young people like the central girl. Are they friends, relatives, or schoolmates? Whoever they are, the picture suggests that the girl in the window is not alone. She is ensconced in networks of affect and affiliation.

The image that drew the world's attention to Chibok differed in several key ways. In the first place, the new image is a stark black-and-white photograph. The contrasts between the foreground and the background are heightened such that one's eyes are drawn to the brightest points, the girl's face and eyes, and away from the darkened areas where the other people are clustered. Furthermore, a single teardrop was added under her left eye to dispel any ambiguity about how she might be feeling. The hashtag that underlines her face, #BringBackOurGirls, could be read as a cry that she is sending out for the return of the missing girls. But much more likely, the new image positions her as one of the missing girls, dejected in her abduction, silent, and looking intently to the world for salvation from the hands of the Boko Haram kidnappers. Addressed to the internet, and therefore primarily international audiences, the face of the campaign invites the viewers to see themselves as saviors, whose actions might rescue the missing girls.

The historian Pamela Scully (2013, 21) has argued that the figure of the violated African woman has circulated as a trope in Western humanitarian circles since at least the eighteenth century. Despite or perhaps because of the familiarity of the image of the vulnerable and violated African woman, #BBOG's initial photographic campaign strategy worked. By the time the campaign logo had been changed to a simple crimson red background featuring bold white or black text, Vitale's photo—or rather the edited version of it—had done its job. The world had claimed the Chibok girls as OUR girls. More important, all the negative global attention had pushed the Nigerian government to finally heed the cries of the Chibok parents and articulate some sort of official plan of rescue.

Executing a rescue proved to be an intensely slow process.[3] One effect was that it proved difficult to sustain the initial mobilizing feeling of the girls being all of *our girls*. At one point Boko Haram released a video of a large group of girls, uniformly dressed in dark hijabs. In an era of intense Islamophobia, this gesture placed the sympathetic image of the familiar schoolgirl into a complicated relationship with a new image of homogeneous anonymous Muslim others. The challenge campaigners faced in maintaining a global focus on a rescue mission was reflected in negative attitudes toward the Chibok girls that emanated from both international and national publics. Although wealthy governments like the United States remained involved, offering technological and logistical support to the Nigerian government's search efforts, and neighboring nations like Cameroon and Niger, whose populations were also targeted by Boko Haram, saw several military successes against the group, the massive amount of attention and encouragement that millions of people across the continent and around the world had directed toward northeastern Nigeria, the town of Chibok, its girls, and its waiting parents steadily dissipated after weeks and months passed with no verifiable rescues.

Within Nigeria, signs of the limits of the uses of the vulnerability-centered campaign began to be displayed in the form of popular resentment toward the Chibok schoolgirls. Nigeria is a paragon of neoliberal governance, where households are accountable for their own water and electricity supplies, where transportation, healthcare, and education are supplied according to the pay-on-demand maxim, and where none of these basic social goods is equally distributed by the government. In a nation where most incidences of violence, from the exceptional to the everyday, went unresolved and even unnoticed, one of the penalties of a successful awareness-raising campaign was simmering resentment. In the print and online press, Nigerians began expressing skepticism about the abduction. Elected officials joined the chorus of skeptics, further facilitating public disengagement from the case.

More challenges were to come as girls who had escaped from Boko Haram camps began appearing in northern Nigeria. The escapees exceeded in problematic ways the portrait of the vulnerable girl that the campaign had built on. Escapees were no longer simple thwarted science students available for universal sympathy. Abducted girls began appearing in northern Nigeria in two troubling forms: as pregnant rape survivors and as invisible sacrificial bombers; both figures would pose serious organizing challenges for the BringBackOurGirls campaign. The first escaped girl, and several since, appeared back in society marked with a pregnancy or what some began calling a Boko Haram baby. This was a morally contaminating baby who was not easily claimed by any part of society. Activists debated whether or not the pregnant girls should abort; they debated whether or not the girls' families were responsible for raising the babies, and what the Bible, the Qur'an, and Nigerian laws had to say about abortion. A tiny minority argued that the debates among activists over the girls and their bodies mirrored the stance that Boko Haram had taken toward girls and their bodies in the sense that no one seemed to be foregrounding the wishes of the girls themselves.

Abducted girls also began to be described as enemies of the state. Worse than being a "Boko Haram wife" or a "Boko Haram mother," abducted girls were increasingly viewed as partners in crime with their abductors, who terrorized the public with random bombings. As early as July 2014, Boko Haram was deploying girls as suicide bombers to population centers in northern and central Nigeria. In Nigerian newspapers, people's anxiety about their own security replaced the focus on the rescue of OUR girls or the salvation of Chibok science students, to construct the girls as dangerous and untrustworthy and as targets of mob violence.

In the international sphere as well, the vulnerable universal girl was being redrawn using long-standing racist paternalist tropes. For example, a cartoon that ran on the cover of the October 22, 2014, issue of the infamous French political magazine *Charlie Hebdo* depicted four identical and heavily pregnant black women in evident need of dental surgery.[4] With their hands on their bellies, their distended mouths loudly exclaimed in unison, "Do not touch our welfare allocations!" These four pregnant black women sporting Muslim headscarves were, the caption told us, the sex slaves of Boko Haram. The cartoon drew on French right-wing ideas about the black woman, the Muslim, African immigrants, and people on government assistance. The Chibok girls, like their cartoon distortions, were to be considered neither real girls nor OUR girls. The violence that their pregnancies offered testimony to disappeared as they were drawn into racist, sexist, and Islamophobic narratives of the Other. The line between the abject and the contemptible was a thin one.

Nonetheless campaign organizers continued working on how to provide support for survivors, families, and affected communities. The question of psychological support in coping with the trauma of the abductions presented itself as an important focus of organizing and advocacy by Nigerian activists. Around this, initiatives emerged to fund scholarships for Chibok girls, to demand counseling services from the Nigerian government, to support girls who escaped from Boko Haram captivity, and to demand that the government provide security to girls' schools and vulnerable communities. These initiatives were met with a mix of support and resentment. In newspapers these signs of resentment against the Chibok girls, and the fissuring of the united ethos the campaign had initially created, took various forms. One was the renaming of the girls as Boko Haram wives. Another was criticism of demands from the BringBackOurGirls campaign that social, psychological, and financial support be put to the disposal of the Chibok families and any girls who were recovered. By their insistence that the rescue and support of schoolgirls from so-called remote communities of northern Nigeria was as important to the nation as it would have been had the girls been the daughters of state governors and oil moguls in the nation's central cities, the BringBackOurGirls campaign was upsetting the normal order of things in neoliberal Nigeria.

The timing of the *Charlie Hebdo* cartoon is important because it was published months after there had been a sustained global #BringBackOurGirls campaign. All around the world, people had claimed the Chibok girls as theirs, bore witness to their abductions and the violence they suffered, and demanded that the Nigerian government and other agents act decisively to rescue the girls and restore them to their families and, hopefully, to their childhoods. The problem was that the call that went around the world required that the girls be girls, specifically schoolgirls, and not mothers, women, or welfare recipients. As abject subjects they had been made available for sympathy and solidarity; deviations from that role would be penalized. While the face of abjection enables the mobilization of salvation projects, it envelops girls within a universal community by way of a gift. The danger of the universalizing gift, which underlies the girl-saving project, is that the gift is not a contract and, as the *Charlie Hebdo* cover pointed out, could be withdrawn at any time (Mauss 1990).

There are important similarities between the #BringBackOurGirls campaign and a girl-saving campaign of an earlier era. These continuities underscore the question of whether girl-saving campaigns inevitably rely on a narrowly gendered idea of *girl* whose defining feature is vulnerability to sexualized violence. The earlier campaign took place at the opposite end of Nigeria, in the urban southwestern capital of what was still a British colony. In the first half of the twentieth century, Lagos was a West African port city in the British Empire. It had a diverse population made up of indigenous Aworis, Yorubaphone settlers from various towns of the former Oyo Empire, communities in the southwestern region of contemporary Nigeria, Ewes, Hausas, Krus, Europeans, and, starting in the nineteenth century, repatriated freed people from Sierra Leone, Brazil, and Cuba. Between the mid-1920s and the early 1950s, Lagos experienced a growth spurt that doubled the population of the city. Two key factors contributed to that growth. First, a depression weakened the viability of rural agriculture-based economies. Second, during the war years of the 1940s, the building of new infrastructure projects to support the war effort was centered on cities such as Lagos and their ports, attracting job seekers from throughout West Africa. Given the primarily economic causes behind the city's growth in the 1930s and 1940s, it should be safe to say that the new urbanites were concentrated in the ranks of the city's poorer classes.

Unlike the nearby town of Ibadan, Lagos was not an agricultural city. It was a city of sellers—they seemed to be everywhere. In 1932 the Lagos Town Council estimated that four thousand so-called squatters and itinerant petty traders or hawkers had gathered at specific points in Lagos. Others considered four thousand to be a conservative estimate and pegged the number of sellers in Lagos Township closer to ten thousand (Lawrence 1932). The Haitian anthropologist Suzanne Comhaire-Sylvain (1951, cited in Coquery-Vidrovitch 1997, 95–96), who conducted research in Lagos in 1948, estimated that there were eight thousand market women in the city, "plus all their assistants and apprentices . . . four or five to one nominal market woman." The 1950 census listed almost thirty-two thousand "petty traders, hawkers, and shop assistants" between the ages of five and sixty-five (Nigerian Department of Statistics 1951, 75). Of these, census takers counted about fifteen hundred (1,451) "petty traders, hawkers, and shop assistants" (74–76), most of whom would have been girl hawkers.

Girl hawkers were itinerant sellers of petty goods: snacks, cigarettes, pencils, and other necessities. Hawking was an apprenticeship in market trading and a component in the socialization of ordinary girls. It was a physically demanding activity. Girls navigated Lagos's streets carrying the weight of their wares upon their heads. The practice required loudly advertising goods for sale. Announcing goods and prices in a melodic voice was part of the cultural imagery of girl hawkers that we find in novels, for example. Despite their noisiness, girl hawkers contributed to the quality of life in their communities. They were part of Lagos's casual labor class and were vital contributors to the incomes of working-class households. For many Lagosians, girl hawkers may also have embodied valued aspects of local cultures: a strong work ethic, household cooperation, youth's respect for their elders, children as household assets, economic independence, and entrepreneurship. While none of these ideals was gendered in any particular way, girl hawkers did personify them in a juvenile female form.

Not everyone had such a benign view of girl hawkers, however. Because of their noisiness, their itinerancy, and, most important, their female gender, girl hawkers captured the negative interest of elite Lagosian women, who routinely engaged in volunteer social service projects. Elite women viewed hawking by girls, in contrast to hawking by women or boys, to be a morally questionable activity and one that hampered girls' education and the advancement of women in the country. Their response to what they perceived as a girl hawker problem was to campaign for stringent restrictions against hawking by girls in the city of Lagos.

Beginning in the early 1920s elite women reformers had been writing petitions to the Lagos Colony government to "prohibit children of both sexes from hawking about the streets until boys have attained the age of 12 and girls 16." In a letter from Charlotte Obasa (1926), a leading figure in the elite women's community, she explains that the prohibition is necessary due to the "stealing and immoral practice to which they are daily [exposed]." In this period, high-ranking colonial officials were well aware of the concerns of elite Lagosian women. Yet they did not take any action until the voices of local elites began to be echoed by those of imperial liberals.

During the 1930s, what one might call the age of imperial liberalism, colonial governments began to interest themselves in the affairs of formerly marginalized subjects such as prisoners, children, and delinquents. The discipline of social work was ascendant, and a new kind of colonial expert, who applied universal theories of human well-being, descended on colonial cities. The liberal turn of the 1930s heralded a complex de-othering of the African child through various empire-wide humanitarian or social work programs. Formerly, African children had been structurally invisible to the colonial state and enveloped within the unit of the patriarchal African family. Yet through universalist discourse, African children in this period became disaggregated from the family and were inserted into a global class of children.

As stated earlier, elite women's views of girl hawkers had a long history. Yet although they were politically influential, they could not write policy outright. Not until the advent of the colonial social worker were elite women reformers able to find a cognate within the colonial administration who could put their moral critiques into the form of legal policy. When social work started in Lagos in 1941, it was at first focused on the category of juveniles, meaning young boys. Elite Lagosian women who had worked for decades on welfare issues related to women and girls could not fail to remark upon the unequal attention the state devoted to problem boys and problem girls. Shortly after the new chief welfare officer arrived in town, women reformers scheduled a meeting to impress on him their sense of the importance of girls in the welfare vision for the city and to inform him about their girl hawker project.

The relationship between elite women reformers and colonial social workers was a rocky one, marred by race, gender, and class conflicts. But the activists finally triumphed in their campaign with the 1943 passage of Street Trading Regulations, a subsection of something known as the Children and Young Person's Ordinance. The street trading regulations prohibited all children under fourteen from selling petty goods in the street and from "playing, singing, or performing, for profit." Girls between ages fourteen and sixteen were subject to further restrictions dictated by the time of day, their relationship to their employers, and the social geography of the city. They were prohibited from hawking *unless* they could supply evidence on demand that they were working for their parents and not for a guardian, employer, or other non-blood relative. All children were prohibited from hawking after 6:30 p.m., and "young females" were specifically prohibited from hawking in the central business district, heavily European neighborhoods, and in the vicinity of bars, brothels, and military barracks—in short, wherever military men or foreign men were easily found (Nigeria 1948). The ordinance thus sought to impede sexual contact between young girls and men, and interracial contact between Africans and Europeans. Penalties for violating the street-trading regulations could be applied to either children or their adults and could take the form of fines of up to £50, imprisonment for up to six months, or a combination of fines and imprisonment. The 1943 Street Trading Regulations were the first of a series of laws passed in the second half of the twentieth century that would make itinerant trading or hawking by children a punishable offense (see Lawal 2004).

In theory, the antihawking ban was gender-neutral, but in practice it was so strongly associated with girls and the threat of sexual violence that for heteronormative Lagosians it seemed illogical and unfair to regulate boy hawkers under the provisions of the law. Although much fewer in number, boy hawkers did exist and were depicted in the press as young students working to earn money for their education. Where boy hawkers were seen as struggling valiantly to lift themselves out of ignorance, girl hawkers were variously constructed as rape victims or young prostitutes, both in need of saving.

Elite women focused the attention of colonial social workers on the growth of the girl hawker population. These girls, they concluded, were morally imperiled by being and working in Lagos. Either they had to be sent out of the city, as they were presumed to be non-Lagosians, or they should be contained within schools and related institutions.

The moralistic underpinnings of elite women's activist work with girl hawkers were laid bare at a public panel discussion that was held on August 8, 1944. At that public meeting, they discussed what they saw as the most pressing moral dangers facing the city of Lagos: underage prostitution and hawking by girls. Elite women activists did not regard hawking by girls as a normal aspect of Lagos social life or the socialization of girls; rather they challenged the colonial state and the Lagos public with the question of why girls were on the streets being exposed to moral danger instead of sitting in schoolrooms advancing toward modern womanhood. For elite women, the girl hawker phenomenon itself was a problem.

What might ordinarily be regarded as two very distinct issues, the exploitative commodification of youthful sexuality and the itinerant peddling of petty goods, were closely linked in the minds of panelists. Several panelists explicitly "attributed much of the moral laxity or prostitution among girls to the habit [of] hawking of goods about the streets" (Daily Service 1944). Panelists also charged working-class women, the mothers and guardians of girl hawkers, with promoting child prostitution. One panelist declared, "A girl would be asked that she must sell all the goods handed to her within a specific period. If she could not get people to buy them she would somehow find ways and means of obtaining money to give to the mother or the guardian" (Daily Service 1944). It is important to note panelists' disaggregation of girls from their households and demonization of working-class parents.

The key outcome of the August 8 meeting was that it placed girl hawkers at the center of Lagos's moral problems. Wartime Lagos formed the backdrop to elite women reformers' dark view of girl hawkers. As a port city in the British Empire, Lagos experienced a ballooning of its military population during the Second World War. Soldiers from various parts of the country, West Africa, and more far-flung places in the British Empire passed through the city. Supporters of the antihawking ban defended the restrictions on hawking by arguing that sexual violence against young girls was rampant in Lagos and the only way that girls could be saved from the clutches of male predators, which meant foreign men, military men, and alcohol drinkers, was if the girls were carefully restricted from coming into contact with them. At the same time as they cast girl hawkers as easy prey for sexual predators, they also charged girl hawkers with being of easy virtue. They were a danger to themselves.

Over the years the hawking ban had a mixed record of success in keeping girls off the streets. The welfare office records show that the number of girl hawkers declined from a high of 684 girls who were apprehended for violations in 1946, to a low of 152 girls who were apprehended in 1951 (see Nigeria 1949, 1950, 1954; Federation of Nigeria 1955, 1956; Western Region of Nigeria 1955, 1956). A new trend was clearly in evidence. Fluctuations in the number of girl hawker arrests could be read as a reflection of the shifting jurisdiction of the Welfare Office or as an indicator of the changing welfare service staff's variable capacity to enforce street-trading regulations. The unambiguous testimony of the rising number of girl hawker arrests is that the ideology of the girl hawker campaign—which viewed hawking as a social ill, girl hawkers as imperiled, vulnerable, and dependent children in need of cloistering, and the prohibition of hawking as an effective response to illicit sexualization of girls—was not supported by the general Lagos public. Significantly, in the late 1950s, when Lagos was made into the Western Region capital and later the federal capital, and the jurisdiction of the welfare office was extended, the idea of girl hawkers as imperiled and vulnerable failed to extend beyond the city. Going into the independence period, hawking by girls was never considered an offense outside of Lagos. The criminalization of hawking by girls and the ideology of girlhood that criminalization relied on would remain peculiarities of life in the city.

In the girl hawker project and the #BringBackOurGirls campaign, girls were made subjects of salvation by being attributed a specific kind of vulnerability. The experiences of young people are here considered separately from how the experiences are understood. I ask us to think about vulnerability as a certain kind of narrowly constructed idea of peril that can only be attributed to a certain specifically delineated kind of girl. Vulnerability as a political attribute assigns a quality of imperilment combined with dependency. In so doing, it forges a relationship between subjects and a state from which they can expect protection or salvation from harm and the threat of harm. In this sense, vulnerability sifts populations into at least two categories: those for whom peril or precarity will be tolerated and even normalized and those who will be endowed with an expectation of safety, whether or not safety is actually achievable. The right or ability to expect succor from the state is thus a political attribute that is unevenly distributed across populations and dependent on contextually specific markers of social difference such as race, sex, class, generation, ability, gender, sexuality, religion, ethnicity, caste where relevant, and so on.

The girl-saving projects under discussion required for their operations a narrowly gendered idea of *girl* whose defining feature is vulnerability to sexualized violence. Everything but a very tightly drawn portrait of the vulnerable subject, a modern girl at risk of sexualized violence, is made to fall away. The modern *school*girl defines even more sharply the outline of those who will not be fit within the circle of succor—the ones who are beyond salvation. For example, even as abducted girls are rarely and very reluctantly framed as child soldiers, boys in Boko Haram strongholds are readily reimagined as enemy terrorists. The portrait of the vulnerable girl that campaigners outline is intended to draw sympathy from audiences and inspire a salvationist impulse within them. Yet in its reliance on certain restrictions, gendered and otherwise, it inadvertently prompts disidentifications as well. The similarities across space and time raise certain questions for us to consider: Is it inevitable that girl-saving projects will rely on a gendered notion of vulnerability that centers the image of the sexually violated body? Can we imagine girl-saving projects in which sexual integrity is not the standard for recognizing peril or offering succor? Can the potency of girl-saving projects be disentangled from their sexist, paternalist, colonial origins, and if so, under what conditions?

....

Abosede George is an associate professor of history at Barnard College and Columbia University in New York. She teaches courses in urban history, the history of childhood and youth in Africa, and the study of women, gender, and sexuality in African history. Her book *Making Modern Girls: A History of Girlhood, Labor, and Social Development* was published in 2014 by Ohio University Press and received the Aidoo-Snyder Book Prize in 2015 from the Women's Caucus of the African Studies Association, as well as Honorable Mention from the New York African Studies Association. She is currently at work on the Ekopolitan Project, a digital forum dedicated to historical research on migrant communities in nineteenth- and twentieth-century Lagos, West Africa.

Notes

1   Not the person's real name.
2   A slide show in the *New York Times* shows the edited black-and-white image as well as the original color photo (Estrin 2014).

3   At the time of the abduction, fifty-seven girls managed to escape when they
    realized the supposed military men were really insurgents in disguise. Over the
    course of the following two years, two more girls somehow returned to society
    on their own. In October 2016 the Nigerian federal government, under Muham-
    madu Buhari, was able to negotiate for the release of twenty-one more Chibok
    girls, and further releases were promised. More recently, in May 2017, eighty-
    two Chibok girls were released through a prisoner-swap program involving the
    Nigerian government and Boko Haram. These cases notwithstanding, the pace
    of progress was widely perceived to be quite slow. For a complete timeline of
    escapes and releases, see *Medium* 2017.

4   *Charlie Hebdo* does not appear to have an online presence. However, there
    have been several analyses of this particular cover. See, for example,
    Manilève 2015.

Works Cited

Comhaire-Sylvain, Suzanne. 1951. "Le Travail des Femmes a Lagos Nigeria." *Zaire:
    Revue Congolaise* 5, no. 2: 168–87.

Coquery-Vidrovitch, Catherine. 1997. *African Women: A Modern History*. Boulder, CO:
    Westview Press.

Daily Service (Lagos). 1944. "Women's Welfare League's Protest Meeting against Moral
    Dangers Proves a Big Success: Govt Will Be Asked to Forbid Hawking by Girls of
    Tender Age." August 10.

Estrin, James. 2017. "The Real Story about the Wrong Photos in #BringBackOur-
    Girls." *New York Times*, May 8. https://lens.blogs.nytimes.com/2014/05/08/the-real
    -story-about-the-wrong-photos-in-bringbackourgirls/.

Federation of Nigeria. 1955. *Annual Report of the Federal Department of Social Welfare for the
    Year 1954–55*. Lagos: Government Printer.

Federation of Nigeria. 1956. *Annual Report of the Federal Department of Social Welfare for the
    Year 1955–56*. Lagos: Government Printer.

George, Abosede. 2014. *Making Modern Girls: A History of Girlhood, Labor, and Social Devel-
    opment in Colonial Lagos*. Athens: Ohio University Press.

Lawal, Bayo A. 2004. "Markets and Street Trading in Lagos." In *Nigerian Cities*, edited
    by Toyin Falola and Steven J. Salm, 237–54. Trenton, NJ: Africa World Press.

Lawrence, C. T. 1932. "Idumagbo Markets." AdminCol File no. 1368 vol. 1, Market &
    Street Trading in Lagos, April 2 Nigerian Archives Ibadan.

Manilève, Vincent. 2015. "*Charlie Hebdo* n'est pas raciste, mais n'est pas irréprochable
    non plus." *Slate.fr*, January 14. http://www.slate.fr/story/96825/etats-unis-charlie
    -hebdo-raciste.

Mauss, Marcel. 1990. *The Gift*. New York: Routledge.

Medium. 2017. "Chibok Girls: A Timeline." https://www.firstpost.com/world/chibok
    -missing-schoolgirls-a-timeline-of-events-after-the-boko-haram-abduction
    -3428362.html. Accessed August 1, 2018.

Nigeria. 1948. "Children and Young Persons Street Trading Regulations, 1946, Made
    under the Children and Young Persons Ordinance, 1943." In *Annual Volume of the*

Laws of Nigeria Containing All Legislation Enacted during the Year 1946. Lagos: Government Printer.

Nigeria. 1949. *Annual Report on the Colony Welfare Service, 1949.* Lagos: Government Printer.

Nigeria. 1950. *Annual Report of the Federal Department of Social Welfare for the Year 1949–50.* Lagos: Government Printer.

Nigeria. 1954. *Annual Report of the Department of Social Welfare Services, Western Region (Including Lagos) for the Year 1953–54.* Lagos: Government Printer.

Nigerian Department of Statistics. 1951. *Population Census of Lagos 1950.* Kaduna: Government Printer.

Obasa, C. Olajumoke. 1926. Letter to Resident of the Colony, August 6. "Comcol. I." No. 498, Lagos Women's League 1924–50. Nigerian Archives Ibadan.

Scully, Pamela. 2013. "Gender, History, and Human Rights." In *Gender and Culture at the Limit of Rights,* edited by Dorothy Hodgson, 17–31. Philadelphia: University of Pennsylvania Press.

Western Region of Nigeria. 1955. *Annual Report of the Social Welfare Department of the Western Region of Nigeria for the Year 1954–55.* Ibadan: Government Printer.

Western Region of Nigeria. 1956. *Annual Report of the Social Welfare Department of the Western Region of Nigeria for the Year 1955–56.* Ibadan: Government Printer.

Anne Moraa

Smoke Is Everywhere, but No One Is Running
A Kenyan Activist Speaks Out

Abstract: The essay explores, through the author's work in developing educational content for adolescent girls, the importance of listening to girls' distinct voices and looking beyond the numbers when seeking to create impact.

There is fire on the mountain,
and nobody seems to be on the run.
Oh there is fire on the mountain top,
     and no one is'ah running.
—Asa, "Fire on the Mountain" (2008)

A fire breaks out in a dorm at Moi Girls High School in Nairobi. A dorm that is overcrowded—partly because the funds raised to refurbish the dorm were used for a chapel instead, partly because the girls do not matter. A fire breaks out in an overcrowded dorm locked from the outside. The matron with the key is gone, and the lock is too strong. A fire breaks out in a locked, overcrowded dorm with sealed windows. It is common to have grills on windows, keeping both intruders out and children in, but school regulations dictate that dorms should have windows that open. A fire breaks out in a locked, overcrowded dorm with sealed windows, where girls are sleeping. And nine girls died (Onyango 2017).

MERIDIANS · feminism, race, transnationalism   17:2 November 2018
DOI: 10.1215/15366936-7176472 © 2018 Smith College

Working with girls and women is simple, a passion. Frankly, the elevator pitch is easy. I work at ZanaAfrica as the managing editor of *Nia Teen* magazine and comics that target girls ages ten to fourteen, empowering them with engaging resources on menstrual health and reproductive rights. We envision a world where girls and women in East Africa are educated and live healthy, productive lives. ZanaAfrica also creates menstrual pads and engages in activist and policy work. Our driving mission is to realize a world in which menstrual health management is recognized as a human right, and the onset of puberty as the most effective time to educate girls on personal health decisions.

Consider these figures. Only 46 percent of women in Kenya report having adequate supplies to manage their menstruation (PMA 2020 2017). Sixty-five percent of them cannot afford sanitary pads at all (FSG 2016). Ten percent of fifteen-year-old girls claim they have had sex for pads (Phillips-Howard et al. 2015). Despite these sobering statistics, many consider Kenya a pioneer in menstrual support for girls. The government removed the value-added tax on menstrual pads and tampons in 2004, and pads for schoolgirls have been part of the national budget since 2011 (Hallet 2016). While important, I question whether these actions do enough to help girls thrive. Do Kenyan girls know enough about their bodies, about themselves?

Reports suggest that the girl who started the dorm fire had attempted to commit suicide at least twice (Momanyi 2017). Twice. We do this work because of the fire. A recent study found that 26.4 percent of school-going adolescents in Kenya showed clinically significant depressive symptoms, with more girls exhibiting symptoms and suicidal behavior than boys (Khasakhala et al. 2012). Girls cannot speak. Because they are deliberately and carefully taught not to speak. Being a girl in Kenya is to be silent. Meekness, smartness, and politeness are highly prized, except when participating in loud, choreographed shows at debate championships and drama festivals. If lucky, your voice can make it to a presidential stage, singing for peace and the end of corruption. Then you go home and stay silent.

I know this because I was once a girl in Kenya. Unlike many other girls, my first period was as calm, idyllic, and privileged as you could imagine: in my house, on holiday, after lunch, after already knowing about menstruation and pregnancy, with pads at home and access to a phone to call my mother. Unlike many other girls, I was not worried that I would miss school. I had pads to manage my menstrual flow, but many girls do not.

This is not complicated.

The reason girls need pads and education is because they need them both. The end.

The shame, the missing school, the complications of this are more than the numbers, than the studies and the rhetoric and the law. It is a fact. It is a truth. It is a right.

Girls tell you this.

Violence is another important concern.

Numbers from a 2010 study of violence against children show that before age eighteen, 32 percent of girls experience sexual violence and 66 percent experience physical violence (UNICEF 2012). Fewer than 10 percent of them seek help. More than half of young women age eighteen to twenty-four believe it is acceptable for a husband to beat his wife. Forty percent of young women believed that a woman should tolerate spousal violence to keep the family together. In light of these views, how can you make girls believe that they deserve more?

We think it begins by asking them what they need.

ZanaAfrica has constructed a database of over ten thousand girls' questions, which we use to develop our content. During field tests, school visits, and general discussions with students all over Kenya, we have a simple process: At the end of the discussion, the facilitator hands out squares of blank paper. The girls have time to write anonymous questions they want answered. The anonymity grants them freedom to ask questions they may be too scared to ask otherwise. Questions range from basic biology ("What is menstruation?") to advice about school ("For someone to be clever in class, what do you do?"), love ("If you love a boy, what can you do?"), and sexual assault ("If you have been raped, what can you do?"). More often than not, we answer every question and communicate with our partners at the school if a particular girl needs additional help. These sessions drive my daily work.

Part of my job is writing a feature comic called Nia, which is about a young Kenyan girl. With girls in our target area of Kilifi, a large, primarily rural and periurban county along the coast of Kenya, as well as girls across Nairobi, we regularly test the characters, the language, the visuals, right down to whether Nia's shoelaces should be tied or untied. We test every element and continue to do so with each issue. In the third issue, for example, we focus on Shona, a fourteen-year-old schoolgirl. We follow her story from the moment her friends abandon her to the time she meets

Jaymo, a handsome and seemingly kind *boda boda* (motorcycle) driver, and the moment he assaults her, illustrated only by a locked door. The storyline represents a common experience for girls across Kenya.

In a focus group about this issue, we asked the girls, "Who is to blame for what happened to Shona?" The girls overwhelmingly agreed: "Jaymo and Shona." "Why Jaymo?" "He shouldn't have entered her house without permission." "He should not have forced her." "Why Shona?" "Why did she take his *boda*?" "She should have known better." "She shouldn't have spoken to him." "Why did she offer him water?" "Why didn't she say no?"

This final question consistently cropped up. We did not want Shona to scream "No!" and fight her attacker because far too often sexual assault does not look like that. From these conversations with girls, we adjusted our story to meet theirs, from Shona offering a high price for the ride (100kshs, a large amount for an average *boda* ride), to specifically telling Jaymo that he should stay outside, to then watching him walk into the house anyway. The magazine in its current form is part of a large-scale randomized control trial involving more than five thousand adolescent girls in 140 primary schools in Kilifi to determine if providing girls with reproductive health education and menstrual hygiene products will positively affect their education and well-being. The results of the trial will not be available until 2019, but I am hoping it proves our hypothesis right: that focusing on what girls themselves say, instead of us making assumptions about their lives, we can create real, impactful change.

There is an urgent need to get stories to girls representing themselves, about themselves, true to who they are. Not a perfect girl, but a real one. In doing this work, we must step outside ourselves, get beyond the statistics, and ask girls what they want. The girls are why we do it. It is necessary for them to own the content, to speak freely to these issues. In Kenya there are limited spaces for girls' self-expression. Despite the fact that 88 percent of the population has access to a mobile phone, most girls cannot speak out for themselves (Communications Authority of Kenya n.d.). Most parents do not give phones to underage children, particularly in rural areas where phones are very expensive. They see the internet as a gateway to evil, to bad influences.

I love seeing zines like *Rookie Mag*, an online magazine for girls. There are no such spaces in Kenya, yet girls here have just as many questions and thoughts to share. Their opinions are just as valid. Our girls need to be heard, but they also need a space to listen to each other honestly. It is impossible to see yourself if you cannot hear voices of girls like yourself.

This is not an abstract concept to me. I do this work largely for myself. It is for me at age fourteen. It is for the awkward, loud, bullied girl whose breasts came too soon and whose ass came too late, who read too much and could not run at all, who did not know that words could come from her own hands until she was twenty-one. It is personal.

The girls who died in the Moi Girls fire are Esther Neema, Nancy Wamuthuri Thuku, Hanna Jeyso Timado, Hawa Haziz, Mary Njengo Mokaya, Alakiir Malong, Natalie Asiko, Whitney Kerubo, and Marcia Okello. One girl, her name withheld by the courts, has been charged with nine counts of murder (Kiplagat 2017). There are calls for stricter punishments for students, including from a member of Parliament who said the "Ministry of Education has made it difficult for teachers to punish errant students by banning caning" (Oduor 2017). An article was posted on a popular gossip blog titled "Five Shocking Things about Girl with Devilish Tendencies Who Started Deadly Girls Fire That Killed 9 Students" (*Ghafla!* 2017). Court reporters described the fourteen-year-old suspect as "the slim girl with a tiny frame. . . . Chocolate-skinned with her hair pulled back to a neat ponytail, her calm and collected demeanour belied the atrocious charges levelled against her. She did not show any emotion as the prosecutor read the charges against her" (Ochieng and Chege 2017). She was wrapped in cloth, head to toe, to obscure her face.

Silent. Silenced.

I imagine the girl who started the fire as my friend. We would be awkward and outcasts and she would share her struggle. I remember who I was then. I would dismiss her. I would say she was not tough enough. Or maybe I would listen to her, and we would listen to each other, and we would spiral into dangerous, fitful fantasies. Or maybe we would cry and cry and cry together, and laugh at how puffy our eyes were and how silly it all was. Maybe we would smile. All I know for sure is that I would not have known then where to begin because the words were missing. I did not have them.

Neither did she.

If we give them a chance, girls will show you, there is smoke everywhere. Look.

Listen.

....

Anne Moraa worked with ZanaAfrica for five years developing and producing the Nia Teen comics and magazines targeting girls. She is a writer, editor, and performer dedicated to telling compelling stories through an African feminist lens.

Works Cited

Asa. 2008. "Fire on the Mountain." On *Asa: Acoustic Live in Tokyo*. CD.

Communications Authority of Kenya. N.d. "Kenya's Mobile Penetration Hits 88%." Accessed November 8, 2017. http://www.ca.go.ke/index.php/what-we-do/94 -news/366-kenya-s-mobile-penetration-hits-88-per-cent.

FSG. 2016. *Menstrual Health in Kenya: Country Landscape Analysis*. Washington, D.C.: Bill and Melinda Gates Foundation. Ghafla! 2017. "Five Shocking Things about Girl with Devilish Tendencies Who Started Deadly Girls Fire That Killed 9 Students." September 7.

Hallet, V. 2016. "What Kenya Can Teach the U.S. about Menstrual Pads." *Goats and Soda*, NPR, May 10.

Khasakhala, L. I., D. M. Ndetei, V. Mutiso, A. W. Mbwayo, and M. Mathai. 2012. "The Prevalence of Depressive Symptoms among Adolescents in Nairobi Public Secondary Schools: Association with Perceived Maladaptive Parental Behaviour." *African Journal of Psychiatry* 15: 106–13.

Kiplagat, S. 2017. "Girl Linked to Moi Girls School Nairobi Inferno Faces 9 Counts of Murder." *Daily Nation* (Nairobi), September 13.

Momanyi, Bernard. 2017. "Suicidal Girl Sets Moi Girls School on Fire Killing 9: Police." *Capital News* (Nairobi), September 4.

Ochieng, A., and N. Chege. 2017. "14-Year-Old Girl Detained for 7 Days in Fire Probe." *Daily Nation* (Nairobi), September 7.

Oduor, B. 2017. "Moi Girls' Fire Victim Buried as Mourners Lash Out at Ministry." *Daily Nation* (Nairobi), September 16.

Onyango, P. 2017. "Parents of Moi Girls School, Nairobi Demand Removal of School Heads." *Daily Nation* (Nairobi), September 5.

Phillips-Howard, P. A., G. Otieno, B. Burmen, F. Otieno, and F. Odongo. 2015. "Menstrual Needs and Associations with Sexual and Reproductive Risks in Rural Kenyan Females: A Cross-Sectional Behavioral Survey Linked with HIV Prevalence." *Journal of Women's Health* 24, no. 10: 801–11.

PMA. 2020. 2017. *Menstrual Hygiene Management: Kenya, 2016*. Washington, D.C.: Bill and Melinda Gates Foundation.

UNICEF. 2012. *Violence against Children in Kenya: Findings from a 2010 National Survey*. Nairobi: United Nations Children's Fund, Kenya Country Office.

Wambui Mwangi

. . . .

Re-collections
Matter, Meaning, Memory

How do you photograph a memory?

The photographer, the subject of the photograph, and the photograph are bound by the shared space and proximities of the photographic moment, but afterward, they embark on different trajectories to unpredictable else-wheres and else-hows of inhabiting diverse modes of being in the world.

Photographs are not what was photographed. Photographs are themselves re-collections, interpretive memories that grow more distant from that which they represent by circulation and with the passage of time, but "representation" also means "to make present again." As a genre, "still life" is life that is *still* but not stilled. Still life is, still, life. Life perceptible to the stillness of an attentive mind; life collected and re-collected; life present, absent, remembered, re-gathered. Photographs are both here (as object) and not-here—the markers of the absence of what or who is photographed.

Each of these images represents an African woman whom I have known and now mourn or miss because I have lost them in some way. I could not photograph them. They include my mother, my grandmother, my cousin, my friend, and even a younger version of myself. Some died, some moved away, some simply grew and changed. Yet, absence is a form of presence and an active shaping of the now: in memory, in mourning, and in melancholia. Presence is similarly an absence from elsewhere or else-when.

MERIDIANS · feminism, race, transnationalism   17:2 November 2018
DOI: 10.1215/15366936-7258664 © 2018 Smith College

Memories gather and matter by gathering meaning and matter. Sticky objects persist and follow and collect in human lives.

My task was also to think about and through the actions of objects not only as they impact on human lives but also as they go through their own lives, changing and charging their own matter and their own ways of mattering. Matter gathers and assembles. It changes. It moves and can be moved. It morphs and mutates. It too collects and re-collects itself.

The way memories matter is also about the matter of memory, matter that has memory and matter that imparts memory.

Note

These images are excerpted from a larger set of my photographs that were part of a collective exhibition in 2011 in Nairobi, Kenya. The larger exhibition, "Curving the Visual," consisted of photographs of African women by five African women photographers.

"Wambui (portrait of a younger self)"

Beatrice

Phyllis

Ng'endo

Rahavu

Jacqueline-Bethel Tchouta Mougoué

. . . .

Gender and (Militarized) Secessionist Movements in Africa
An African Feminist's Reflections

Abstract: Utilizing interdisciplinary and multimethodological approaches, this essay explores women's roles in buttressing the political cohesion of secessionist movements in postcolonial Africa. It argues that African women have supported the actions of male-dominated secessionist movements in order to garner their own social and political power. Using case studies from Anglophone Cameroon, Western Sahara, Cabinda Province (Angola), and Biafra (Nigeria), the essay historicizes and outlines a new analytical framework that explores women's multifaceted participation in secessionist movements in modern-day Africa.

On January 19, 2017, a Cameroonian woman known as "Mami Margaret" released a six-minute video for YouTube, imploring women in the two English-speaking areas of the country to come together to protest Francophone rule (Ekan 2017a). Speaking in Pidgin English, or Cameroonian Creole, she lamented the disappearance, execution, and imprisonment of male leaders of Anglophone opposition groups over the preceding four months. She also called upon women to support the Cameroon Anglophone Civil Society Consortium's "ghost town" campaigns, in which activists in Anglophone regions would withdraw from everyday activities in public spaces for two days to protest Anglophone marginalization. She further proposed that women protest naked in the streets, referencing a tradition in which the Takumbeng (or Takembeng), a rural-based

MERIDIANS · feminism, race, transnationalism   17:2 November 2018
DOI: 10.1215/15366936-7176483 © 2018 Smith College

traditional secret society of women in their sixties and seventies, protest naked to intimidate and shame men who consider the sight of their vaginas bad luck. Her message was clear: Anglophone women in Cameroon should unify.

Mami Margaret broadcast her video from Tamulong, a section of Bamenda, the capital of the modern-day Anglophone Northwest Region of Cameroon, which is an important stronghold against Francophone hegemony. The Northwest and Southwest Regions were once part of the British Empire, unlike the rest of the country, which was French-ruled. Following a 1961 plebiscite organized by the United Nations, the British Southern Cameroons federated with the (formerly French-ruled) Republic of Cameroon, while the British Northern Cameroons became part of Nigeria. Since that time Anglophones have felt increasingly marginalized by the Francophone-led state, as they account for less than 20 percent of the country's population. In October 2016 the Anglophone regions erupted in protest after the president announced that all Cameroonians must give pride of place to the French language. By November this discontent had evolved into a larger political movement dubbed "the Coffin Revolution" because a key leader appeared in public in a coffin and many declared that they were willing to risk death in order to combat fifty years of socioeconomic marginalization by the politically dominant Francophone state. Some demanded federalism, while others sought secession. The state responded by shutting down the internet in Anglophone towns from January to April 2017 (*Cameroon Concord News* 2017).

Given the internet blockade, Mami Margaret's video was likely uploaded from a Francophone region of the country or even from Nigeria, since Anglophones had become "digital refugees" (*Al Jazeera* 2017; Atabong 2017). The video's reference to the Takumbeng would have been familiar to many Cameroonians. In the early 1990s the group engaged in mass protests after the military tried to arrest an Anglophone political opposition party leader following the reintroduction of multiparty politics (Kah 2011, 75). Takumbeng women surrounded the candidate's compound to thwart his formal arrest and provided him with food and access to supporters. When the military entered his compound, the women disrobed, knelt, and lifted their breasts with their hands. The women successfully repelled the advance of the soldiers armed with guns, tear gas, and grenades. The soldiers feared that the women's exposed vaginas and breasts would become "guns of war" (Kah 2011, 75). The age of the women, all seniors in their community, was a significant aspect of their power, as it gave them authority drawn on maternal associations (DeLancey et al. 2010, 357). Although the Takumbeng did not likely participate in protests in 2016 or January 2017, they did eventually respond to Mami Margaret's call for unity and took part in protests in Anglophone Cameroon and abroad in September and November 2017 (Manunga Studio 2 2017; Ekan 2017b; Yombo 2017).

In this essay, I historicize and explore women's participation in African secessionist movements, such as the one just described in Anglophone Cameroon. I argue that African women have supported male-dominated political organizations that advocate for secession by drawing upon their gendered positioning within communities in order to garner social and political power. They endeavor to draw strict cultural, social, and political boundaries between themselves and the "other" (i.e., the hegemonic state) in an attempt to solidify an "imagined community" within real geographical boundaries vis-à-vis succession (see Anderson 1991). As I explain, women's participation in these types of secessionist movements is wide-ranging, from serving as militants to heading nongovernment organizations and campaigning for women's rights while working for politically dominant governments.

Inspired by Molara Ogundipe-Leslie's (1994) classic work on Nigerian women, I use what I term tri-(neo)colonialism as a lens, based on the understanding that African women in secessionist movements confront three layers of social and political subjugation. Ogundipe-Leslie contends that there are six mountains on African women's backs: traditional or indigenous viewpoints on culture, backwardness because of European colonization, race, patriarchy, external oppression and foreign intrusion, and, most significant, women themselves. I adapt her typology to focus on the multilayered oppressions that women in African secessionist movements face: male-dominated political organizations, hegemonic states, and Western neocolonialism. Using case studies from Anglophone Cameroon, Western Sahara, Cabinda Province (Angola), and Biafra (Nigeria), I historicize and outline a new analytical framework that explores women's multifaceted participation in secessionist movements in modern-day Africa.

My position as a researcher who is Francophone Cameroonian-born drives this comparative research. When researching Anglophone Cameroonian history, my Anglophone interviewees were always slightly suspicious of my interest in Anglophone nationalism, given my Francophone background. But as I explained, having lived most of my life in the United States as a black woman, I identified with the sociopolitical marginalization of Anglophone Cameroonians, even if our grievances differed because of different geographical and historical contexts. This explanation seemed to make my interviewees more relaxed and eager to engage in conversation, seeing me as an ally.

Being myself marginalized piqued my interest in trying to understand the experiences of women in separatist and/or secessionist movements on the continent. As an African feminist who is concerned with the needs and conditions of women on the continent, I was curious to know if liberation struggles (read: secessionist efforts) elsewhere on the continent also suffered from erasure and, if so, whether that erasure was more severe in women's case. My African feminist curiosity compels me to move beyond women's history per se and to connect the histories of women to contemporary political movements. While African feminism seeks to resist multiple axes of oppression, including tradition, the goal is, as the African feminist Minna Salami (2012) points out, is "to enable tradition to adapt to its times so that rather than stagnate, it can enrich society, as customs and culture should do."

With this in mind, my African feminist interjection endeavors to illuminate some of the distinct strategies that African women have used to advocate for gender and political equality within volatile political landscapes, such as utilizing centuries-old traditional women's organizations to demand change. Such insight might illuminate key strategies—often dismissed by the selective gaze of some scholars—that women have adapted in order to preserve authority (and survival) in turbulent (militarized) political landscapes. Thus this work and these reflections are meant to start a conversation about how feminist scholars—particularly those identifying as African feminists—can begin to analyze secession through the lens of gender.

Theorizing Gender and Secessionist Movements in Africa

Since the 1960s Africa has seen the rise of political resistance movements, including separatist and secessionist movements, which are rooted in beliefs about sociopolitical, ethnic, cultural, and even linguistic differences. According to Jean-Pierre Cabestan and Aleksandar Pavković (2012), separatism is "a political objective that aims to reduce the political and other powers of the central government of a state over a particular territory and to transfer those powers to the population or elites representing the population of the territory in question." Secessionism, on the other hand, seeks to remove all power from the central government (1–2). They argue that separatist movements often develop in a secessionist direction and caution that the distinction between them often blurs because some political movements waver between both political goals. This is certainly the case with English-speaking Cameroon, where some of the separatist intentions have transformed into secessionist movements, while others have ambiguously wavered between the two political objectives, depending on the given political climate.

Political scientists, sociologists, and economists have attempted to explain the causes and effects of secessionist and separatist movements, as well as state reactions to them, while political theorists have focused on the politics and political legitimacy of secessionist governments (Buchanan 2017). Thus far, most of this research has not had much to say about women's roles in secessionist or separatist movements across the world. There is also "surprisingly little feminist scholarship on militarism in Africa," according to Amina Mama and Margo Okazawa-Rey (2008, 2). However, as this work will show, women and gender have been central in shaping African political identities, particularly within secessionist movements, which are often heavily militarized.

In contrast to many decolonization movements, which often garner widespread political support, secessionist movements usually face obstacles in their efforts to mobilize populations (Pavković 2015). Consequently gender roles and conduct, specifically for women, fluctuate more in secessionist movements than they did in independence movements, as women face challenges accessing social, political, economic, and educational rights in such volatile environments. Such movements are often highly militarized, and as Alicia Decker's (2014) work on Uganda clearly illustrates, gender profoundly influences women's (and men's) understandings and experiences of military rule and militarized events. Secessionist movements often face opposition from powerful states that want to protect their own political interests and territorial integrity with military force, which has the potential to displace thousands of people. Displacement can expose women to heightened levels of gender-based violence, particularly within refugee camps, where local and national authorities, as well as international peacekeeping forces, may prey on them (Clarke 2008). Women can also experience new opportunities and challenges if war breaks out during or after secession, which suggests that we must carefully examine the entire secession process through a feminist lens.

Feminist political theory allows us to understand how women in secession and separatist movements have used various strategies to garner greater political, social, and economic authority. As the political scientist Valerie Bryson (2016, 1) explains, "Male political theorists ignore the existence of ongoing gender-based inequalities and injustices, or treat these as marginal issues, irrelevant to mainstream political theory . . . [while] most feminist political theory sees women and their situation as central to political analysis." Thus, using feminist political theory as a tool of analysis can illustrate how women are active agents who challenge larger political systems of inequality rather than merely passive subjects in secessionist movements (Allen 2013). As the feminist political scientist Jill Vickers (2016) observes, such "narratives portray women as passive victims of male violence and few consider women's active participation in separatist projects." And Decker (2017, 102) writes, "Women are not simply victims of militarism. They can employ a number of different strategies to mediate the violence." She notes that women exhibit "strategic agency" even when navigating a militarized setting.

This work also builds upon Stephanie Urdang's (1979) groundbreaking book, *Fighting Two Colonialisms: Women in Guinea–Bissau*, which discusses the parallel struggles of women for independence and for their rights as women. I see postcolonial secessionist movements as similar to anticolonial movements in that they seek to combat a foreign other in order to achieve self-determination. Like anticolonial movements, African women in secessionist movements are frequently asked to ignore gender concerns until after "liberation" (e.g., Geiger 1997; Lyons 2004; Schmidt 2005). However, contemporary examples of persistent patriarchy in many African countries reflect the fact that liberation from colonialism does not necessarily result in gender equality, belying the argument that the triumph of secessionist movements will make space for women's concerns. As the protracted conflict in South Sudan illustrates, secessionist movements may face long and bloody decades of struggle, even after "victory." Ignoring women's voices and stories from past and current secessionist movements only serves to obscure our understanding of internal forms of colonization, or intracolonization.

Secessionist movements are part of a larger pattern of (militarized) political movements on the African continent. Mama and Okazawa-Rey

(2008, 1–2) contend that when "political transitions to African rule came, the institutions of state bore the marks of a patriarchal and militaristic history. . . . Individual nations found themselves variously enmeshed in Cold-War politics and the arms race, and embroiled in a series of deadly proxy wars." Moreover "the vast majority of these conflicts were carried out within nations, with increasingly devastating impact on civilian populations and rising casualties among women and children" (1–2). Secessionist movements in postcolonial Africa reflect this pattern of internal civil strife, and women are often the chief casualties. By examining secessionist movements through the lens of gender, we can clearly see that women experience the quest for self-determination in very different ways than men.

Militarization and Womanhood

This section explores how women in two contemporary secessionist movements have experienced militarization and how they have challenged, renegotiated, and reinterpreted various ideas about gender and femininity in military-occupied environments. It also examines how militarized secession movements have used women to advance their larger political goals.

The Sahrawi

The Polisario Front has led the separatist movement of the indigenous Sahrawi of Western Sahara, who have sought liberation from Morocco through active resistance since 1976. A stalemate in the mid-1980s led to a 1991 truce and ceasefire, supervised by the United Nations Mission for the Referendum in Western Sahara (MINURSO). Although Morocco initially promised a referendum on independence, this vote has yet to take place, ostensibly due to disagreements about Sahrawi voter rights. The ceasefire remains, but the Polisario Front have repeatedly threatened to recommence fighting because of Morocco's failure to hold a referendum. While the Moroccan government considers membership in the Polisario Front illegal, the United Nations recognizes the organization as the Sahrawi people's legitimate political representative and contend that the Sahrawi have a right to demand the referendum promised in the ceasefire agreement (Vasquez 2014).

Feminist scholarship overwhelmingly demonstrates that ideals of "normal" family life and adherence to rigid gender roles are often suspended during times of conflict (e.g., Geiger 1997; Lyons 2004; Schmidt 2005). For Sahrawi women, however, disruption of this kind has been normal for the past four decades. This complicates scholarly understandings of gender role reversals during politically tenuous times. In fact, for indigenous Sahrawi women, playing a role outside of the home represents a continuation of tradition. Sahrawi women have always run camps when men traveled for battle or for trading, taking up key responsibilities that bolstered their social and political control within the home and their communities (Morris 2013). Women also governed their family's tents—making, repairing, and moving them—and took care of their family's animals and children. Traditional Sahrawi society is matrilineal, and women can inherit property. They can thus survive independently of their fathers and husbands (Lippert 1992).

Just as Sahrawi women have managed nomadic camps for generations, they have also managed refugee camps in Tindouf, Algeria. These camps are home to the Polisario Front and thousands of exiled Sahrawi. Many able-bodied men who joined the fight died, leaving women as camp leaders. The Sahrawi in Tindouf have struggled to rebuild their communities in their extended period of exile, and women have played an integral role in this process. Erica Vasquez (2014) has explored women's leadership roles in these camps. She has found that some women head up community-building projects that support the education of Sahrawi youth, while others work in clinics and schools. Still other women work as journalists and police officers. Vasquez's study demonstrates that Sahrawi women have expanded their authority in exile, forming new strategies to garner social and political power even as they support the actions of male-dominated political organizations that are fighting Moroccan occupation in their home region. As citizens of a state-in-waiting, these women ensure the survival and continuation of their communities, renegotiating their citizenry in powerful ways. Community-building projects make them important decision makers for their exiled communities, suggesting that women can obtain social and political power, even in volatile landscapes. Whether women will retain this power after "liberation" is unclear. Nonetheless, as Vasquez concludes in her study, the ability of Sahrawi women to find ways to maintain and extend their social and political authority "shows the elevated roles of women in the movement, their organization, and the discrimination inflicted upon them by the Moroccan forces. It also challenges orientalist narratives about the subjugated Muslim woman" and illustrates how different cultural contexts can enhance power for women, allowing them to participate in secessionist movements differently from their male counterparts (5).

In fact women are often the most visible figures of secessionist movements. A 2013 *Washington Post* interview with a prominent Sahrawi activist, Sultana Khaya, clearly reflects this (Morris 2013). In this interview Khaya remembers how a police officer brutally beat her face during a 2007 protest, crushing her eye socket and leaving her blind in one eye. She refused to back down, insisting that such great strength was normal for Sahrawi women. "The Sahrawi woman is very great; she's very powerful," she says. Khaya articulates a militarized ideal of womanhood, noting, "I don't even think about getting married until the Sahrawi women become independent." By emphasizing a militarized femininity, women like Khaya disassociate themselves from their bodies and gendered expectations by postponing marriage and motherhood (Saltman and Gabbard 2011; Hentz 2014). Similar to what Decker (2014, 11) discovered in Uganda, "new constructions of masculinity and femininity . . . emerged from militarist practices, which significantly influenced gender roles and relations." In proclaiming that they did not want to marry until all women were free, women like Khaya embraced a militarized femininity that justified the sacrifice of wifehood and motherhood. Within this context women's support for secession defined a new version of womanhood that was militarized, altering extant perceptions of ideal womanhood during times of war.

On the other hand, evidence belies the claim of Sahrawi women like Khaya that they have achieved gender equality in exile (Saltman and Gabbard 2011). Women do not occupy the highest political posts in Tindouf camps. Moreover, because the Algerian government does not police the camps, gender-based violence often goes unchecked. A recent Human Rights Watch (2014) report describes the failure of some intergovernmental organizations to prioritize combating gender-based violence in militarized environments such as refugee camps. While noting that the United Nations "maintains a permanent presence in the refugee camps in Tindouf and Western Sahara," the report finds that MINURSO is the most prominent UN entity and that it "has no human rights mandate and conducts no ongoing human rights monitoring or reporting" (5). Human Rights Watch describes the Moroccan state's opposition to such a mandate, in spite of Polisario's support. Thus multilayered neocolonial influences and policies—by Algeria, Western Sahara, and the UN—shape and influence Sahrawi women's daily access to security and human rights while in exile.

The lack of protection for Sahrawi women exists against the backdrop of heightened violence because of pre-displacement norms as well as disturbed gender relations. Militarism can strengthen the equation of masculinity with violence and create an environment that seems to encourage violence against women (Mama and Okazawa-Rey 2008, 3). Susanne Buckley-Zistel and Ulrike Krause (2017, 4–5) assert that men sometimes react violently to displacement and encampment "in order to maintain their social status as patriarchs." The authors therefore find higher levels of "domestic violence [and] sexual abuse . . . by fellow refugees." They likewise describe gender-based violence by officials empowered to keep order in refugee camps. Imprisoning women for adultery or other "honor crimes," such as having children out of wedlock, has been documented in Tindouf (Human Rights Watch 2008, 2014; Amnesty International 2016). Larger narratives about the ongoing conflict often eclipse reports of such gender-based violence. Thus, while women are recognized as critical to the secessionist movement, they must also navigate multiple layers of political, social, and violent physical subjection in support of the movement.

Cabinda, Angola

The gender-based violence that women encounter in highly militarized spaces is also evident in Cabinda, a region of Angola that is separated from the rest of the country by the Democratic Republic of Congo. The Front for the Liberation of the Enclave of Cabinda (FLEC) has sought independence from two external powers since 1963: from Portugal until 1975 and, after that, from the Luanda government after Angolan independence. Activists contend that Cabinda has a culture and history distinct from the rest of Angola. Soldiers in the armed wing of FLEC have waged a low-level guerrilla war for independence for forty years. They operate in exile with branches in Congo-Brazzaville and Paris as well. The Luanda government, however, has resisted giving up Cabinda because the province accounts for more than half of the country's oil production (Koné 1998; Reid 2015).

European and North American petroleum companies have also endeavored to exercise economic and political control in Cabinda since the discovery of oil in 1966. For instance, France supported separatist intentions in the country for decades by providing military and arms support to FLEC fighters to protect the interests of Total, a multinational integrated oil and gas company and the largest French company in Angola (Koné 1998). Such external meddling declined after the international Angolagate scandal (1993–2000), in which individuals in the French and Luanda governments were exposed for corruption and illegal arms deals (*The Economist* 2008). Yet interference likely continues through the same channels; as research on the illicit arms trade in Africa has demonstrated, it is "opaque, amorphous and dynamic," and thus it is impossible to determine which entities supply the arms that fuel conflict (Schroeder and Lamb 2006, 69).

The persistence of the conflict certainly has an impact on women's lives. A 1996 press release reveals that although most FLEC fighters are men and teenage boys, women also actively participate. According to Silou, one of approximately fifty women who are part of the armed wing of FLEC, "Our role as women who have joined up is to increase the fighting capacity of Cabinda's women. . . . There are nearly 80,000 women in Cabinda and we are trying to make them understand the meaning of mobilization. . . . We devote ourselves totally, body and soul, to keeping the Cabindese cultural patrimony alive" (Ngangoue 1996). She explains that she is a teacher of children and does not ask for a salary to "improve the intellectual capacity of Cabindese children who will continue this liberation struggle" (Ngangoue 1996). Many women also help to feed combatants and see the involvement of their sons as an important contribution to the political movement. An elderly woman, whose twenty-one-year-old son fights for FLEC, stated, "By producing cassava, yams, bananas and other crops we feed our fighters, our husbands and sons. . . . In this way we give them the courage to face our Angolan enemy. . . . By accepting to send our young sons to the front, we are sacrificing ourselves for the independence of our country. We accept this with heavy hearts, but we have to do so in the interest of future generations" (Reid 2015). While some Sahrawi women delay marriage and motherhood, Cabindese women sacrifice their sons to a greater cause and seek to preserve some semblance of patriarchy (or "cultural patrimony" as Silou puts it), demonstrating the varied ways that women, drawing on their gendered positioning as mothers (or potential mothers), support male-dominated secessionist movements.

Women in Cabinda face gender-based violence as well. A 2003 report from the Institute of Security Studies mentions that Angolan soldiers frequently rape women and girls in the province (Porto 2003). A 1997 report on human rights violations in the province by the Ad-Hoc Commission for Human Rights in Cabinda also reveals systematic gender-based violence. It shows that both the Angolan Armed Forces and the National Police of the Republic of Angola failed to investigate or prosecute the army's abuses against civilians. The report notes that the army responded to accusations of gender-based violence and human rights violations by transferring suspected perpetrators to different areas of Cabinda or to another province of Angola (Human Rights Watch 2004). Although rape is a common tool of war, it is not always recognized as a war crime. As Helen Scanlon (2008, 31) asserts, rape is "often simply viewed as an 'unfortunate' consequence of war even though it has been integral to war strategies." Deeming gender-based violence an "unfortunate" consequence of violent militarized movements sidelines women's experiences and ignores the fact that secessionist movements are entrenched in larger patriarchal societies. As feminist political theory emphasizes, acknowledging women's experiences during war and seriously interrogating them provides an opportunity for change.

Womanhood in Public Protest

Women have led protests in several African countries in the postcolonial period, adapting colonial-era strategies to resist other Africans (vis-à-vis intracolonization) rather than imperial authorities. Next I discuss some of the complex political and embodied strategies that such protesting women have used.

Biafra, Nigeria

In May 2017 Nigerian soldiers chased the attendees of an Indigenous People of Biafra women's conference from the stadium they were using as a venue. A nineteen-minute video circulated on YouTube depicting the ensuing protest as women disrobed to the waist or completely, marching to the house of a chief in the Abiriba community in southeastern Nigeria to protest the attack. The chief told them he would stand up for them. "Everybody has a right to associate with anything or any organization. It's a free world," he said. He implored the women to "conduct themselves in a peaceful manner" and noted, "This is a fight that doesn't require guns but wisdom. We don't want the Biafra [War] that killed people. I urge you to use diplomacy to follow this struggle" (Onyeji 2017). In this instance, women used public spaces to protest in a way that may be distinct from men. Women figuratively and symbolically stage and embrace national belonging, emphasizing varied public rituals and performances. At the same time, this makes women's activities ripe for co-optation by otherwise male-dominated secessionist movements.

The women's protests were the culmination of long-standing secessionist intentions in eastern Nigeria. Nigeria gained independence from British rule in 1960, and a violent conflict began six years later when rioting erupted after General Yakubu Gowon seized power in a military coup in September 1967. A massacre (many scholars say it was an attempted genocide) of Igbo people in the North followed. Many Igbo fled to the Eastern Region for protection. In response, Chief Chukwuemeka Ojukwu, the governor of the region, launched plans for secession, declaring the independence of the Eastern Region and the establishment of the Republic of Biafra on May 27, 1967. Fighting broke out less than two months later between federal and Biafran forces; the ensuing war resulted in high casualties, as well as widespread starvation and famine in Biafra (Falola and Ezekwem 2016). Civil conflict between the federal government of Nigeria and the secessionist Republic of Biafra lasted until January 1970. Much of the fighting took place along the Bight of Biafra, the southeastern coast of Nigeria.

While much has been written about the Biafran secessionist movement—the civil war has been the subject of novels, plays, and poems as well as academic literature—scholars have not fully addressed the participation of women and girls. Making their case based on human rights norms, pro-Biafra activists have called on the international community for help. Most recently, in 2017, acting through the Organization of Emerging African States (OEAS), they sought help from the European Union, calling on the High Representative of the Union for Foreign Affairs and Security Policy, Federica Mogherini, to conduct a referendum for Biafra's independence (Akpan 2017). In response, the chief administrative officer of OEAS, Jonathan Levy, stated that the "protection of human rights and fundamental freedoms remains a priority for the EU," calling on Nigeria to respect such rights (quoted in Akpan 2017). He also cautioned the OEAS and Biafra agitators that established international law might limit their claims, and that armed secession could not lead to the establishment of an independent state (Akpan 2017).

Against this backdrop, Biafran women resurrected traditional methods of social protest. For example, their actions recalled those who protested British colonial activities in 1929 by "sitting on a man," a form of shaming practice traditionally used only by (Igbo) women of Nigeria when confronting serous grievances (Van Allen 1972). "Sitting on a man" "could include singing vulgar songs outside the home of a man who had violated women's rights and activities" (Sheldon 2016, 17). In 1929 the colonial government had undertaken measures to impose direct taxation on women, which women strongly resented. Many of those who protested the taxes worked in markets and thus had significant economic and political control in society. Subsequently women collectively mobilized to express their discontent with the erosion of their political and economic authority in what became known as the "Women's War." The widespread protests included attacks on local African male authorities; the protesting women saw such men as collaborators in the colonial system. Women also attacked the British court building and sang insulting songs to male colonial officials. The women demanded their exemption from taxes, the removal of corrupt chiefs, and the introduction of female judges. The tradition of "sitting on a man" was well established and women had periodically used it against local African men as a mechanism to protect their rights (Van Allen 1972). The May 2017 protest reflects a pattern in which African women reinterpreted traditional forms of protest to fit modern times. Their protest reflects a pattern in which women use their bodies to participate in contemporary liberation struggles, providing a useful alternative to navigating the complexities of secessionist movements that seek help from international organizations that do not always prioritize women's experiences and grievances.

Few local Igbo men dared interfere in the 1929 women's protest. By contrast, when Nigerian women launched a traditional protest against the state in 2017, male leaders issued a warning calling for peaceful protests only. They sought to enforce male authority, demanding that the protesting women behave "civilly." At the same time, as they had in 1929, Pro-Biafra Igbo men generally did not interfere with the protest to any great extent because it aligned with their interest in asserting political power against the hegemonic state.

Anglophone Cameroon

Men's co-optation of women's political activities also took place in neighboring Cameroon, where they urged women to support male-dominated Anglophone opposition organizations. The YouTube video featuring Mami Margaret represented an attempt by the male-dominated Anglophone Civil Society Consortium to co-opt women's protests against national celebrations of International Women's Day (IWD) that had taken place the prior March. IWD, which takes place annually on March 8, is typically a significant event for women in Cameroon, as they celebrate and participate in seminars and networking events over the course of several weeks. Bertrade Ngo-Ngijol Banoum and Anne Patricia Rice (2015, 5) observe that IWD involves "a rich web of interrelated programming including seminars, debates, capacity-building workshops, arts and craft fairs, theater, music and dance performances, political rallies, commemorative parades, and business conferences and networking events." They write that the wearing of the IWD *pagne*, a colorful wrapper, which features images and phrases related to the year's global theme, is the most visible sign of women's unity on IWD. Yet in 2017 many Anglophone women did not purchase it because they joined a boycott to protest Francophone domination, taking to heart the year's theme, Be Bold for Change. In Bamenda, an Anglophone opposition stronghold, local newspapers reported that there were so few participants that the IWD march lasted less than an hour rather than the usual two to three hours (*Cameroon Concord News* 2017).

The outlawed Anglophone Civil Society Consortium had requested that citizens in the Northwest and Southwest regions observe a "ghost town" on March 8. The choice of the date represented an attempt to co-opt women's political power, as their abstention from IWD would make a bold statement. Some women protested by going about their usual activities in lieu of participating in IWD. In a video circulating on social media, Tassang Wilfred, a male program coordinator of the outlawed consortium, thanked women who boycotted, saying, "You have told the government that you want your husbands and your children to come back home [from detention] and you have told the world that you are unhappy" (*Journal du Cameroon* 2017). He urged citizens to be steadfast in the protest and warned they would suffer greater marginalization if they gave up "the struggle" for equality with Francophones.

The rhetoric Wilfred employed crossed linguistic and cultural boundaries. Edith Kah Walla, a Douala-based Francophone female politician and social activist, called on both Anglophone and Francophone women to boycott Women's Day (Enow 2017). She reminded women that children had been killed during protests and that children had lost the ability to go to school. She called on them to protest a government that arrested leaders of peaceful protests and violated their rights to communicate (by shutting down the internet), pointing out that the Cameroonian economy was in a slump. Wallah endeavored to unify women around mutual grievances. Thus she implied that women could not be truly free if they did not focus on freeing *all* Cameroonians, regardless of social, cultural, linguistic, and political cleavages.

Although women's participation has been critical to the Anglophone male-dominated movement, the international community has largely ignored their concerns. In 2009 the African Commission on Human and Peoples' Rights rejected a case filed for Anglophone independence by a leading Anglophone self-determination organization, the Southern Cameroon National Council. In their decision they noted that the state should abolish "all discriminatory practices against people of Northwest and Southwest Cameroon, including equal usage of the English language in business transactions" (23). At the same time, they affirmed the status quo by concluding that comprehensive national dialogue, rather than secession, must address Anglophone concerns. Similarly, when Sam Egbe, a Cameroonian living in the United Kingdom, asked the British government to offer assistance in early April 2017, Tobias Ellwood, a British Parliament member in charge of relations with Africa and the Middle East, declined, saying that the 1961 referendum should stand. He recommended "broad-based dialogue with a range of interlocutors and a return to normalcy in [Anglophone] regions" (*Pretoriavibe* 2017).

While men have protested Anglophone subjugation on both sides of the Atlantic by appealing to the international community, women have used traditional forms of protests, like their Nigerian counterparts, to draw attention to the situation in their own unique ways. In September 2017, for example, Anglophone Cameroonian women in the United States mobilized Takumbeng, surrounding the hotel of the Cameroonian president Paul Biya during his recent visit to New York to participate in the 72nd Ordinary Session of the United Nations General Assembly (Aliguena 2017). The women used traditional forms of protest and transnational networks to foster political solidarity, Anglophone inclusion, and nationalist aspirations.

Failure to analyze how women, individually and collectively, serve the goals of secessionist movements that are embedded in larger patriarchal orders leads to an incomplete picture of how gender shapes such movements. By not participating in IWD and by protesting in public spaces that make their collective agency visible across national boundaries, Anglophone women focused on the broader political goals of secession. As the political scientist Aili Tripp maintains, such co-optation of women's sociopolitical activities is a recurring pattern in postcolonial African states where women's organizations are co-opted by their governments and encouraged to applaud the actions of male-led organizations (Tripp 2000; Tripp et al. 2012). Hence Anglophone Cameroonian women chose to sacrifice a political unity that traversed ethnic, political, linguistic, and social boundaries to support male-dominated political organizations that advocated for secession. Even more, as Aliguena (2017) demonstrates, women turned their attention to demanding the release of imprisoned Anglophone male political dissidents, which may further marginalize their political unity and sideline issues of gender equality in Cameroon more generally. At the same time, a limited and technocratic approach to "women's issues" is often used strategically by postcolonial elites to obscure patriarchal control over the state, such as the use of IWD celebrations to bolster nationalist aims.

Conclusion

While Western and African media and academic literature continue to diminish women's participation in past and present secessionist movements, this essay shows that African women have found new and varied strategies to access social and political power in politically turbulent environments. While there are many active secessionist movements in contemporary Africa, this work serves as an entry point from which to understand African women's roles and activities in postcolonial liberation struggles. While most scholarship has ignored women in secessionist movements, this has begun to change. Most recently, Sondra Hale (2001) examined South Sudanese women's activism in exile during the secessionist struggle, and Nada Mustafa Ali (2015) conducted an extensive study of women's experiences during the South Sudan secessionist movement and the plight of women in the initial state-building process afterward. Yet there is much more work to do on gender and secessionist movements in contemporary Africa. I hope these reflections serve as an entry point to a larger conversation. Key questions remain unanswered, such as how religion and gender intersect to drive secessionist movements forward. The role women play in movements such as that of Uamsho (means "awakening"), a Muslim religious group in Zanzibar advocating for secession from mainland Tanzania, might be different from that of Muslim Sahrawi women in Western Sahara.

Another important issue to explore relates to the alliance of secessionist movements that cross geographic boundaries. The closeness between English-Speaking regions of Cameroon and Nigeria, based on geography and the legacy of shared European rule, may add another layer of political challenges that women must navigate within secessionist movements. Recent international news reports have suggested that the West African coast could be further destabilized if Anglophone Cameroonians and pro-Biafrans join forces to seek self-determination (Iaccino and Murakoshi 2016). What it means for women if transnational secessionist movements attempt to unite politically and militarily remains unclear. As many of these movements are still active, their effects on women's lives, and the ways that women negotiate within them, remains unclear. It is evident, however, that women and gender will continue to play a significant role in secessionist movements across the continent.

....

Jacqueline-Bethel Tchouta Mougoué is an assistant professor in the Department of History at Baylor University. An interdisciplinary feminist scholar, Mougoué is interested in the gendering of identities in modern Africa. Her research interests particularly focus on the gendering of identities in state politics, body politics, and religious politics in Cameroon.

Works Cited

African Commission on Human and Peoples' Rights. 2009. "266/03: Kevin Mgwanga Gunme et al. / Cameroon." Decision on Communications, 45th Ordinary Session, May 27. http://www.achpr.org/communications/decision/266.03/

Akpan, Jeremiah. 2017. "European Union Replies Pro-Biafra Agitators over Calls for BiafrExit." *Naija*. https://www.naija.ng/701259-european-union-replies-pro-biafra-agitators-calls-biafrexit.html#701259.

Ali, Nada Mustafa. 2015. *Gender, Race, and Sudan's Exile Politics: Do We All Belong to This Country?* Lanham, MD: Lexington Books.

Aliguena, Honore. 2017. "Takumbeng at Dictator Biya's Hotel in New-York." YouTube, September 25. https://www.youtube.com/watch?v=9_qY9eg6HLc.

Al Jazeera. 2017. "Cameroon Shuts Down Internet in English-Speaking Areas." January 25. https://www.aljazeera.com/news/2017/01/cameroon-anglophone-areas-suffer-internet-blackout-170125174215077.html.

Amnesty International. 2016. "UN Must Monitor Human Rights in Western Sahara and Sahrawi Refugee Camps." April 26. https://www.amnesty.org/en/latest/news/2016/04/un-must-monitor-human-rights-in-western-sahara-and-sahrawi-refugee-camps/.

Anderson, Benedict. 1991. *Imagined Communities: Reflections on the Origin and Spread of Nationalism*. London: Verso.

Atabong, Amindeh Blaise. 2017. "'Digital Refugees,' Repression and the Death Penalty—Cameroon's Escalating Language Conflict." *Equal Times*, February 21.

Banoum, Bertrade Ngo-Ngijol, and Anne Patricia Rice. 2015. "Embodying African Women's Epistemology: International Women's Day in Cameroon." In *Writing through the Visual and Virtual: Inscribing Language, Literature, and Culture in Francophone Africa and the Caribbean*, edited by Renée Larrier and Ousseina Alidou, 3–14. London: Lexington Books.

Bryson, Valerie. 2016. *Feminist Political Theory.* Basingstoke, U.K.: Palgrave Macmillan.

Buchanan, Allen. 2017. "Secession." In *The Stanford Encyclopedia of Philosophy,* edited by Edward N. Zalta. Stanford: Stanford University Press. http://plato.stanford.edu/archives/sum2013/entries/secession/

Buckley-Zistel, Susanne, and Ulrike Krause. 2017. *Gender, Violence, Refugees.* New York: Berghahn Books.

Cabestan, Jean-Pierre, and Aleksandar Pavković, eds. 2012. *Secessionism and Separatism in Europe and Asia: To Have a State of One's Own.* New York: Routledge.

Cameroon Concord News. 2017. "Southern Cameroon Women's Day: Attendance Noticeably Less Than Expected." March 9.

Clarke, Yaliwe. 2008. "Security Sector Reform in Africa: A Lost Opportunity to Deconstruct Militarised Masculinities?" *Feminist Africa* 10 (August): 49–66.

Decker, Alicia C. 2014. *In Idi Amin's Shadow: Women, Gender, and Militarism in Uganda.* Athens: Ohio University Press.

Decker, Alicia C. 2017. "What Does a Feminist Curiosity Bring to African Military History? An Analysis and an Intervention." *Journal of African Military History* 1, Issue 1-2: 93 – 111.

DeLancey, Dike, Rebecca Neh Mbuh, and Mark W. DeLancey. 2010. *Historical Dictionary of the Republic of Cameroon.* Lanham, MD: Scarecrow Press.

The Economist. 2008. "Angola-gate." November 19. https://www.economist.com/news/2008/11/19/angola-gate.

Ekan, Gil. 2017a. "Southern Cameroons Woman Calls for All Women to Protest Naked." YouTube, January 19. https://www.youtube.com/watch?v=Xu4ozsNrhtw.

Ekan, Gil. 2017b. "Southern Cameroonians Women in New York Unleashed Takumbeng at Paul Biya's Hotel." YouTube, September 22. https://www.youtube.com/watch?v=Yw5GXmgQidI.

Elombah News. 2017. "Biafra: Those Calling for UN Intervention Will Have a Long Wait." September 18. https://elombah.com/biafra-those-calling-for-un-intervention-will-have-a-long-wait-expert/.

Enow, Tabi Marriane. 2017. "Women's Day 2017: Women Implored to Speak Up against Injustices." *Journal du Cameroun*, September 3.

Falola, Toyin, and Ogechukwu Ezekwem, eds. 2016. *Writing the Nigeria-Biafra War.* Suffolk, U.K.: James Currey.

Geiger, Susan. 1997. *TANU Women: Gender and Culture in the Making of Tanganyikan Nationalism, 1955–1965.* Portsmouth, NH: Heinemann.

Hale, Sondra. 2001. "Alienation and Belonging—Women's Citizenship and Emancipation: Visions of Sudan's Post-Islamic Future." *New Political Science* 23, no. 1: 25–43.

Hentz, James J. 2014. *Routledge Handbook of African Security*. London: Routledge.

Human Rights Watch. 2004. "Angola: In Oil-Rich Cabinda, Army Abuses Civilians." December 22. https://www.hrw.org/news/2004/12/22/angola-oil-rich-cabinda-army-abuses-civilians.

Human Rights Watch. 2008. "Human Rights in Western Sahara and in the Tindouf Refugee Camps." December 19. https://www.hrw.org/report/2008/12/19/human-rights-western-sahara-and-tindouf-refugee-camps.

Human Rights Watch. 2014. "Off the Radar Human Rights in the Tindouf Refugee Camps." October 18. https://reliefweb.int/report/algeria/radar-human-rights-tindouf-refugee-camps.

Iaccino, Ludovica, and Sho Murakoshi. 2016. "Biafra and Southern Cameroons Might 'Join Forces to Achieve Independence.'" *International Business Times*, February 25.

Journal du Cameroon. 2017. "Consortium Acclaims 'Resounding Boycott of Women's Day' in NW, SW Regions." September 3.

Kah, Henry Kam. 2011. "Women's Resistance in Cameroon's Western Grassfields: The Power of Symbols, Organization, and Leadership, 1957–1961." *African Studies Quarterly* 12, no. 3: 67–91.

Koné, Elizabeth M. Jamilah. 1998. "The Right of Self-Determination in the Angolan Enclave of Cabinda." Working paper, African Studies Center, University of Pennsylvania, Philadelphia. https://www.africa.upenn.edu/Workshop/kone98.html.

Lippert, Anne. 1992. "Sahrawi Women in the Liberation Struggle of the Sahrawi People." *Signs* 17, no. 3: 636–51.

Lyons, Tanya. 2004. *Guns and Guerilla Girls: Women in the Zimbabwean National Liberation Struggle*. Trenton, NJ: Africa World Press.

Mama, Amina, and Margo Okazawa-Rey. 2008. "Editorial: Militarism, Conflict and Women's Activism." *Feminist Africa* 10 (August): 1–8.

Manunga Studio 2. 2017. "Takumbeng Relief 18 11 2017 London." YouTube, November 12. https://www.youtube.com/watch?v=hdZ_ucLvgho.

Morris, Loveday. 2013. "In Western Sahara, Women Play Large Role in Forgotten Struggle for Independence." *Washington Post*. July 7.

Ngangoue, Nana Rosine. 1996. "Angola-Women: Living with War in the Forests of Cabinda." Inter Press Service: News Agency, May 27.

Ogundipe-Leslie, Molara. 1994. *Re-creating Ourselves: African Women and Critical Transformations*. Trenton, NJ: Africa World Press.

Onyeji, Ebuka. 2017. "Nigeria: Pro-Biafra Women Protest Half-Naked against Soldiers." *AllAfrica*, May 20. https://allafrica.com/stories/201705210015.html.

Pavković, Aleksandar. 2015. "Secessionism and Separatism Monthly Series: Secession and Secessionism." *H-Net*. https://networks.h-net.org/node/3911/discussions/90459/secessionism-and-separatism-monthly-series-secession-and.

Porto, João Gomes. 2003. "Cabinda: Notes on a Soon to Be Forgotten War." Working paper, Institute for Security Studies, Pretoria. http://archive.niza.nl/docs/20030819121948283.pdf.

Pretoriavibe. 2017. "Shocking Discovery!!! Common Wealth Totally against Federalism or Secession; So." September 15. https://africanarguments.org/2015/12/08/the-crackdown-in-cabinda-the-hidden-politics-of-angolas-exclave/.

Reid, Helen. 2015. "The Crackdown in Cabinda: The Hidden Politics of Angola's Exclave." *Africanarguments*, December 8.

Salami, Minna. 2012. "7 key issues in African Feminist Thought?" *Msafropolitan*, August 16. https://www.msafropolitan.com/2012/08/7-key-issues-in-african-feminist-thought.html.

Saltman, Kenneth J., and David Gabbard, eds. 2011. *Education as Enforcement: The Militarization and Corporatization of Schools*. New York: Routledge.

Scanlon, Helen. 2008. "Militarization, Gender and Transitional Justice in Africa." *Feminist Africa* 10 (August): 31–48.

Schmidt, Elizabeth. 2005. *Mobilizing the Masses: Gender, Ethnicity, and Class in the Nationalist Movement in Guinea, 1939–1958*. Portsmouth, NH: Heinemann.

Schroeder, Matt, and Guy Lamb. 2006. "The Illicit Arms Trade in Africa." *African Analyst* 1, 3rd quarter: 69–78.

Sheldon, Kathleen E. 2016. *Historical Dictionary of Women in Sub-Saharan Africa*. Lanham, MD: Rowman & Littlefield.

Tripp, Aili Mari. 2000. *Women and Politics in Uganda*. Madison: University of Wisconsin Press.

Tripp, Aili Mari, Isabel Casimiro, Joy Kwesiga, and Alice Mungwa. 2012. *African Women's Movements: Transforming Political Landscapes*. Cambridge, U.K.: Cambridge University Press.

Urdang, Stephanie. 1979. *Fighting Two Colonialisms: Women in Guinea-Bissau*. New York: Monthly Review Press.

Van Allen, Judith. 1972. "'Sitting on a Man': Colonialism and the Lost Political Institutions of Igbo Women." *Canadian Journal of African Studies* 6, no. 2: 165–81.

Vasquez, Erica. 2014. "Living under Occupation in the Western Sahara: Women, Resistance and Self-Determination." Working paper, School of Foreign Service, Georgetown University, Washington, D.C.

Vickers, Jill. 2016. "Secessionism and Separatism Monthly Series: Gendering Secession." *H-Net*, March 20. https://networks.h-net.org/node/116427/pdf.

Yombo, Catherine Muring. 2017. "Takumbeng Unleash." *Southern Cameroon National Council UK*, September 23. http://ukscnc.co.uk/2017/09/23/454/.

Makhosazana Xaba

· ·

Three Women

Three women step out of the Calabash hotel
The sudden wave of freezing raindrops-filled winds
Hits them. They hug in haste, run to the two cars
Midnight approaches, sounding louder & louder

The youngest woman, alone in her car smiles
Unstoppably, to herself, as she drives into the night
The voices of the two women still alive in her head
In bed, her smile becomes the conductor of her dreams

In the black Mercedes Benz, C180 the oldest woman
Turns on the heater before they take off
They see the stories of Grahamstown on the
Architecture of buildings as they drive out of town

The younger of the two, the driver of the Benz,
Steadies the car on the road while her mind jolts,
Crosses over, skips, stretches, scatters & returns
To the single holding thread: the warmth of sisterhood

The oldest woman runs into her B & B on Harry Street
After saying goodbye, goodnight, thank you for everything
In her room she turns on the heater, the electric blanket
The kettle & the ultimate dream: a world of women of wisdom

MERIDIANS · feminism, race, transnationalism   17:2 November 2018
DOI: 10.1215/15366936-7176494 © 2018 Smith College

In bed she returns to the topics of conversation
With the two women while a chorus plays in her heart
    "Hold on, hold firm
    Enjoy the joys of sisterhood,
    The joys of sisterhood
    The tangible joys of sisterhood"

Makhosazana Xaba is a poet, short story writer, and anthologist. She is the author of two poetry collections and *Running and Other Stories* (2013), which won the SALA Nadine Gordimer Short Story Award in 2014. Her poetry has been anthologized extensively, translated into Italian, Mandarin, and Turkish and is available from the Cambridge Poetry Archive. In 2017 her poem "Twenty one houses" was nominated for the Pushcart Prize, and in 2014 she was nominated in the poetry category of the Mbokodo Awards. In 2016 she edited *Like the Untouchable Wind: An Anthology of Poems*.

Selina Makana

Contested Encounters
Toward a Twenty-First-Century
African Feminist Ethnography

Abstract: This essay reflects upon both the predicaments and the promises of feminist ethnography in contemporary Africa from the position of an African feminist researcher. Two key questions guide the analysis: What are productive ways to respond to feminist critiques of representing the African woman "other"? What are the promises, if any, of African feminist ethnography documenting the histories of women on the continent? This essay argues that African feminist ethnography is a productive methodology that helps to highlight knowledge production about women's lives in their specific sociopolitical, ethnolinguistic, religious, and economic contexts. To highlight the significance and limits of reflexivity and the idiosyncrasies of ethnographic research, this essay calls for a different way of naming the encounters between researchers and their participants. It therefore proposes naming this energy the *ebb and flow of fieldwork research* because this metaphor helps to destabilize and move beyond the rigid binaries of insider/outsider that have traditionally characterized power relations in fieldwork.

On a sunny Friday morning in mid-September, three security guards usher me into the National Assembly building in Luanda, the capital city of Angola. I confidently greet them in Portuguese. Two of the three security guards smile and try to make small talk. The third asks for my identification, but before I pass it to him, the other two, almost in unison, say, "There is no problem. She is one of us." They then ask if I am from the province of

MERIDIANS · feminism, race, transnationalism 17:2 November 2018
DOI: 10.1215/15366936-7176516 © 2018 Smith College

Bié. I hesitate before I shake my head. "But where are you from, *a senhora*?" I respond in my poorly constructed Portuguese that I am from Kenya. "Kenya?" comes another unison reply. "But, what are you doing here?"

At this point I hand them a copy of my passport, including my consent form. After they look over the documents, one of the guards hands them back to me and says, matter-of-factly, "You look like one of us. You could be Angolan." I look at my watch, and as if reading my mind, the second guard quips, "I know you have to go, but you could really become Angolan if you marry one of us. You look very young too." I laugh and say that I am already taken. The joke—at least that is how I chose to see it—puts all of us at ease. They let me into the building. I am taken to a boardroom for a meeting with former female guerrillas of the opposition party União Nacional para Independencia Total de Angola (National Union for Total Independence of Angola; UNITA).

As I wait for the president of the League of Angolan Women, the women's branch of UNITA, the receptionist introduces herself. "From the phone I thought you were American and white, but you are black," she said. "I also thought you work for a non-governmental organization. So, who are you?" I smile and respond politely, trying to hide my frustration. This was the fifth time since I had arrived in Luanda in August that I have confronted this question. "I am a doctoral student and I am also Kenyan. I am here to conduct research about Angolan women and their involvement in the armed struggle and the civil war." I give her a copy of my bio as proof of my identity. She glances over it and with a look of mistrust retorts, "But you speak English? I still think you are American and a journalist. It is rare to see black people come to do research here. Are you really African or African American?" I smile again, nodding and shaking my head at the same time.

The skeptical look on the receptionist's face makes me uncomfortable and agitated. I want to say I understand her suspicion, but I also want to tell her how disappointed I am— disappointed that she believes that only Americans or whites from the West are capable of doing academic research. My frustration melts away when my research partners walk into the room. "I hear you are Kenyan and American, just like Obama," says my interviewee, shaking my hand. I respond that I am not American, but I don't think she hears me.[1]

As researchers, we position ourselves with various markers, including race, gender, sexuality, age, class, ethnicity, nationality, language, and religion. In my case, the multiple identities I embody as a thirty-something-year-old, unmarried, English-speaking Kenyan woman at an elite university in the United States inevitably influenced my fieldwork in Angola. This essay contributes to the growing literature on methods and techniques for conducting qualitative research in Africa, as well as to feminist research methodologies more generally. I build on the works of several African feminist scholars, Black feminists, and other women of color ethnographers transnationally who have written about unequal relations of power in fieldwork but also how identity remains a contested and negotiated sphere in which ethnographers struggle to cultivate research strategies that allow them to name and describe their unique experiences in the field (see Abu-Lughod 1990; Bennett 2008; Davis and Craven 2016; McClaurin 2001; Mullings 2000; Tamale 2011).

I draw upon examples and anecdotes from my own experiences while conducting interviews with women ex-combatants and civilians in Angola to examine the ways that cross-cultural perceptions, interactions, and representations influenced my fieldwork and the outcome of my data collection. The field as a site of power reveals the dynamic way in which identities and their attendant power relations are created, contested, and transformed when a researcher encounters her research partners. I argue that for those of us who identify as African feminist ethnographers, it is important that we fashion research practices that embody creativity, that foster empathy with our research partners, and that destabilize relations of power. In fleshing out the messiness of African feminist ethnography, I am reminded of Chandra Mohanty's (2003, 226) assertion that it is crucial for transnational feminist scholars to acknowledge differences and particularities of our research in order to "better see the connections and commonalities because no border or boundary is ever complete or rigidly determining. The challenge is to see how differences allow us to explain the connections and border crossings better and more accurately, how specifying difference allows us to theorize universal concerns more fully." It is my belief that an awareness of these underlying elements of our research contributes to a more engaged field experience for feminist ethnographers as we attempt to capture the particularities and nuances of African women's lives.

I began this essay with a personal anecdote to emphasize how fieldwork for African feminist ethnographers can be a messy process fraught with contradictions. The encounters I described beg the question: Given that Africa and Africans are not a monolithic group, how do the multiple identities that we inhabit as scholars affect and/or transform our research? It is worth noting that I define African feminist ethnography as a decolonized ethnography in that it acknowledges and promotes the development of theories based on non-Western assumptions. Taking a cue from Faye V. Harrison (2011, 5), who observes that a decolonized anthropology ought to be "directed toward the empowerment of its studied populations," I posit that African feminist ethnography flips the script of Western ways of writing African women's lives as "othered subjects" and redresses this history through a process of recovery and historical analysis. As a contextual and experientially based approach to the production of knowledge, feminist ethnography challenges the false dichotomies of positivism. To this end, I contend that African feminist ethnography is manifested in our self-conscious positioning as African women who research the lived experiences of women on the continent.[2] Our identities thus become a crucial point of departure for our theorization and, at the same time, a point of entry for our fieldwork.

My ethnographic fieldwork encompassed twenty-five oral interviews (both formal and informal) and participant observation carried out in Angola and Portugal between August 2015 and January 2016. Some of the interviews were highly confidential, as some feared the negative consequences of being identified in any way. My research site was translocal, multilingual, and multisited. Since I chose not to confine myself to a specific city, the multisited nature of my ethnographic experience enabled me to see how gender was politicized and institutionalized within various parts of Angola. I conducted all interviews in a qualitative and semistructured style in Portuguese, although some of the interviewees also spoke some English. Each interview lasted between one and a half and three hours.[3] My interviews went beyond interrogating what roles women played in armed struggles to focus on the why and the how of women's involvement in war. Angolan women's narratives are crucial to my study because they are fundamental to how women understand their lives; as Julia Powles (2004, 20) posits, some issues "can only really be communicated through narrative since they are not readily amenable to generalization."

This essay brings to light some of the challenges and dilemmas I encountered during my fieldwork. I use concrete examples of how I navigated these fieldwork dilemmas in Angola by employing the metaphor of the *ebb and flow of fieldwork research* and reflexivity as a methodological strategy that helped me to move beyond the false dichotomy of insider/outsider

and to explore the complex negotiations of identity, power, and positionality. Acknowledging and naming the dilemmas that arise during fieldwork helps to establish rigor and expose the complexities of the research
process. I argue that the points of information that former women combatants and civilians shared with me, how I gained access to them, the
assumptions they made about me, the uneasy interactions we experienced,
and the context in which they revealed their wartime experiences, were
largely mediated by my own multiple identities.

Positionality in Feminist Ethnography

My interactions with my research partners made it clear that no researcher
is guaranteed a seamless and comfortable relationship with her collaborators because the dynamics of the interviewing process are rife with complex formulations. As Josephine Beoku-Betts (1994) aptly concludes, even
when black feminists conduct research within their own communities,
there are moments "when black is not enough." It is here that we might
recall Lila Abu-Lughod's (1990) work on the dangers of feminist ethnography, in particular, assuming a certain universalism regarding "women's
experience." She was particularly concerned about feminist ethnographic
practices that erased power differentials between the more privileged
researchers and one's research participants. Both Beoku-Betts and Abu-
Lughod alert us to the challenges of identity politics during fieldwork. They
also remind us why researchers must pay attention to intragroup differences. My interactions with the security guards and the receptionist clearly
demonstrate that notions of difference often complicate one's experiences
in the field.

Within feminist ethnography, first-person narratives have continued
to gain traction as a strategy for retelling and interpreting experience. To
this end, researchers emphasize the centrality of positionality as a way to
interrogate the politics of identity and difference in the research process. In
his writing on cultural identity, Stuart Hall (1990, 222) cogently observes,
"Practices of representation always implicate the positions from which we
speak or write—the positions of *enunciation*. . . . Though we speak, so to
say 'in our own name,' of ourselves and from our own experience, nevertheless who speaks, and the subject who is spoken of, are never identical,
never exactly in the same place." Hall's assertion alerts us not only to issues
of authorship and to how our identities are always in flux but also to how
the idea of representation is about relations of power. Enunciating one's

positionality is even more crucial for many of us who conduct research in the field of gender and militarism because that field is embedded in power hierarchies that privilege a certain kind of militarized masculinity and cast doubt upon women's presence in the masculinist arenas of war. Just as women are not expected to be in war zones, they are also not "supposed" to study war.

Positionality in feminist research provides a space for a dialectical relationship between objectivity and subjectivity in one's research. Regardless of whether the researcher situates herself as an insider or an outsider, her positionality always has a bearing on the level of trust and openness she has with her interviewees, as well as how she collects, analyzes, and represents her data. Positionality thus plays a significant role for researchers in and of Africa since notions of difference and similarity on the continent are far from homogeneous; they vary from region to region, from country to country, and from one ethnolinguistic community to another. Therefore, when conducting fieldwork in such a heterogeneous environment, an African researcher carries on her shoulders a huge burden of representation. This weight can push the researcher to ask pertinent questions: Whose story am I documenting, and why does this story matter to the community and the outside world? Social responsibility and accountability become much greater for researchers traveling to cultural settings other than those of their own birth and upbringing. This burden of representation, as Amina Mama and Margo Okazawa-Rey (2012, 8) observe, nurtures a real and intimate engagement with the various manifestations of difference, power, and privilege that characterize the contexts within which researchers are engaging.

African Women in the Field:
Going beyond the Outsider/Insider Divide

When I was confronted with questions such as "Kenya, but what are you doing here?" and "Are you American? It is rare to see black people come to do research here," I quickly realized how unprepared I was to tackle what some may dismiss as "uninformed questions" of our research partners. Yet these questions reminded me of what my driver had said when he came to pick me up from the airport upon my arrival in Luanda: "I saw you several times as I looked around the waiting area. I passed by you three times because I was expecting to see a white woman."[4] These encounters and many others I experienced in the course of my fieldwork reveal the simple fact that the way many communities on the continent experience research is often associated with white-skinned Westerners and their short-term visits. This fact puts pressure on African feminist researchers because we are not always seen as legitimate scholars.

In her interview with Elaine Salo, Amina Mama states, "We have always been part of the early conceptualizations of so-called 'Western feminism,' even if not properly acknowledged as such. More importantly African women have always defined and carried out their own struggles. African feminism dates back in our collective past, although much of the story has yet to be researched and told" (Salo and Mama 2001, 60). Even when African scholars—more precisely African women—document histories of Africans, we have to demonstrate our intellectual prowess in ways that are not expected of white scholars. It is, therefore, not an exaggeration to state that African women are generally ignored as intellectual subjects because our intellectual labor and knowledge production are so easily dismissed in academic spaces.

Prior to my arrival in Angola, the connections I made through academic networks and social media proved useful in the selection of my participants and continued to facilitate my work once I was in the capital city. Friends I made through the local universities in Angola and church-based organizations kindly offered their expertise and helped me to navigate the highly politicized and militarized terrain in Angola. A new friend embraced me as one of her own and led me to other intermediaries who became valued collaborators during the course of my fieldwork. I needed intermediaries not only because of the sensitive nature of my research project but also because of what Marissa Moorman (2008) calls the "political paranoia" of the country, which meant that many participants were not willing to open up for fear of persecution.[5] I quickly embraced the idea of being "one of us"—very delightedly—because it accorded me the insider status every researcher yearns for. I appreciated my insider position because there were times when security clearances for conducting interviews with high-profile politicians were expedited through the connections I had made. I thought that the privilege sometimes accorded to me as an insider was due to my Africanness and that I "looked like an Angolan," a form of unspoken solidarity among African women. Although this was not always the case, I believed that my participants eventually were open with me because I was "one of them."

This "outsider within" position, to use Patricia Hill Collins's (1986 and

1997) phrase, allowed me to ask new questions that brought to light aspects of Angolan women's realties, or truths, that are often concealed, unnoticed, and erased by dominant narratives of the country's history. A case in point: I asked an ex-combatant to describe her experiences in a guerrilla camp in Kinshasa. She replied:

> You have probably been told all the "good" things about the armed struggle. The movement was not one "happy family" as you have probably been told. How could it have been? Some soldiers abused women because of the frustration with the war. The very comrades we supported violated our bodies. Every Angolan woman bears visible and invisible scars of the war. There, feel free to write that down and use it anyway you want because it is the truth. The truth you will never hear because of the shame.[6]

To highlight the fact that not all of her comrades behaved badly, my interviewee often used the phrase "behaved like monsters." She argued that the tough conditions of war brought out the "monster," even within good soldiers. This view is problematic since it dismisses the magnitude of wartime sexual violence by framing it as an isolated event that involved only a few deviant "monsters" and absolves the rest of responsibility. When my interviewees told me, as they often did, how the anger in loss and the murkiness of the war could force their men into "behaving like monsters," I became more aware of my own inability to understand the power of anger in grief and suffering.

To venture into the field of war is to grapple with the ethnography of violence, which is an inescapable part of life for many people across the world. Up until then I had not critically reflected on how the trauma of war, apathy, and death permeated the ordinary everydayness of many Angolan women's lives. That there is scant research on this area no doubt had a direct bearing on my pragmatic ability to carry out feminist research and produce antihegemonic knowledge. Therefore it was encouraging that my research partners willingly retold their traumatic experiences of war and urged me "to feel free to write that down." It could be that they understood the power of the spoken and written word as a way of carving themselves into the history of Angolan liberation struggles. I consider the testimonies of Angolan women as counternarratives that demonstrate women's agency and resilience, as well as their perceived roles in the body politic of the nation.

While the fluidity of my identity allowed me to move effortlessly through some social spaces, and despite the fact that I assumed I had the emic knowledge of insiders due to my Africanness, there certainly were other moments when I bumped awkwardly into the unpredictable web of social entanglements. People read me, almost across the board, as an American. Being acutely aware of the politics of location, identity, and representation forced me to reexamine constantly my location as a researcher in relation to my interviewees. I have to admit that there were moments when I was comfortable being mistaken for an American because of the convenience that came with an American identity. For instance, I appreciated the many doors that were opened as most of the women I spoke with felt that I was better positioned to represent their stories to the rest of the world.

It is here that I would like to suggest another way of naming this energy between my research partners and me. Who we want to be in the eyes of our participants, vis-à-vis how they see us, underlines one of the most complex challenges of conducting qualitative research. In my case, the delicate dance between us led me to understand our intricate relationship as one that is akin to waves of the sea. Rather than see my fieldwork encounters as shaped by rigid binaries of insider/outsider, I call this energy the *ebb and flow of the fieldwork process.*[7]

The Ebb and Flow of the Fieldwork Process

Richa Nagar (2014, 89) addresses the need for reflexive research practices and the challenges of cross-border fieldwork research by observing that "the difficulties of speaking with collaborators across borders are rooted in the structural realities of fieldwork—a research practice that frequently entails disjunctures between the sites of face-to-face encounters with people whose stories we want to tell, and the institutional locations from which we produce knowledge about them." To this end, the tensions arising from unequal relations of power in fieldwork cannot be emphasized enough. The assumption that my Africanness would open most doors and make me feel at home completely underestimated the degree to which my subjectivity was negotiated in nuanced and contradictory ways. Because I went to Angola, naïvely and rigidly, locating myself as an insider—and a reluctant outsider—it soon became evident that this binary failed to articulate the complex and multilayered experience of my research process. I found myself neither a total insider nor an outsider in relation to the women I interviewed because of my back-and-forth engagement with them. Different scholars of native anthropology (Trinh 1989; Narayan 1993) have challenged the belief that "native" researchers are insiders regardless of their complex backgrounds. The extent to which a researcher can be viewed as an insider is questionable because we inhabit multiple subjectivities with many intersecting identifications.

In cases where I needed to use Teresita, my Angolan host and translator, this ebb and flow of fieldwork encounters became even more apparent.[8] Although we had corresponded only via email while I was working on my visa application process, my translator and I developed an instant rapport as soon as I got to Angola. In our first meeting, Teresita, through teary yet distant eyes, told me that I reminded her of her "long lost relative" and she wanted to make sure that my time in Angola went smoothly. I was struck by how much she trusted me. In fact she even offered me a place to stay in her cozy two-bedroom apartment. I asked her why she did not treat me with suspicion, and her response was swift: "You are not like others. You are like my daughter." In my interviews with subjects who spoke Portuguese or other ethno-linguistic registers, such as Kimbundu and Umbundu, my epistemological position as a researcher in relation to my translator and interviewees uncovered the respectful tussle for truth. For example, when older high-ranking government officials treated me with mistrust because of my perceived young age, Teresita negotiated on my behalf. She had an uncanny ability to effortlessly switch between Portuguese and Kimbundu, which my interviewees found reassuring. Over the course of the interviews, I realized that she would interject into our conversations the phrase "We Africans." The phrase reassured my interviewees that I was "one of them" but also served to remind everyone in the room of our shared history as Africans. The role of the translator and the act of translation matter significantly in ethnographic research because the translator is part of the knowledge production process.

Through my positionality as nonwhite/non-Western and nonwhite/ Western researcher in a non-Western research setting, I was able to examine the ebb and flow of energy between my research partners and myself in the context of our multiple identities. Our identities were continuously contested and negotiated on the basis of nationality, ethnicity, age, religion, and marital status. These women were in no way inactive or passive recipients of the fieldwork process; they dismantled the common fieldwork praxis that often positions the researcher as all-knowing. By their simultaneously locating me during interviews as "one of them" and as the "other," a nonhierarchical and reciprocal relationship emerged in which my interviewees and I learned from one another during the research process. My encounters were molded by back-and-forth episodes of solidarity, trust, empathy, and suspicion.

Victoria Sanford and Asale Angel-Ajani (2006) note that in the context of war and violence, scholars have to contend with the difficult challenges involved in the act of representation when they speak on behalf of survivors of war. For instance, my interviewees were aware of the relational dimension of the research process, and therefore many of them demanded to know for whom my research was meant, why their wartime experiences mattered, and how I would represent their narratives. One former militant with Movimento Popular de Libertação de Angola (People's Movement for the Liberation of Angola; MPLA) asked me, "Why are you interested in our stories?"[9] This is a valid question for many ex-combatants who still hope to have their political memories and neglected voices written into the national history and who want to reclaim visibility in the history of the Angolan liberation struggle. We can perhaps surmise that many of the women asked this question because they were simply suspicious and feared being exploited or misrepresented. Margarida Paredes (2015, 46) points out in her interviews with Angolan women guerrillas that many wanted to be assured that sharing their stories was a "means of valorizing their life histories and memories in the public space," and they needed to see "this visibility as a tool for personal and social emancipation."

Some interviewees were aware of the politics of location and knowledge production. For example, after assuring her that I would eventually publish a book based on the interviews, one woman was grateful and relieved to tell her story, admitting, "This was hard for me. I have kept these memories inside me for thirty years. Some of them are good, but most of them were bad. Many Angolan women have learnt to forget. Forgetting is difficult."[10] It is precisely because of such accounts and the lack of an archive of women's experiences in wartime that oral history continues to be an important tool for restoring to the national historiography those marginalized social groups absent or excluded from official archives of war, and thus from master narratives of Angolan nationhood. Alicia Decker (2014) cogently points out that since women are often in the "shadows" of war and militarism, women's memories are crucial in uncovering and reconstructing their wartime experiences, which tend to be left out of historical records. In a politically charged environment such as Angola where voicing the truth or any form of political dissidence has dire consequences, truth is often contested in hushed tones—and my research partners were aware of this. For many women located on the margins of history, there is something politically transformative in the pursuit of truth, especially when this truth speaks to power.

The ebb and flow of fieldwork does not guarantee smooth sailing for the researcher. For me, it meant knowing that there were situations when I would have to be vulnerable to misinterpretation. On several occasions, for instance, I was mistaken for a reporter. With advice from colleagues who had done previous research in Angola, I made a conscious decision not to video-record my interviews. Nonetheless some women still felt suspicious of my tape recorder and even questioned my true intentions. With my tape recorder in hand, my identity was immediately shaped and constructed as a journalist, and rarely as a student researcher, which meant that some of my participants were willing to speak only in general terms. Other women lamented, "You come here to interview us and when you go back to your countries you report bad things about us."[11] Not only did the women recognize the exploitative nature of research, but they also held me accountable for my privileged position as a researcher. These exchanges reveal that because fieldwork is a human experience, research participants can question the motives of researchers, thus making the interview process difficult.

Conclusion

The multiple intersections of my identity allowed me to make several sociocultural and cross-national connections with Angolan women ex-combatants. These connections underscore that identity is salient in determining how the data are collected and what kinds of data are available to researchers. During some informal conversations with my research partners the insider characteristics of my identity enabled me to feel more like a family friend, a little sister, or a daughter than a researcher. For a transnational subject conducting fieldwork in spaces considered "home," there is a futility in imagining that the fluidity of one's identity can enable one to avoid this binary. This is because what lies at the heart of the engagement between a researcher and her participants is the ability of one's research participants to locate her—often in unexpected positions that make one uncomfortable but that can prove insightful in retrospect.

In this respect, reflexivity certainly does not guarantee a solution for dilemmas of critical feminist ethnography. Although as African feminist researchers we aim for an egalitarian, nonhierarchical relationship with our research subjects, this does not mean that we can always achieve it. However, reflexivity does provide us with strategies to deal with the inevitable power relations involved in representing others' experiences and voices. Thus the challenge for African feminist ethnographers is to create knowledge that emerges from the diverse and complex contexts in which we live and work. African feminist researchers must take questions of identity seriously in order to create nonhierarchical relationships with our research partners. This awareness may also enable us to appreciate the fact that our positions within the research process are not static, but contingent and always shifting. It is my hope that this essay will spark a conversation on the nuanced ways that feminist methodologies can account for the experiences of those of us who do not fit neatly into the insider/outsider dichotomy but must carve out alternative—and sometimes messy—ways of being in the field. For African feminist ethnographers, this will allow us to better understand the implications of doing fieldwork in sites we consider home.

....

Selina Makana is a postdoctoral research scholar at the Institute for Research on Women, Gender, and Sexuality at Columbia University. Her areas of research include gender and militarism, African women's social history, transnational feminisms, and African diaspora theory.

Notes

1   Field notes, September 18, 2015.
2   The past ten years have produced exciting scholarship by African feminists documenting experiences and stories of women in different regions of the continent. In particular, projects funded by the Council for the Development of Social Science Research in Africa's annual Gender Institute and the University of Cape Town's African Gender Institute have provided insights on researching African women's lives.
3   Given the vastness of Angola's geography, the ethnographic interviews I conducted in the provinces of Luanda and Benguela do not represent the war politics of the entire nation. I chose Luanda and Benguela for the following reasons: they were significant during the war because of the centrality of the Benguela railway; they received many refugees from rural areas because they were major urban centers; and they represented communities with diverse ethnic, socioeconomic, and political backgrounds.
4   Field notes, August 2015.

5   Recent scholarship underlines the challenges of conducting fieldwork in Angola, including intense government surveillance, the high cost of living, and limited reliable data from government sources. For more on the complexity of Angola as a fieldwork site, see Pearce 2012; Paredes 2015; Soares de Oliveira 2015.

6   Interview with the wife of a former soldier in the People's Armed Forces of Liberation of Angola, October 11, 2015, in Luanda.

7   I am deeply grateful to Ula Taylor for pushing me to think beyond binaries and for suggesting this concept of ebb and flow.

8   Of the twenty-five interviews I conducted, ten were facilitated with the help of a translator who spoke Portuguese, Kimbundu, Umbundu, and Kicongo.

9   Interview with a former MPLA militant and executive member of the Organization of Angolan Women, September 28, 2015, Bairro Popular in Luanda.

10 Interview with Ruth, September 11, 2015, in Luanda.

11 Interview with official in the Organization of Angolan Women, October 3, 2015 in Luanda.

Works Cited

Abu-Lughod, Lila. 1990. "Can There Be a Feminist Ethnography?" *Women and Performance* 5, no. 1: 7–27.

Bennett, Jane. 2008. "Researching for Life: Paradigms and Power." *Feminist Africa* 11: 1–12.

Beoku-Betts, Josephine. 1994. "When Black Is Not Enough: Doing Field Research among Gullah Women." *NWSA Journal* 6: 413–33.

Davis, Dána-Ain, and Christa Craven. 2016. *Feminist Ethnography: Thinking through Methodologies, Challenges, and Possibilities.* Lanham, MD: Rowman & Littlefield.

Decker, Alicia C. 2014. *In Idi Amin's Shadow: Women, Gender, and Militarism in Uganda.* Athens: Ohio University Press.

Hall, Stuart. 1990. "Cultural Identity and Diaspora." In *Identity: Community, Culture, Difference,* edited by Jonathan Rutherford, 222–37. London: Lawrence & Wishart.

Harrison, Faye V. 2011, "Anthropology as an Agent of Transformation: Introductory Comments and Queries." In *Decolonizing Anthropology: Moving Further toward an Anthropology for Liberation,* 3rd edition, edited by Faye V. Harrison, 5. Arlington, VA: American Anthropological Association.

Hill Collins, Patricia. 1986. "Learning from the Outsider Within: The Sociological Significance of Black Feminist Thought." *Social Problems* 33, no. 6: 14–32.

Hill Collins, Patricia. 1997. "How Much Difference Is Too Much? Black Feminist Thought and the Politics of Postmodern Social Theory." *Current Perspectives in Social Theory* 17: 3–37.

Mama, Amina. 2012. "What Does It Mean to Do Research in African Contexts?" *Feminist Review* 98, no. S1: e4–e20.

Mama, Amina, and Margo Okazawa-Rey. 2001. "Militarism, Conflict and Women's Activism in the Global Era: Challenges and Prospects for Women in Three West African Contexts." *Feminist Review* 101: 97–123.

McClaurin, Irma. 2001. *Black Feminist Anthropology: Theory, Politics, Praxis, and Poetics.* New Brunswick, NJ: Rutgers University Press.

Mohanty, Chandra. 2003. *Feminism without Borders: Decolonizing Theory, Practicing Solidarity.* Durham, NC: Duke University Press.

Moorman, Marissa. 2008. *Intonations: A Social History of Music and Nation in Luanda, Angola, from 1945 to Recent Times.* Athens: Ohio University Press.

Mullings, Leith. 2000. "African-American Women Making Themselves: Notes on the Role of Black Feminist Research." *Souls* 2, no. 4: 18–29.

Nagar, Richa. 2014. *Muddying the Waters: Coauthoring Feminisms across Scholarship and Activism.* Urbana: University of Illinois Press.

Narayan, Kirin. 1993. "How Native Is a 'Native' Anthropologist?" *American Anthropologist* 95, no. 3: 671–86.

Paredes, Margarida. 2015. *Combater duas vezes: Mulheres na luta armada em Angola.* Lisboa: Verso da História.

Pearce, Justin. 2012. "Control, Politics and Identity in the Angolan Civil War." *African Affairs* 111, no. 444: 442–65.

Powles, Julia. 2004. "Life History and Personal Narrative: Theoretical and Methodological Issues Relevant to Research and Evaluation in Refugee Contexts." New Issues in Refugee Research: Working Paper No. 106. Geneva: UNHCR. www.unhcr.org/research/RESEARCH/4147fe764.pdf.

Salo, Elaine, and Amina Mama. 2001. "Talking about Feminism in Africa." *Agenda: Empowering Women for Gender Equity* 50: 58–63.

Sanford, Victoria and Asale Angel-Ajani, eds. 2006. *Engaged Observer: Anthropology, Advocacy, and Activism.* New Brunswick, NJ: Rutgers University Press.

Soares de Oliveira, Ricardo. 2015. *Magnificent and Beggar Land: Angola since the Civil War.* New York: Oxford University Press.

Tamale, Sylvia, ed. 2011. *African Sexualities: A Reader.* Cape Town: Pambazuka Press.

Trinh Minh-Ha. 1989. *Woman, Native, Other: Writing Postcoloniality and Feminism.* Bloomington: Indiana University Press.

Chipo Dendere

Finding Women in the Zimbabwean Transition

Abstract: This essay is a feminist response to the 2017 coup in Zimbabwe that brought to an end Robert Mugabe's thirty-seven-year on power. Mugabe came into power in 1980 after his party, the Zimbabwe African National Union–Patriotic Front (ZANU PF), successfully negotiated for an end to the civil war. The male-dominated ZANU PF has stayed in power because they consolidated power around Mugabe's leadership. However, as the aging Mugabe became frail and his fifty-two-year-old energetic wife found her political voice, ZANU PF became deeply fractured and was facing electoral defeat in the 2018 elections. Grace Mugabe's rise to power became the rallying point for ZANU PF to evict their longtime leader. Her fall from power has been used to restrict the voices of women even in this new era of political openness.

On November 21, 2017, after thirty-seven years in power, Robert Mugabe resigned as president of Zimbabwe. Mugabe had been the central figure in Zimbabwean politics, in our homes, our education, and the narrative of even the most intimate details of our lives. I was born in the mid-1980s, a few years after independence, and in that sense I am part of the born-free generation. Being a born-free meant that our generation was free of the burdens of colonial rule and white minority rule, free from curfews and everyday policing of places where black bodies belonged. It was also generally understood that civil liberties were limited. In Mugabe's Zimbabwe there was freedom before speech but not after; therefore our generation was brought up not to speak or think politics. The day Mugabe resigned

MERIDIANS · feminism, race, transnationalism   17:2 November 2018
DOI: 10.1215/15366936-7176505 © 2018 Smith College

brought relief among millions of Zimbabweans who had followed the events leading to his ouster with much trepidation.

The suddenness of the Zimbabwean coup created a unique opportunity to place black Zimbabwean voices at the center of the storytelling. Unlike in past Zimbabwean moments of crisis, the majority of narrators were not white British experts. In this unlikely space, I found my voice via social media to provide my academic and personal take on the events in Zimbabwe. The conversation was also framed by other young women based in Zimbabwe, including Fadzai Mahere, a lawyer and political candidate. Mahere's entry into politics represented a new type of engagement by a cohort of middle-class youth who had been largely absent from politics prior to the 2016 citizen uprisings. The voices of veteran activists Priscila Misihairambwi, Maureen Kademaunga, and Margaret Dongo in different forums gave additional legitimacy to the demands for Mugabe's resignation. Female Zimbabwean journalists working for international news agencies—Haru Mutasa with *Al Jazeera*, Robyn Kriel at CNN, and Shingirayi Nyoka at the BBC—kept the world informed on the hour-by-hour events happening in Harare.

For a short time during the coup-not-coup events, Zimbabwe was truly open for freedom of expression. Among the many messages I received from Zimbabweans feeling freed from oppression was one from a rural teacher who said, "Today I shouted Mugabe must go, in my home and I did not feel afraid." Outside observers commented on the jubilation and sense of Uhuru (new beginnings, independence) that shaped this truly Zimbabwean experience. Away from home, I encouraged the women in my life, many of whom are in their late twenties and early thirties, to march for the first time in support of the military decision to oust Mugabe. The world watched as hundreds and thousands of black, brown, and white Zimbabweans marched in solidarity toward a new, post-Mugabe Zimbabwe.

The toxicity that has characterized Zimbabwean politics for the past decade appeared to have been placed on hold. And yet, even in these moments of reprieve, female acts of celebration were still under scrutiny. Female voices on television were acceptable only to the extent that they too placed the blame for Zimbabwe's woes on the former first lady Grace Mugabe. In the new dispensation narrative woven by the military and war veterans, the coup had been initiated to cure the "bedroom coup" that had been staged by Grace Mugabe against Robert Mugabe. When a group of young female activists pulled down pictures of Robert Mugabe from a hotel

lobby, their act of celebration was heavily criticized online and in print
media. Critics said their behavior was reminiscent of Grace Mugabe–style
politics, never mind that male activists and policemen all around the
country had been praised for pulling down the same pictures and trashing
them. When we spoke up in solidarity with the female activists and pointed
out the double standard, we were told that there was no room for women
like Grace Mugabe, who spoke out of turn. The overt sexist and misogynis-
tic tone of Zimbabwean politics did not die with Robert Mugabe's exit.
Instead the fall of Grace Mugabe legitimized the exclusion and silencing
of women in the political space.

Each cycle of Zimbabwean politics comes with a theme. The themes are
often infused with language of the liberation struggle. In 2002, when the
government initiated the land reform program, they called it the Third
Chimurenga War. In 2005, when the government implemented an overnight policy that displaced over 700,000 urbanites from their homes, they
called it Operation Clean Up the Dirt. In 2008, after Robert Mugabe lost the
election to Morgan Tsvangirayi, the run-off campaign theme was Operation How Did You Vote? The ruling party's economic policies have been
equally militaristic. In an effort to revive the failing agriculture sector, the
ruling party introduced *command agriculture*, a policy that oversaw the distribution of agriculture inputs to party loyalists. The theme for the coup
and the transition is Operation Restore Legacy. On November 15, 2017,
when the military took over the national broadcasting compound and
television, they informed the world that Robert Mugabe was safe and that
their only goal was to deal with the criminals around the president. Generation 40, the Zimbabwe African National Union–Patriotic Front (ZANU
PF) faction led by Grace Mugabe, was accused of violating liberation
struggle ideals. Thus, to understand the Zimbabwean coup and the post-
transition politics, it is important to analyze the role of gender politics in
the liberation struggle narrative.

While the coup gained the endorsement of ordinary citizens, it is also
true that the military intervention was not motivated by the need to find
solutions to the twin economic and political crises. Grace Mugabe had
succeeded in isolating war veterans and placing herself as the next in line
to succeed her husband. She capitalized on the already existing sexist narrative of Zimbabwean politics to eliminate political opponents, including
former vice president Joice Mujuru. Mujuru's war credentials are as solid as
those of her male counterparts, including General Constantino Chiwenga

and Emmerson Mnangagwa, but her ouster did not ignite their ire. Instead, after Mujuru's expulsion from ZANU PF, the state-run media dedicated months to attacking her war credentials and sexuality. There was no coup to cure Grace Mugabe's open involvement in politics then. Grace Mugabe's problems with the old guard escalated when she forced the expulsion of war veteran leaders and Mnangagwa. The army generals and other key male politicians felt exposed and worried that their standing in the regime was no longer safe with Grace Mugabe at the political helm.

When it became clear that Mnangagwa would take over the presidency, one of his advisors tweeted that the new first lady would stick to traditional roles of charity work and being mother of the nation. Indeed, in the early weeks of her husband's presidency, Auxillia Mnangagwa was the main focus of state media. She toured state hospitals and was even pictured making an unplanned stop to buy tomatoes from roadside vendors. Shortly after the inauguration, the new president announced that his wife would resign from her seat in Parliament to focus on the job of being mother to the nation. During the announcement, a group of well-placed elderly women wailed so loudly that the president had to pause to give the women room to express their deeply felt loss. The president placated their cries with the promise that as mother of the nation his wife was in a better position to do more for them. For her part, the new first lady cried silently in a corner. She was seen but not heard. The politics of the new dispensation is one in which women must be seen to support the goals of their husbands wholeheartedly, and they must never betray a desire for personal ambition. They must not become Grace Mugabe.

Even with the uncertainty of the coup and the role of the military there was some expectation that Mnangagwa's presidency would be a step forward for all Zimbabweans, including women. The Zimbabwean Constitution is clear on gender equality. However, women are still underrepresented in political parties, in the legislature, and in the executive. Mnangagwa's new cabinet has less gender diversity than Mugabe's 1980 cabinet. Mnangagwa appointed only 13 percent of women to executive positions, a far cry from the 50 percent constitutional requirement. When women raised these issues in the public domain, two common responses were that we must shut up and that the president could not appoint women because there were not enough qualified women in Parliament. Mnangagwa also had the opportunity to appoint a woman for one of the two vice presidential positions. Instead he appointed General Chiwenga and

Kembo Mohadi, a critically ill individual who has spent the majority of his tenure in hospital abroad.

Vice President Chiwenga's thirty-three-year-old wife, Marry Chiwenga, has been subjected to relentless attacks on her person because of her looks and style of dress. The attacks have come from both sides of the political divide. The irrational fear that a young, beautiful, vocal woman will become a Grace Mugabe has intensified existing tensions between men and women in politics. After the death of Morgan Tsvangirayi, his widow was a public victim of cultural norms that allow families to bully widows. Elizabeth Tsvangirayi was accused of cheating on her husband and threatened with disinheritance. Female activists and academics followed the events closely. Some proposed that we write statements in solidarity with her, but, in the end, we decided to remain silent because we did not want her to be further harassed. At Tsvangirayi's funeral, Thokozani Khupe, the vice president the Movement for Democratic Change, the opposition party, was violently attacked when she pointed out that according to her party's constitution, she was the rightful heir to the presidency. Khupe was eventually elbowed out of the party. Only fifteen female parliamentary candidates will represent ZANU PF in the general elections for the 210 seats.

The new dispensation is exciting and yet exhausting. The women's movement is spread too thin and the challenges are insurmountable. Social media has created a new avenue for women to engage in politics and express ourselves freely, but it has also empowered sexist bullies. Excessive online bullying has forced women to retreat from engagement. The majority of attacks against women focus on their looks and sexuality. On February 28, 2018, I testified before the U.S. Congress on Zimbabwe after Mugabe. I was the first black Zimbabwean woman to do so in recent years. In my testimony I emphasized that the United States must support local efforts to strengthen democracy and bring youth out of poverty. I also asked the United States to provide clarity on sanctions placed on Zimbabwe and political elites. I asked political elites under targeted sanctions to show their commitment to democracy. I expected that I would experience some backlash, but I had not anticipated the avalanche of death and rape threats that I received. In response to the attacks, like other women I shut down my social media accounts and disengaged.

The good news is that there is some opening up of political space and women are creating safe communities to support engagement. In the event President Mnangagwa wins the forthcoming election, it is very unlikely that his government will willingly give women more room to participate in politics. Most female activists are aware of this possibility, and they have already begun building strategies to counter executive repression.

. . . .

Chipo Dendere is a Zimbabwean-born political scientist and a Consortium for Diversity Fellow in the Political Science Department at Amherst College. She researches African politics, migration, and democratization and is working on a book manuscript on the impact of voter exit on the survival of authoritarian regimes. Dendere received her Ph.D. from Georgia State University.

Toni Stuart

....

my mother's trousseau

is not filled with bed spreads and sheets. i have no hand embroidered pil-
low cases. no lace frilled table cloths or curtains. i have been collecting my
own sheets. i inherited linen from her cupboard. but the linen is not linen,
it is polyester and synthetic. polycotton blends of machine designed prints.
no hand-woven. no hand-stitched. no passed down cloth that's lived on the
beds of all the women in my family. i have no hand-carved wooden chest,
no brass lock and key to keep things safe. no mothballs, no lavender to keep
the intimacy of my sheets fresh. the intimacy of our sheets is not fresh. it is
fraught with frayed dreams hung from the wispy hairs of my mother's
temples. it is softly packed away in the folds of her arms. it is wafting
silently through her curtains on sunday afternoons, when the light
remembers to fall through her lounge windows. my mother's home is no
longer my home. i have been learning to leave since i first learnt to walk.
unlearning her fear: unwrapping it from my skin. unlearning her shame to
set both of us free. unraveling all that ties us up tight, and fat, in our bones
and skin. and waiting, waiting, for the ease to return to our joint breath.
i have been learning to leave since i first learnt how to breathe. on my own.

....

Toni Stuart is a South African poet, performer, and spoken word educator. Her work
has been published in anthologies, journals, and nonfiction books locally and
abroad. She has an M.A. Writer/Teacher (Distinction) from Goldsmiths, University
of London, where she was a 2014–15 Chevening Scholar. She lives in Cape Town and
works in both Cape Town and London.

MERIDIANS · feminism, race, transnationalism   17:2 November 2018
DOI: 10.1215/15366936-7176527 © 2018 Smith College

Msia Kibona Clark

Feminisms in African Hip Hop

Abstract: Women hip hop artists in Africa have created spaces for themselves within hip hop's (hyper)masculine culture. They have created these spaces in order to craft their own narratives around gender and sexuality and to challenge existing narratives. This research uses African feminism as a broad lens through which to examine how these women artists present challenges to patriarchy, gender norms, and the politics of respectability that may or may not align with African feminist ideologies. In addition to resistance, this research examines how these artists use their art to construct their own dynamic and multidimensional representations in ways that find parallels within African feminisms. In this study, more than three hundred songs produced by women hip hop artists were surveyed. The study revealed diverse expressions of feminist identities, implicit and explicit rejections of patriarchy, and expressions of sexuality that included agency and nonconformity.

In the United States we have seen Black feminist scholarship engage hip hop studies in conversations around the experiences of Black women in hip hop culture. Hip hop studies in Africa have considered questions of women in hip hop, but they have not fully engaged in conversations with African feminist scholarship. Meanwhile women in African hip hop communities create music that reflects the cultural and political environments in which they live and that often contain important social commentary. These songs by female hip hop artists (or MCs) in Africa are important because they challenge existing social norms and present narratives of gender that are nonconforming. In this essay I examine the lyrics of African female hip hop

MERIDIANS · feminism, race, transnationalism   17:2 November 2018
DOI: 10.1215/15366936-7176538 © 2018 Smith College

artists for evidence of African feminist discourse. I argue that the work of these MCs often aligns with African feminist thought as well as hip hop feminist thought. What becomes clear is that women in Africa use hip hop as a form of cultural resistance that is often in line with African feminist ideals. My analysis also shows how these artists have created spaces within masculine hip hop cultures. Women enter hip hop recognizing the use of hip hop culture as an important space for creating one's own narratives and for challenging existing narratives. This study contributes to African feminist scholarship by detailing how these female artists present challenges to patriarchy, gender norms, and the politics of respectability. Through their work, female MCs construct representations of African women that are complex and multidimensional.

This essay presents an analysis of the major themes that emerge in songs produced by female hip hop artists cross-continentally. These themes engage with feminism, patriarchy, and sexuality, themes that run parallel to conversations occurring within African feminist thought. In fact songs performed by female artists can carve out space for African feminist dialogues in hip hop cultures, which challenge distorted narratives about African women. This is most impactful for young female fans, who are then able to conceptualize gender in different ways. This also affects young male fans, challenging them to think of gender differently. At the very least, these songs inspire more conversations around gender.

Much of my data comes from a survey of music produced by African female hip hop artists. The largest proportion of songs (38 percent) came from South Africa, which corresponds with the number of active women hip hop artists in the country. The large number of South African female artists is due in large part to their having greater access to resources. South Africa also has one of the oldest hip hop scenes in Africa, with hip hop artists emerging about a decade earlier than the rest of Africa. While the first female hip hop artists in South Africa did not emerge until a decade after the first male artists, women have always been participants in hip hop culture as rappers, DJs, graffiti artists, and break-dancers. Other songs came from Nigeria (14 percent), Kenya (11 percent), and Ghana (10 percent). Other countries included in the study were Zambia (7 percent), Tanzania (5 percent), Zimbabwe (5 percent), Botswana (4 percent), Senegal (2 percent), Uganda (2 percent), Namibia (1 percent), and Rwanda (1 percent). With the help of student assistants, I analyzed 324 songs for specific themes using SPSS software. Although most of our analysis focused on English-language songs, we were able to translate a limited number of songs into French, Portuguese, and Arabic. The songs focused on seven major themes: social and political issues, sexuality and relationships, women and gender, sexism and violence against women, braggadocio and disses, identity, and emotional struggle. These themes are also commonly found in African feminist scholarship.

Feminist Identities

There are several strands of African and diaspora feminisms that could be used, in part, to analyze the music of female hip hop artists in Africa. These strands include African feminism, Black feminism, hip hop feminism, motherism, womanism, transformative feminism, and third world feminism. These feminisms are tied to the needs of African and diaspora women to distinguish their struggles from Western feminists. Hip hop feminism emerged when diaspora feminist scholars felt that Black feminism conflicted with their relationship to Black female sexuality. In the United States, it emerged as a way to confront misogyny in hip hop and to challenge broader exploitations of Black women. Hip hop feminism challenges existing power structures and is rooted in the racial and economic oppressions of people of color (Durham et al. 2013). It is related to Black feminism, but as Durham and colleagues point out, it differs by challenging respectability politics.

The term *respectability politics* is often used in discussions of the experiences of diaspora and African women. It comes from the self-policing that happens within these cultures. Diaspora and African women are expected to behave in ways that are socially acceptable, or respectable. Confrontations with respectability politics is a major theme in hip hop feminism. According to Durham et al. (2013, 725), "There are often serious reprisals for people of color, and women of color in particular, when we freely express sexual agency and desire. Engagement with respectability politics, then, continues to be vitally important to hip-hop feminism." While hip hop feminism is tied to the Black experience in America, there are several points of overlap in Africa.

There is no shortage of feminisms that can be employed as a lens through which to examine the work of female hip hop artists in Africa. African feminism, with its own substrands, proves the most useful. There is a temptation to coin a new term that, like hip hop feminism in the United States, shows a departure from African feminist thought in African hip hop communities. Rather than adding new feminist labels, it is most helpful, at least at this stage, to utilize African feminist lenses for this research. There are several African feminist perspectives, and attempting to provide a comprehensive definition is difficult. There are diverging views among African feminist scholars on the primacy of motherhood, gender categories, and the inclusion of diverse sexualities in the African feminist agenda. There are, however, some common threads. African feminist scholars often challenge patriarchy and attempts to control women's bodies. African feminism does not have an antagonistic relationship with men. African feminist scholars largely acknowledge the intersections between gender, class, and race. Images of African women as powerless, oppressed, and needing intervention, or as feisty, tough, and exotically sexual have been perpetuated within and outside Africa, and African feminist scholars challenge this. The Sierra Leonean scholar Filomina Chioma Steady (1987, 4) attempted to define African feminism when she wrote:

> African feminism combines racial, sexual, class, and cultural dimensions of oppression to produce a more inclusive brand of feminism through which women are viewed first and foremost as human, rather than sexual, beings. It can be defined as that ideology which encompasses freedom from oppression based on the political, economic, social, and cultural manifestations of racial, cultural, sexual, and class biases. It is more inclusive than other forms of feminist ideologies and is largely a product of polarizations and conflicts that represent some of the worst and chronic forms of human suffering.

Most of the artists in this study do not expressly identify as feminists. Many see themselves as far removed from the term, which is often seen as grounded in academic discourse or European culture, and therefore irrelevant to their lives. While many artists do not expressly identify as feminists, however, they do articulate feminist concepts in their music, and for their mostly young fans this is often their first exposure to feminist thought.

Overall, 10 percent of the songs surveyed mention feminism or expressions of female empowerment. Of that group, more than 50 percent were produced by South African artists like Godessa, Miss Nthabi, Devour Ke Lenyora, Kanyi, Yugen Blakrok, Gigi Lamayne, and Dope Saint Jude. Gigi Lamayne identifies as a feminist in her music, and in a 2017 interview she reiterated her identification with feminism, recognizing the "fluidity" and evolving nature of feminism (Clark 2017a). She is also very aware of the impact of her music on young girls and consciously pushes back against patriarchy in both South African and hip hop culture (Clark 2017a). Dope Saint Jude also employs a feminist identity in her music, but distances herself from the feminism of academia. In a 2016 interview she stated:

> I think I provide a type of feminism that's a lot more accessible to people because I am hesitant about the academic rhetoric that's inaccessible to people like my cousins, because feminism is for all of us. I dislike the inaccessible discourse that can be seen as limited to the elite. People living in the slums can also understand feminism, it shouldn't be an exclusive club. With my music, I provide a more accessible, fun, easier approach that celebrates our complexities as women. There are so many types of women who are feminists and don't feel like they can call themselves feminists because the idea is so exclusive, academic, that is far-removed and doesn't interact with who they are as a person. (Odunlami 2016)

In her song "Realtalk" Dope Saint Jude raps, "Your brand of feminism, to my world, is so outdated / Please update it for the rappers, for the fly girls, for the girls who like to f*ck / For the sisters, for the mothers." In "Xxplosive," she raps, "I'm changing the mold of a mad Black woman / matriarchy chastise when we hear them say yo massa / patriarchy hates cause we own our space like brasse." The "mad Black woman" trope can be utilized to dismiss the grievances of Black women, something that has been extensively discussed in Black feminist scholarship. Here Dope Saint Jude mentions the "mad Black woman" and places the trope in a South African context. The line "matriarchy chastise when we hear them say yo massa," appears to refer to women-led communities chastising men who take up a submissive stance in relation to white men. *Massa* is a derivative of the word *master*. In the next line, the term *brasse* is Cape Town slang for a crew of guys. Dope Saint Jude is therefore saying that it upsets patriarchy and patriarchal structures that she and her female friends are occupying male spaces. She identifies as a feminist but offers a feminism that she feels is more accessible and relevant to those outside of academia.

Kanyi, another South African artist, rejects the feminist label. She feels that being called a feminist comes with a set of definitions that one is then expected to consistently live up to (Clark 2017b). While her music is in line with many feminist ideals, she rejects the label. In her music, and in our interview, Kanyi embraces the dominant themes found in African feminism.

She brings her Xhosa identity into her music and aesthetic, and uses that voice to speak out against sexism and patriarchy within South African culture. Other artists in the study who may reject feminist identities have also produced songs that articulate feminist ideals. The artists Stella Mwangi (Kenya), Cleo Ice Queen (Zambia), and Cindy Rulz (Tanzania) produce primarily apolitical music, but these artists also produce music with feminist themes. When we examine the songs for evidence of African feminist ideas, we find rejections of attempts to control women's bodies, rejections of patriarchy, expressions of female agency, acknowledgments of class and race intersections, and feminist approaches to engagements with men.

In looking at the works of three diverse artists, Burni Aman and MsSupa of South Africa and Cindy Rulz of Tanzania, we find lyrics that do not express feminist identities but that express sentiments that could be in line with African feminist frameworks. In "Femme de Combat" Burni Aman (an original member of the group Godessa) speaks to the intersecting oppressions of race, gender, and class in her verse about the struggles of Black and Coloured mothers from the townships who labor in factories and as domestic workers. In the song she raps:

scrubbing the floors, known as Black and Coloured
women who work in factories where dreams are gutted
walk home tired to their households corrupted
one parent alone she stands, no husband to hold her
no money education, means you destined to suffer.

In "The Game," MsSupa speaks to the challenges of being a female in a male-dominated culture. She speaks to sexism in hip hop and the attempts to dictate how female artists should rap, and how they should sound:

The game has been bitter to me back from the start
Yo, it broke my heart but I never gave up
The fact that I'm a female didn't help me either
The whispers, the gossips, on how I made the cover . . .
Rap a certain way, then I'm too hardcore
I rap a certain way, then I sound like porn
I rap about the streets, and still I get scorned
Should I sound wack and just rap some poems?
I'm starting to think that if I had a penis I would make it

Or if I was ugly enough, no guy would even date me
Or if I was in with the conscious clique
Or just stay underground and let the main make it
Then I'll be it, y'all.

In "Unstoppable," Cindy Rulz also brings up the fact that she is a female artist and is challenging the idea that hip hop is for men. In this excerpt from her song, she refers to herself as unstoppable, but also as having more talent than the average male artist:

Female rapper hiyo ndo last name
Unstoppable inaweza ikawa nickname
Nachofanya inaweza take hata two men
You gotta be scared cause yeah I'm the best
Bars zangu zinachoma niite assassin
Cindy ameua beat tayari murder kesi.
Unstoppable can be my nickname
What I do can take two man to do it
You gotta to be scared cause yeah I'm the best
My bars burn call me assassinator
Cindy murder the beat murder case.

The distance between African feminist scholars and African women outside of the academy is not new, and these artists represent that distance. It is worth noting that both Gigi Lamayne and Dope Saint Jude, two artists who have expressed feminist identities, attended university in South Africa. The former graduated from the University of the Witwatersrand and the latter from the University of Cape Town.

Women, Patriarchy, and Hip Hop

Discussions of gender and sexism appear in 20 percent of the songs. In some songs, this is a dominant theme, such as "Wakilisha Madame" ("Represent Madame") by Nazizi (Kenya) and Rah P (Tanzania) and "Femme de Combat" by Burni (South Africa). Several of these songs focus on emotional struggle, highlighting the impact of sexism and patriarchy. In "Wakilisha Madame," Nazizi and Rah P celebrate women in East Africa and call for them to be strong, saying that they are in solidarity with these women. In the song "Soeur" ("Little Sister"), Moona (Senegal) raps about a teenage girl who wants to grow up too fast and is willing to do anything to get what she wants. Moona talks about a teenage girl who thinks she is a woman, with a woman's wants and needs, and who almost has a woman's body. Many of these songs are written to inform, comfort, and inspire. They inform the listener of the diverse and complex experiences of women on the continent. These songs do this in a way that conveys a sense of "us" rather than "them." These songs also speak to women who have lived these experiences. In the songs, the artists occupy the same cultural spaces as the women they sing about, and they often acknowledge shared experiences in their lyrics.

My survey found that songs by female hip hop artists are more likely to deal with violence against women and sexual harassment than songs by their male counterparts. Of the songs in this study that address violence against women (VAW), 27 percent also deal with both VAW and love and relationships, 27 percent discuss VAW alongside female empowerment, and 53 percent discuss VAW alongside the lives of African women. The songs from Botswana, Nigeria, and Tanzania discuss violence against women the most. Of the few songs analyzed from Senegal, 50 percent have lyrics focusing on the lives and experiences of African women in general. In no other country do discussions of African women show up as frequently. In Senegal, the artists Sister Fa, Coumbis Sorra, and Toussa Senrap have all penned songs that depict the conditions of women.

There are also songs in which female artists challenge patriarchy directly, using much stronger language. These songs do not come from a place of struggle but from a place that is meant to warn against attempts to impose patriarchy. In many of these songs, artists boast about their lyrical skills. In fact elements of bragging (about the artist's skills, looks, etc.) are in many (35 percent) of the songs surveyed. Almost every artist had at least one song in which they boasted about their skills as artists. Braggadocio is an important way for artists to announce their credibility. Like the song "I'm Ready" by Abena Rockstar (Ghana), braggadocio establishes the presence of an MC in hip hop culture (Clark forthcoming). Braggadocio is a direct challenge to patriarchy and should be seen as a rejection of gendered social expectations. "I'm here to sit my ass upon the f***ing throne," sings Devour Ke Lenyora (South Africa) in her song "The Storm." That one line says she has the skills to be a hip hop MC, and her place on the throne rejects the idea that thrones are only for men, or that women should occupy only spaces next to men.

While bragging is a theme that appeared frequently, most of the bragging focused on the artist's skills as an MC. By contrast, in the United States, bragging often includes boasts of an artist's skills as well as their looks and material possessions. African female MCs focused more on skills than on material items. Songs that take the space that women have made within hip hop culture and use it to confront patriarchy include "How We Do It" by Keko (Uganda), "HERoes" by Sampa the Great (Zambia), "Kaboom Shots" by Gigi Lamayne (South Africa), "Female Dog" by MsSupa (South Africa), and "Queen Kong" by Pryse and Eva Alordiah (Nigeria). All provide explicit rejections of patriarchy. For example, in "Female Dog," MsSupa challenges both patriarchy and male masculinity, first by using the word *herstory* instead of *history*, and then by repeating in the chorus, "You rhyme around me, you'll feel like less of a man / other MCs ain't got a chance at all." This line is a reference to the emasculation of a man by his peers that often occurs if he loses a hip hop battle to a female MC. An important part of hip hop culture is battling. In a battle, rap artists stand on opposing sides with a crowd of spectators surrounding them. The artists take turns saying verses, and the audience determines who has the best verses and is thus the winner of the battle.

The politics of respectability are challenged in the lyrics of many of these songs. Wanjiru Mbure (2013) discusses respectability politics in her analysis of social media spaces in Kenya. Her discussion of the sex blog *Nairobi Nights*, written by a female sex worker in Nairobi, reveals the expectations placed on women and the social consequences for violating these expectations. In "Kaboom Shots," Gigi Lamayne uses strong, "unladylike" language in her direct confrontation with sexism in the music industry. She raps, "I ain't paying for no favors in my birthday suit / A female could never get to top place my nigga / Still the same vote riggas in the game my nigga / . . . You got to be the bosses hoe to be the man my nigga?" In the same song, she takes on the role of both mother and MC with the lines "I'm going into labor with my mic in my hand / Writing lyrics for the future that you barely understand." In the song, she challenges hip hop as a masculine culture by using the metaphor of motherhood to signify her connection to hip hop.

Many female MCs in Africa depart from some African feminists who privilege motherhood. Of African feminism Oyeronke Oyêwùmi (2003, 12–13) says, "The privileging of motherhood in the African family organization contrasts with the ambivalence about motherhood in feminism." The subject of motherhood did not show up in most of the songs surveyed.

Only 6 percent address the artist's own mother, and only 1 percent address the artist being a mother. This is despite the fact that many of the artists are also mothers. This is not interpreted as disregard for motherhood, or even ambivalence toward it. In conversations with artists who are also mothers, the subject of their children often came up. Those conversations focused on navigating careers and motherhood and the presence of their children at many of their professional events, including our interviews. The songs that deal with women and motherhood do privilege motherhood and present multidimensional depictions of motherhood that are not limited to mothers being the bearers of tradition or the queen mother trope often found in hip hop music produced by men. Limited focus on motherhood, as well as social issues more generally, means that the works of African female MCs may differ from most African feminist scholarship.

While patriarchy is constantly challenged, few (6 percent) of the songs deal with social issues. Of the songs that do, most are from South Africa. Of the 7 percent of songs dealing with corruption, 70 percent are from South Africa. Of the 6 percent that deal with poverty, 62 percent are from South Africa. And of the 4 percent that deal with conflict, 68 percent are from South Africa. Conflict was not limited to wars but also included street violence. Some of the songs with strong social and political content are "Africa Rise" by Lness (Kenya), "Revolution" by Moona (Senegal), "Social Ills" by Godessa (South Africa), "Fees Will Fall" by Gigi Lamayne (South Africa), and "Brown Baas" ("Brown Boss") by Dope Saint Jude (South Africa). Both "Revolution" and "Fees Will Fall" address the need for social change in their respective countries. In "Revolution," Moona specifically addresses the need to end social divisions, as well repression of the masses by the state. She says (English translation), "Revolution with a capital R like RAP / And raffle all the ideas received without getting off track / Revolution with a capital R like religion / With interpretations that only create divisions." Gigi Lamayne, who graduated from university in the midst of the #FeesMustFall movement, released "Fees Will Fall" right after graduation. The song is a direct attack on the postapartheid African National Congress government. Her first stanza:

> Our parents barely get a wage
> But they slave for this nation
> The black child will never ever
> Gain emancipation

I wonder if King Biko would agree to this shit
The forefathers of our land wouldn't sign to this shit
And fat cats walk around they got nothing to lose
Except a few bad comments on the evening news.
We're all haunted by race and class
The roots of the grass
And so they treat us like trash
And even though we complain
As dropouts and explain
Our parents scream for the day
We'll get degrees but then hey
We still lose in the last resort
Are we ever gon have the qualification in hand?
They grabbed the spoon from our hand
And so we shouldn't be mad?
They control through the cash
On who's broke and who's stacked
So let the students attack!! FEES WILL FALL.

In her song "Brown Baas," Dope Saint Jude comments on racism in South Africa with lines like "I'm representing the voiceless and don't you ever forget it / I've got power and passion and I don't need to defend it." In reference to race and racism in South Africa, she raps, "they keep us in chains while they keep on building their towers," while deliberating on her Coloured identity, saying, "do you know what it's like to be brown for a girl like me?"

In an interview with Okay Africa, Dope Saint Jude discusses her place in the racial politics of South Africa:

> My Coloured identity has always been a difficult thing for me to deal with. I am a first generation Coloured person, as I come from a mixed-race family. I recognize my blackness, even though I am Coloured. I feel a great sense of responsibility to my community and to young women, to be a role model and to work hard. I think it is so important for us to have our voices heard, to change [the] voice of the media and to create the climate we want in South Africa! (Mazaza 2015)

Many of the songs that explicitly address social and political issues came from South African artists. Both Gigi Lamayne and Dope Saint Jude are among the South African artists that have presented the most content that contains commentary about social and political issues.

Love and Sexuality

Attempts to control or repress female sexuality have roots in the colonial system, in which Europeans created narratives of African women that depicted them as primitive and highly sexual in comparison to European women (Hames 2008, 2010; Tamale 2011; Mbure 2013). These depictions helped to rationalize some of the sexual violence committed against African women. African women and their "insatiable" sexual appetites contrasted with the perceived conservatism of European women. Within African cultures, we have also seen attempts to define and suppress female sexuality. While assertiveness in men is socially rewarded, women are expected to remain submissive (McFadden 2007; Mbure 2013). Social norms seek to regulate what women can wear, how women can talk, how women present themselves in public, and how women interact with men. This has been reinforced through religion (Christianity and Islam), statutory laws, customary laws, rape, corrective rape, and public shaming (Oloruntoba-Oju 2006; Vincent 2008; Kwenaite and Van Heerden 2011; Makoni 2011; Shipley 2012; Decker 2014).

Female hip hop artists dismantle respectability politics in two ways: through their lyrics and through their aesthetics. Several of the songs in this survey present celebrations of sexuality, expressions of sexual desire, and rejection of passive personas. Twenty-five percent of the songs surveyed address sex, sexuality, love, and relationships. These songs overwhelmingly depict romantic relationships in which women show agency and are not passive participants. Different regional trends also emerge in the songs. West African (with the exception of Senegal) artists talk the most about sex (heterosexual), sexuality, love, and relationships. South and East African artists have more songs that exclusively talk about sex, sexuality (heterosexual), love, and relationships.

In the songs "Me Gye Wo Boy" ("I Am Your Boy") by Abena Rockstar (Ghana), "Wobejeimu" by Amaa Rae (Ghana), "Stella Stella Stella" by Stella Mwangi (Kenya), "Only One" by Sasha (Nigeria), and "If You Want Me" by Mo'Cheddah (Nigeria), the artists present more assertive sexualities in which they discuss their own prowess. This "unapologetic pro-sex stance" is seen as a battleground between hip hop feminism and other feminisms in the academy (Durham et al. 2013, 724). In African feminist scholarship, we do see some discussion of the importance of African women being free to explore and express sexual desire and celebrate sexual pleasure (McFadden 2003; Tamale 2011; Sopitshi 2012). The explicit representations of sex by female hip hop artists in Africa elicit debates on whether these artists are internalizing their own oppressions or showing agency by challenging patriarchy.

Stella Mwangi's song "Stella Stella Stella" presents a sexy, confident, urban woman. She boasts about her sexual dominance and skill and presents herself as a street-smart Nairobi woman. In the first stanza she sings:

> I'm a sexy mother***er
> Go and ask your brother
> I keep them boys coming
> L'L'L'L'Like no other
> They could never stop me even if they tried to block me
> Shooting threes on these suckers like I'm Kobe on the
>   court.

In this verse she boasts about her skills and her sexuality. In the music video, she wears shorts and a crop top that shows her stomach. She is rapping and dancing in an urban setting with Nairobi's famous *matatus* (buses) in the background. The image Mwangi presents contrasts with the real social repercussions for women who dress "inappropriately." There have been instances of women being jeered at for wearing shorts or short skirts. In Nairobi in 2014, for instance, a woman was physically attacked for wearing a miniskirt, sparking protests over the attack (*BBC News* 2014). Laws in Uganda and other countries have sought to codify how women can dress (Makoni 2011; Decker 2014). In many urban areas in Africa, women may face public shaming for wearing miniskirts. Thus the miniskirt has become a contested battleground over the policing of women's bodies. In Pryse's (Nigeria) song "Na Still Woman," the artist raps, "No matter how much smarter or how much harder you work / society may not know this, they're measuring your skirt." In making conscious choices to talk and dress in a manner that challenges patriarchal customs, these artists are also aware of the social consequences. Their choice to challenge these customs has impacts on the real lives of young women, especially those in urban Africa.

In South Africa, women artists also express their sexuality. According to Gigi Lamayne, in today's South Africa, young women are being "unapologetically sexy" (Clark 2017a). She feels that they are doing this on their own terms, even when those expressions confront cultural norms. South African artists Devour Ke Lenyora, Dope Saint Jude, MsSupa, Nadia Nakai, Rouge, and Miss Celaneous are all rappers who have written lyrics that unambiguously express their sexuality. In the songs "Envy" and "Say My Name," Devour Ke Lenyora describes intimate scenes with her partner. In "The Storm," she raps, "I'm your boyfriend's mentor, girlfriend's secret / I trust you will keep it."

Female hip hop artists often use subtext to create representations of diverse sexual identities and sexualities. In Tanzania, where homosexuality is illegal, female MCs present diverse sexual identities in the subtext of their lyrics and videos (Clark 2014). Homosexuality is illegal throughout most of Africa, making it difficult for artists to express sexualities that are not heterosexual. In South Africa, artists have been able to be more diverse in their expressions of sexuality. This is not to say that being gay in South Africa does not come with its own social repercussions. There have been an estimated thirty murders of gay and lesbian South Africans between 2012 and 2016 (Fletcher 2016). The rape and/or murder of Black lesbians in South Africa is often done as a "corrective" measure or as a punishment for their homosexuality (Hames 2008; Livermon 2012; Morrissey 2013). The murder of gay, lesbian, and transgender people is a global issue that affects countries where homosexuality is a crime, as well as countries where there are laws protecting gay, lesbian, and transgender communities. Female artists in South Africa who express queer sexualities understand the cultures in which they live. Many choose to use subtext, while others, such as Cape Town's Dope Saint Jude, are openly gay.

In her song "Real Talk," Dope Saint Jude raps, "for the mothers with the baby daddy and baby mama / for the girls who also boys, please update it, make it smarter." In this line she references women in both heterosexual and homosexual relationships who have children with their partners. She also references transgender identities and acknowledges their lack of recognition. In the song "Xxplosive," she proclaims that she's "down with my dykes, down with my queers / I'm down with my boys, I'm ripping drying tears." Dope Saint Jude often raps in a queer slang called Gayle, which developed in Cape Town's gay community and is used mostly among English- and Afrikaans-speaking gay men (Cage and Evans 2003). Her emergence in South Africa's hip hop scene may represent one of the first Africa-based queer female artists to openly represent their sexuality in their music.

Adam Haupt (2016, 1) says that Dope Saint Jude is "transforming South African hip-hop by queering a genre that has predominantly been male and heteronormative."

Conclusion

Female MCs in Africa, as well as globally, confront patriarchy in their music. It is often couched in harsh language that is infused with urban slang. Because of this, in many African countries, female MCs can be labeled troublemakers (because of hip hop's confrontational nature), lesbians (because of hip hop's masculine culture), and whores (when female artists do not express their sexuality in socially approved ways). These sometimes serve as a preventative measure, barring many women from actively participating in local hip hop communities (Prince 2011; Shipley 2012; Clark 2014). Additionally pressures from family often oblige women to make a choice between their roles as daughters, wives, and mothers and their ambitions as MCs (Prince 2011; Clark 2014; Neff 2015). These pressures and expectations affect career paths and often include disruptions and delays in production, performances, and career opportunities. Mbali Langa's (2010) study of female hip hop artists in South Africa, namely QBA, Arazen, and Zephmetric, found that the pressures faced by female MCs cause many of them to drop out of the culture completely.

In Africa, and globally, hip hop culture seeks to place women in a box. They are either categorized as honorable, respectable women or as dishonorable whores. The categories of honorable and respectable are based on heteronormative constructions of womanhood that use shaming as a method of policing women's behavior. This research establishes the fact that female hip hop artists cross-continentally resist patriarchy and do not relinquish their right to define themselves as women and as sexual beings. This research also establishes the presence of African feminist ideals in their music.

African feminist scholars have for decades provided frameworks for studies of gender in Africa. Through their scholarship, we understand that gender constructs throughout Africa were greatly influenced by the presence of Europeans in Africa. Many of the colonial policies in Africa stripped women of social, economic, and political power and codified patriarchy in national institutions and structures (McFadden 2001; Tamale 2011). African women continue to grapple with unequal social power and resource allocations. Women's access to education, capital, and power structures remains unequal. African feminism confronts these power imbalances.

There now needs to be more dialogue between African feminism and hip hop. Dialogue in the United States between Black feminism and hip hop (or hip hop feminism) began in the 1990s. Similar scholarship slowly began emerging about Africa in the 2000s, thanks in large part to the work of Adam Haupt at the University of Cape Town. There is need for additional research, done in a way that conveys an understanding of the artists' voice and that recognizes their agency. Ali Coleen Neff (2015, 450) suggests that too often scholars "seek to 'discover' or 'give exposure to' emerging global undergrounds." Mary Hames (2010, 2) says, "Feminist researchers should therefore be vigilant not to speak on behalf of the other which is often the case in the academy." This has been the approach of numerous scholars of hip hop in Africa. There is now a need for more scholarship that engages hip hop and African feminism from an understanding of both the academy and hip hop culture.

. . . .

Msia Kibona Clark is an associate professor in the Department of African Studies at Howard University. Her research focuses on popular culture in Africa. She is the author of several scholarly publications on hip hop's intersections with gender, migration, and politics in Africa, including the 2018 book Hip Hop in Africa: Prophets of the City and Dustyfoot Philosopher. Clark also produces the *Hip Hop African* blog and podcast.

Works Cited

BBC News. 2014. "Kenyans Protest over Nairobi Miniskirt Attack." November.

Cage, Ken, and Moyra Evans. 2003. *Gayle: The Language of Kinks and Queens: A History and Dictionary of Gay Language in South Africa.* Johannesburg: Jacana Media, 2003.

Clark, Msia Kibona. 2014. "Gendered Representations among Tanzanian Female Emcees." In *Ni Wakati: Hip Hop and Social Change in Africa*, edited by Msia Kibona Clark and Mickie Koster, 144–69. Lanham, MD: Lexington Press.

Clark, Msia Kibona. 2017a. "HHAP Episode 7: Gigi Lamayne on Feminism and Politics in South Africa." *Hip Hop African*, podcast, February 6. https://hiphopafrican .com/2017/02/06/hhap-episode-7-gigi-lamayne-on-feminism-politics-in-south -africa/.

Clark, Msia Kibona. 2017b. "HHAP Episode 15: Kanyi Mavi on Hip Hop, Xhosa, and Rap Culture in South Africa." *Hip Hop African*, podcast, October 1. https: //hiphopafrican.com/2017/10/01/hhap-episode-15-kanyi-mavi-on-hip-hop-xhosa -rap-culture-in-south-africa/.

Clark, Msia Kibona. Forthcoming. *Hip-Hop in Africa: Prophets of the City and Dustyfoot Philosophers*. Athens: Ohio University Press.

Decker, Alicia C. 2014. *In Idi Amin's Shadow: Women, Gender, and Militarism in Uganda*. Athens: Ohio University Press.

Durham, Aisha, Brittany C. Cooper, and Susana M. Morris. 2013. "The Stage Hip-Hop Feminism Built: A New Directions Essay." *SIGNS: Journal of Women in Culture and Society* 38, no. 3: 721–37.

Fletcher, James. 2016. "Born Free, Killed by Hate: The Price of Being Gay in South Africa." *BBC News*. April 7.

Hames, Mary. 2008. "Lesbians and the Civil Union Act in South Africa: A Critical Reflection." In *To Have and to Hold: The Making of Same-Sex Marriage in South Africa*, edited by Melanie Judge, Anthony Manion, and Shaun de Waal, 258–67. Johannesburg: Jacana Media.

Hames, Mary. 2010. "Se(x)ation, Sensation or Research? Interrogating the Research Gaze." *BUWA!* 1, no. 1: 53–55.

Haupt, Adam. 2003. "Hip-Hop, Gender and Agency in the Age of Empire." *Agenda* 17, no. 57: 21–29.

Haupt, Adam. 2016. "Queering Hip-Hop, Queering the City: Dope Saint Jude's Transformative Politics." *M/C Journal* 19, no. 4. http://journal.media-culture.org.au /index.php/mcjournal/article/view/1125.

Kwenaite, Sindi, and Ariana Van Heerden. 2011. "Dress and Violence: Women Should Avoid Dressing Like 'Sluts' to Avoid Being Raped." *South African Journal of Art History* 26, no. 1: 141–55.

Langa, Mbali. 2010. "Lyricism and Other Skizims." M.A. thesis, University of the Witwatersrand, Johannesburg.

Livermon, Xavier. 2012. "Queer(y)ing Freedom: Black Queer Visibilities in Postapartheid South Africa." *GLQ: A Journal of Lesbian and Gay Studies* 18, no. 2: 297–323.

Makoni, Busi. 2011. "Multilingual Miniskirt Discourses in Motion: The Discursive Construction of the Female Body in Public Space." *International Journal of Applied Linguistics* 21, no. 3: 340–59.

Mazaza, Shiba Melissa. 2015. "Dope Saint Jude: Hip-Hop, Feminism, Race Politics and Cape Town Queer Culture." *Okay Africa*, March 27.

Mbure, Wanjiru G. 2013. "Busted Cultural Myths and Nairobi Nights: A Critical Analysis of Gendered Social Media Spaces in Kenya." *Africa Media Review* 21, nos. 1–2: 63–87.

McFadden, Patricia. 2001. "Cultural Practice as Gendered Exclusion." In *Discussing Women's Empowerment: Theory and Practice*, edited by Naila Kabeer, 58–72. SIDA Studies, no. 3.

McFadden, Patricia. 2003. "Sexual Pleasure as Feminist Choice." *Feminist Africa* 2: 50–60.

McFadden, Patricia. 2007. "African Feminist Perspectives of Post-Coloniality." *Black Scholar* 37, no. 1: 36–42.

Morrissey, Megan E. 2013. "Rape as a Weapon of Hate: Discursive Constructions and Material Consequences of Black Lesbianism in South Africa." *Women's Studies in Communication* 36, no. 1: 72–91.

Neff, Ali Coleen. 2015. "Roots, Routes and Rhizomes: Sounding Women's Hip Hop on the Margins of Dakar, Senegal." *Journal of Popular Music Studies* 27, no. 4: 448–77.

Odunlami, Antonia. 2016. "Gal-Dem in Conversation with Dope Saint Jude." *Gal-Dem.com*, April 9.

Oloruntoba-Oju, Taiwo. 2006. "'Dèdè n dẹ ku ikú n dẹ Dèdè': Fe/male Sexuality and Dominance in Nigerian Video Films (Nollywood)." *Stichproben: Wiener Zeitschrift für Kritische Afrikastudien* 11: 5–26.

Oyêwùmi, Oyeronke. 2003. *African Women and Feminism: Reflecting on the Politics of Sisterhood.* Trenton, NJ: Africa World Press.

Prince, Emma. 2011. "Rwanda: Gender Equality through Hip Hop." *AllAfrica.com*, May 16.

Shipley, Jesse Weaver. 2012. "The Birth of Ghanaian Hiplife: Urban Style, Black Thought, Proverbial Speech." In *Hip Hop Africa: New Music in a Globalizing World*, edited by Eric Charry, 29–56. Bloomington: Indiana University Press.

Sopitshi, Athenkosi. 2012. "Won't Nobody Even Try to Reach Her Mind . . ." *Feminist Africa* 17: 129–32.

Steady, Filomina C. 1987. "African Feminism: A Worldwide Perspective." In *Women in Africa and the African Diaspora: A Reader*, edited by Rosalyn Terborg-Penn and Andrea Benton Rushing, 3–22. Washington, D.C.: Howard University Press.

Tamale, Sylvia, ed. 2011. *African Sexualities: A Reader.* Cape Town: Pambazuka.

Vincent, Louise. 2008. "Women's Rights Get a Dressing Down: Mini Skirt Attacks in South Africa." *International Journal of the Humanities* 6, no. 6: 11–18.

Neo Sinoxolo Musangi

. . . .

Homing with My Mother /
How Women in My Family Married Women

Abstract: Recent activist and academic work regarding same-gender marriage and relationships has brought to the fore supposed precolonial archives that seem to suggest that something we might call homophobia is as colonial in Africa as is the notion of the nation-state. While this archival work might be important in creating space for African queers, it fails to engage fully with what it might mean to be both African and queer, in the *here* and *now*. So what, if there were no *ancestral queers*? What do these archives concretize and block out of queer possibilities? While thinking with, and against, this archival record, this essay centers one family's recent history as a calculated exercise in both memory and method. Putting older black women on the agenda evokes their and others' freedom and the intellectual contributions of black women who have, over the years, constituted the survival of black theory and a logic of care. This is an exercise in how *else* one could choose to arrive at blackness and queerness and feminism by way of narration.

"How are you called?"

Nĩtawa Mũsangi, Mũsangi wa Katũnge, Katũnge wa Ngũkũ, Ngũkũ wa Ngũnda, Ngũnda wa Kĩseve, Kĩseve wa Manzi, Manzi wa Ndete, Ndete wa Ndete wa Nzĩ, Nzĩ wa Wathiũtune, Wathiũtune wa . . .

We have always introduced ourselves.

When we do we do not begin with, "My name is"; instead we introduce ourselves as *how* we are called: I am called Mũsangi, Mũsangi of Katũnge,

MERIDIANS · feminism, race, transnationalism   17:2 November 2018
DOI: 10.1215/15366936-7176549 © 2018 Smith College

Katūnge of Ngūkū, Ngūkū of Ngūnda, Ngūnda of Kīseve, Kīseve of Manzi,
Manzi of Ndete, Ndete of Ndetewanzī, Ndetewanzī of Wathiūtune,
Wathiūtune of. . . . To tell this story in English, in the way that I do, makes
me a fraud, or perhaps a seemingly pretentious archivist of a people to
whom one only has remote connection. To translate *wa* to "of" creates a
want, a want for a noun, a gendered noun: son of, daughter of. This want is
neither real nor imaginary but it is no less present. It is a creation of my
Englishnesses, a creation that calls for an insertion that, although not
particularly useful for this exercise in translation, is made necessary for
the internal workings of a language that does not take politely to "direct
translation" and political omission.

Throughout my life whenever I have encountered my mother's people in
my grandmother's village, the question arises, "How are you called?" It is
in the repetition of this question that I want to reimagine introductions
and to enter this archaeology of my family's equally repeated genealogy:

I am called Mūsangi *of* Katūnge—and that is important.

"How are you called?"

Part of how I am called is also about self-identifying as a feminist
(located within particular geohistories) and the decision to start from a
place of *selfing*. As a black nonbinary feminist located in Africa and of no
particular disciplinary formation, my research nonmethods are most likely
the kind that Achille Mbembe (2001, 2) would categorize as "opus dogmas
and empty dreams."[1] According to Mbembe, African modes of self-writing
have only produced "dead end" nativism and Afro-radicalism. In this way,
Mbembe implores us to resist the urge to act from our thinking. Several
Black feminists, on the other hand, continue to show us that our lived
realities come with as much intellectual rigor as research conclusions to
which we might arrive via different methods. Christina Sharpe (2016, 13),
writing on the problem that "traditional" research methods present to
Black academics, quotes Patricia Saunders: "For Black academics to produce legible work in the academy often means adhering to research methods that are 'drafted into the service of a larger destructive force' thereby
doing violence to our own capacities to read, think, and imagine
otherwise."

Following the Jamaican writer Sylvia Wynter (1994), Sharpe (2016, 13)
implores us to resist our participation in the reproduction of our "narra-
tively condemned status" and instead "become undisciplined." In a similar
argument, Danai Mupotsa (2010, 3) asks, "When will African women get to

study interiorities without displaying self-indulgence and privilege?" Sharpe's becoming "undisciplined" is what Mupotsa calls being "undutiful daughters"; Pumla Gqola (2017) uses becoming "rogue" and Sara Ahmed (2010), speaking of what she calls "living in proximity to a nerve," calls the undisciplined "killjoys."

In this essay I privilege the *how*—rather than the *what*, or perhaps even the *why*—of my family life through a generation of women beginning with my grandmothers, by way of my mother. I use the question "Wītawa ata?" or "How are you called?" as an entry point for an inquiry into the thing now known as woman-to-woman marriage, its relationship to a logic of care, and how this relationship could potentially enable us to rethink community formation beyond kinship and family ties.[2] The research I present here is decidedly "unconventional" as it emanates from what has become, for me, an urgent need to tell these stories. By so doing, I want to take seriously the lives of these women as both method and theory. I attempt to foreground these networks of care as central to my coming to feminism and as a significant contribution to black intellectual life and thought. Through this memory-work and narration, the essay also addresses (without joining in) an aspect of the social world that has become even more visible with the rise of human rights frameworks—mostly of the LGBTI variety (see, for example, Nyeck and Epprecht 2013; Epprecht 2013) or the West's obsession with "salvage anthropology," and the unrestrained search for African baskets of absurdities. Of salvage anthropology, Kath Weston (1991, 341) writes, "The story is a familiar one in the annals of the discipline: well-meaning ethnographers rush out to record 'traditional' practices and rituals before the latter change or disappear. At their worst these efforts repackage colonial discourses (e.g., 'primitive' societies) for consumption by Anglo-European audiences."

Some things are worth repeating: This is not an experiment in kinship or a thing called woman-to-woman marriage or even a thing called marriage. This is an exercise in how *else* I could choose to arrive at blackness and queerness and feminism. By putting the older black women in my family on the agenda, I imagine not only my own freedom and that of others, but I also, quite deliberately, want to take seriously the intellectual contributions of black women who have, over the years, constituted the survival of something I want to call black theory and a logic of care. By inviting my mother into this conversation, I also seek to invite her into my world-making project through memory-work. Between the many unspoken hi/stories between my mother and I, this genealogy-mining over WhatsApp is pleasurable (albeit labor-intensive), but for the few days that we do this, we (my mother and I) become coauthors of a story that constitutes history as present, history as an intricate witnessing of our own experiences of living, then and now. This exercise is to home both my mother and I without the overbearing disingenuousness and obligations of consanguinity, or the anthropological weight of the thing often called kinship or family ties.

Keguro Macharia (2015) speaks of how he has found family unusable as a beginning place for understanding the human (and those who get unhumaned) because, he says, families are not only toxic places but also, like "tradition," tend to dwell on root-identity. Similarly I find myself struggling with the beginnings of my exploration given that the family (including mine) and kinship are some of the most visible sites for the theater of heteronormativity (Steyn 2009). I choose to begin from, and with, the women of, and in, my family nevertheless because, as Bibi Bakare-Yusuf (2003, 10) argues, by seeing women as automatic victims "we fall into the trap of confirming the very systems we set out to critique."

"How are you called?"

From Wambui Mwangi and Frantz Fanon I learn to begin from where I am standing. And this also means returning to where I started. (Macharia 2017)

Over a text message I ask my mother why my grandmother Mūkūta left her husband's home in Ikomoa in the late 1960s.³ She is quick to correct me. She says, "She did not leave, she was returned because she had no sons." My mother is named after my sūsū Mūkūta and she is called Katūnge, the one who was returned. What does it mean to "return"? What does it mean to return someone? What do people do with people who are returned? Here, I return, with Keguro and Wambui and Frantz, to where I started, with stories woven around my grandmothers.

First, a footnote: I am immensely grateful for Keguro's friendship and the many ways his intellectual generosity has allowed me to think with ideas that I initially did not perceive as academic enough, ideas that have always seemed to run wild in ways that did not sit in well within academic disciplines. Here I deliberately call Keguro and Wambui by their first name, not to take away from the titles that carry their surnames but to acknowledge their contribution to black thought and to briefly point to the place of friendship in intellectual work coming from parts of Africa—intellectual work that has beautifully morphed into a network of friendships and affirmation in a world in which Africans are to be studied while taking the place of academic tour guides. Both Keguro and Wambui, separately and together, continue to teach us that thinking with gender and queerness is central to the way we think about blackness as well as in the production of intellectual work deeply rooted in our realities. Keguro's ongoing book project, which has brought together Fanon and homosexuality through the idea of "frottage," gives me permission to call Fanon by his first name, Frantz, because he is among my friends, and in that way, I could even claim him as a friend, in the hope that this creates an intimacy and in so doing allows for a thinking with, a building with, a starting with, that does not rely on unusable bibliographies.

"How are you called?"

The autobiographical example is not a personal story that folds onto itself; it's not about navel-gazing, it's really about trying to look at historical and social process and one's own formation onto social and historical processes, as an example of them. (Saidiya Hartman quoted in Sharpe 2016, 8)

Here, the partial story:

Mūkūta: My grandmother Mūkūta was the third-born child of Ndūkī and Ngūnda wa Kīseve.[4]

But let's begin at least somewhere further down, just before the beginning of this new beginning!

My great-grandfather Ngūnda wa Kīseve had four houses: Katoto, Ndūkī, Mwale, and Kaniki.[5] Sūsū Mūkūta and my grandfather Ngūkū came from the second house, the house of Ndūkī. Between them there were two brothers and a sister: Kīmanga, Kamaū, and Mwila. My grandfather Ngūkū, Kamaū, and Mwila lived rather uneventful lives except for their individual madness, which had become something of a family reputation and which many people in my extended family are believed to still carry: *Iwa Mbaa Ngunda,* "They are from the Ngūnda clan," is a phrase used often around Kyamboo and Migwani to explain my relatives' insatiable appetite for meat, quarrel, and alcohol.[6] My sūsū Mūkūta's brother Kīmanga is said to have gone out to sea on a ship, and when he did not return, he was assumed dead. When someone is assumed dead, my people will bury a banana plant to appease the gods and to settle the uncertainty.

But—this is not my story to tell (at least not now). There was no body to bury when Kīmanga died, but one must be buried, and so my grandfather Kīmanga is dead—and buried.

Nizilibel'uba nizalwa ngobani
    (Oh nizalwa ngobani)
Nizilibel'uba nizalwa ngobani na
    (Oh nizalwa ngobani).[7]

Facebook, June 1, 2016

My grandfather's sister, my susu Mukuta, had a story about a child that she and my mother found abandoned under a thorny bush while they tended to my grandfather's goats. "Kana kaitu i ka malithiani," she'd sing in Kikamba. I did not know what "malithiani" meant till I was old (and deliberate) enough to figure out the genealogy of invented Kikamba words. "Malithiani"—used in this song as a noun—is from the verb "kuithia/kuithya," which means to graze.

My aunt Anne would at times go to kuithya. She hated it. All of my grandmother's ten children took turns to look after umau's (Grandpa's) goats, but my aunt Anne complained about it the most. My aunt Anne hated the goats because they did not let her love Jesus fully. She missed church to tend to the goats because Jesus or no Jesus, my umau's goats must be taken care of and Jesus gave him children exactly for that. A story is told of how my aunt Anne would go to look after the goats and instead of watching over them, she'd get to the fields and spend the entire day crying and praying that the goats would be dead by the time she opens her eyes: "Ngai nivoya ngusalukya nithie mavuli aa makw'ie," she'd pray. Still, the goats would be there, bleating and humping.

So my susu Mukuta was married and then she wasn't and then she was again. When my mother was born, my susu Mukuta had already been unmarried. She had come back to her father's home and moved in with my mother's mother and her children. Our umau had given her sister, my susu Mukuta, a small plot of land and built her a small hut. He even gave her some goats of her own. What no one said was that all of my grandmother's ten children would now take turns to tend to my susu Mukuta's goats too. No one talks about where my susu Mukuta's own children were at the time. She lived alone in this little hut. But we know my susu Mukuta got unmarried because her womb bore no sons. Not only did she not have sons, her uterus only carried two children. Only two daughters. My granny had a whole twelve children, two of whom died young and four others in the last few years. But my susu Mukuta was beautiful with that double lip of hers and when she found herself a woman to marry, she had her own goats to use for the bride price.

My susu Mukuta had two girls and two other girls by her wife. She couldn't be a man's wife so she found herself a wife! My umau and granny named my mother after my susu Mukuta. Later the two would bring home an abandoned baby with jaundice!

This memory comes back to me every May. It's been many years since this story by and of my susu Mukuta became entangled with my mother's and that of my own. I descend from a lineage of intricate, complex, and survivor women who have molded me and allowed me to reinvent myself—without contradiction.

Upon the death of sūsū Mūkūta's husband Mwangangi, sūsū Mūkūta would go back to her marital home in Ikomoa and marry a younger woman called Kakonge, who gave them two daughters. Years later sūsū Mūkūta's "wife" would die and the daughters would get married, leaving her with no one except for two graves on a small farm. During the final years of her life, sūsū Mūkūta would circulate between the homes of her two daughters (with her husband Mwangangi), those of her grandchildren, and for a very long time would come back to her brother Ngūkū's home and live with my mother's mother, sūsū Ndolokasi.

o o o

My great-grandfather's first house with Katoto did not yield much. By the time Katoto married my great-grandfather, she already had a daughter (by another man). Ngūnyū, Katoto's only daughter, had three dead siblings and an adopted brother, Mwendwa. No one in my family seems to remember where Mwendwa came from before he became part of our family. I suspect that this memory exercise is unnecessary. Mwendwa was my great-grandfather's child and that is all we choose to remember (at least for now). Having been married and having borne children of her own, our sūsū Ngūnyū would come to live with my mother's mother, sūsū Ndolokasi, around about the same time that our sūsū Mūkūta reappears at my grand-father's home. For the first time, we have three elderly women of no blood relation sharing a setting still construed as home-by-kinship. My great-grandfather's third house by Mwale gave them five children: Ngula, Simba, Kalundu, Mũtwa, and Nzore. I like to see this house as the most interesting. At about 110 years, Mũtwa, the only daughter from the house of Mwale, is the only surviving child of my great-grandfather and the only one who took up my great-grandfather's tradition as a healer. I remember Mũtwa's brother Simba as an unusually quiet man who wore only khaki and Kalundu as the quarrelsome one whose house had become known for night screams from his wife and children.[8] Out of all the Mwale sons, I remember Nzore with much more clarity as I was already a young adult by the time he died. He was a genuine child of my great-grandfather and had forged a great friendship with my sũsũ Ndolokasi. Their older brother Ngula, of whom I have no memory, had several wives, one of whom was Syondũrĩa.

> **Syondũrĩa:** Married to Ngula as Kĩvĩvya, my sũsũ Syondũrĩa is said to have
> been spitefully renamed as such having come back from neighboring
> Kikuyu with exaggeratedly stretched earlobes, one of which would
> later tear in a fight with her co-wife. Having had only one daughter,
> Losa, sũsũ Syondũrĩa would later marry a younger woman, Kavula,
> who would bear them three children. For most of their marriage
> years, Kavula did not stay with sũsũ Syondũrĩa; she lived in Juja,
> Kiambu, where she worked. My mother and I do not remember exactly
> when and why Kavula left for Juja, but I do remember her coming
> home much later as an older woman in her fifties speaking a mixture
> of Kĩkamba and Gĩkũyũ. Kavula, it is said, came back to take care of
> her "mother-in-law," sũsũ Syondũrĩa, who was already aging.[9] When
> Kavula came back, however, sũsũ Syondũrĩa rejected the care she
> offered. Moving out of the two-bedroom house the Catholic church
> had built for them as part of a program to assist older and poorer
> women in the parish, sũsũ Syondũrĩa lived alone in the hut that was
> the kitchen. One of my later memories of this rejection of care revolves
> around passing by their home with my younger cousins and finding
> our sũsũ Syondũrĩa sitting by the open fire on a chilly July morning
> with the corner of her *khanga* slowly catching fire. After quickly putting
> out the fire, we walked back home bothered by how a frail person like
> our sũsũ Syondũrĩa could refuse to be cared for by the clearly capable
> and willing woman that she chose to marry. It was incomprehensible
> to all of us that this marriage between our sũsũ Syondũrĩa and Kavula

had failed! Later Kavula would become one of my sũsũ Ndolokasi's best friends and her companion and caregiver.

"How are you called?"

In this narration I focus on the relationships that my sũsũ Ndolokasi had with her sister-in-law sũsũ Mũkũta, her wife/daughter-in-law Kakonge and her daughters, as well as the relationship with sũsũ Syondũrĩa, by way of her wife/daughter-in-law Kavula. Earlier researchers of woman-to-woman marriage have focused on the reasons why women among the Akamba and other black peoples married women.[10] In this exploration I have neither the urge nor the inclination to pursue or confirm that record. This is because a quest of this kind would not only simplify, at least for me, what I have experienced as a rather calculated logic of care, but would also regurgitate old utility arguments devoid of a careful consideration of the nature of these relationships. Since the early 1970s and 1980s, when woman-to-woman marriage seems to have warranted the attention of legal and social science scholars, there has resurged a different kind of interest emanating from studies of sexualities and human rights. In these studies and activist work, these marriages are seen as a way of arguing for lesbian rights as a "culturally acceptable" way of forming relationships across Africa. While understandable, this search for cultural archives risks distorting not only ideas of being queer and African now, but also sexualizes—without sufficient evidence—relationships between women that might not otherwise have been sexual. Ifi Amadiume (1987) discards this argument in what could be seen as a rather homophobic commentary, as offensive to the women who joined in these sorts of marriages. Woman-to-woman marriage as lesbianism, Amadiume says, would be "totally inapplicable, shocking and offensive to Nnobi women since the strong bonds between them do not imply lesbian sexual practices" (7). Christine Obbo (cited in Zabus 2013, 50), in response to Herskovits's suggestion that women in these relationships might have had some sort of sexual relationship through mutual masturbation, cautions against such assumptions, even as we acknowledge the possibility of sexual intimacy. Fascinating and useful as they are, these debates are beyond the scope of this essay and my interest. It is important to state, however, that whether or not women in the women-to-women marriages had sexual relationships is becoming more and more unuseful and unusable as I become comfortable with unknowable worlds. In other words, I am not interested in the totality of these relationships, or, to borrow from Édouard Glissant (1990, 191), the urgency for transparent lifeworlds makes me clamor even more for the right to opacity:

> The opaque is not the obscure, though it is possible for it to be so and be accepted as such. It is that which cannot be reduced, which is the most perennial guarantee of participation and confluence.

"How are you called?"

Instead I want to pursue, through these relationships, the idea of care as shared work and as shared affect rather than as an economically or legally binding practicality. The logic of care, seen this way, is not constitutive of volition or will but is embedded in a shared understanding of practical normativity by those involved in care-sharing.[11]

"How are you called?"

Toward a conclusion: Admittedly the logic of care here is not only about the women of and in my family; it is also about my own obsession with remembering as a projection of anxieties around memory loss as my body decays and as I anticipate complications that might have to do with my temporal lobe epilepsy and other conditions of the brain. This exercise in memory is as crucial to my mother as it is to me and my siblings, with whom I have shared bits of this hi/story.

And this is how I arrive at care: In a conversation about how much I miss my sũsũ Ndolokasi, an older cousin reminds me about how much sũsũ cared about people whom no one else seemed to give a damn about! My cousin Diana mentions sũsũ Mũkũta and our sũsũ Syondũrĩa's wife/ daughter-in-law Kavula in particular. Diana uses the word *care*, not *love*, not *kindness*, not generosity, but *care*. But care has often been seen as the business of fragility and vulnerability. Care work is that which nurses and family members (often called kinkeepers and primary caregivers) do with and for patients, the elderly, some persons with disabilities, and children. Often not thought of as affect, care is seen as work, as something underpaid hands do to ease the lives of those who are often not economically useful or usable themselves. Care is something that African migrants might do for economic survival in Europe and America. Care, seen this way, is either a value project or a legal battleground but not a network of ethical being(s). But what does it mean to think of narrative as care? What is made possible by this attempt to remember the people we care about as people who cared about others? Could this memory-work be care-work? And if so, what is the value of this labor in feminist terms?

Avishai Margalit (2002) tells us that although there is an ethics of memory, there is very little morality of memory. Ethics, Margalit argues, is defined by the thick social relations we have with those nearest and closest to us. Morality, on the other hand, is characterized by thin social relations with people to whom we are not bound by any special ties. In other words, both an ethics and a morality of this sort would require some form of shared memory, which is "the cement that holds thick relations together" and without which caring is not possible (27).

"The relation between memory and caring . . . is . . . an internal relation—a relation that could not fail to obtain between these two concepts since memory is partly constitutive of the notion of care" (Margalit 2002, 27–28). Margalit's thesis, as Janelle Taylor (2010) has shown in reference to her mother's dementia, is solely dependent on cognitive recognition. In the absence of such recognition, caring is not possible because one may simply not remember names, which Margalit sees as a metonym for remembering the people themselves. But what is the nature of this obligation to remember names and perhaps events from the past? Do we still care if we do not or cannot remember? Of course we do! However, while we still can, my mother and I are trying to remember to, in many ways, make caring possible, for ourselves and for others in ways that are human and make living possible.

. . . .

Neo Sinoxolo Musangi is an independent researcher and artist based in Kajiado, Kenya. Musangi studied at the University of the Witwatersrand, Johannesburg, and has previously worked at the British Institute in Eastern Africa, Nairobi.

Notes

1   Increasingly I am becoming jaded about and dissatisfied with gender categories that seem to expand the possibilities of gender identity while paradoxically cementing and concretizing "new" gender categories. I use *nonbinary* here not as an arrived-at place of gender totality but as a pointer to the possibilities of thinking and living with and in gender beyond male/man and female/woman.

2   I borrow *logic of care* from Mol 2008.

3   Hereafter sũsũ (Kĩkamba for "grandmother").

4   Our sũsũ Ndolokasi would later correct us and insist that there was no Kĩseve in our family lineage. Kĩseve, sũsũ Ndolokasi claimed, was an invention of my

grandfather Ngũkũ wa Ngũnda, who liked to distort things because he was cunning and corny and liked to tease children. Sũsũ Ndolokasi further claimed that Ngũnda's father was Manzi. I think of my grandfather exactly like this: the person who would create his own grandfather figure and want his own grandchildren to believe (in) his little creation. With all due respect to sũsũ Ndolokasi, I'll stick with my grandfather's version of his family tree. I honor my grandfather's distortion of events to indulge his imagination but also to pursue my own interests in the invention of self.

5   I say *houses* and not *wives* because that is what we called ourselves—the house of Ndũkĩ, the house of Ndolokasi, and so on—to clarify from which wife, among many, we descend.

6   Mbaĩ (clan), used in this way, does not refer to the often large subgroups of the Akamba people, such as the Aombe, Anzaũnĩ, Atangwa, but rather to a three- to four-generation family identified by a renowned patriarch. My great-grandfather Ngũnda wa Kĩseve, the chief patriarch, was a man of no small means. We don't know whether when he arrived at the place now called Kyamboo he had already been practicing as a witchdoctor or whether the idea came to him upon arrival. He came, it is said, from Masakũ through Kĩtui with his friends, Kanuku wa Ngolanye and Kĩmanyi wa Ngĩla, who for whatever reason settled somewhere along the route. No one seems to know why these three left their families and walked miles away, but we know that, like the protagonist in Dambudzo Marechera's (1978) *House of Hunger*, they packed what they had and left and in many ways changed the landscape of wherever they settled.

7   These lyrics are borrowed from the chorus to Thandiswa Mazwai's 2006 song, "Nizalwa Ngobani," which is both a question and a reminder of "where we come from." Here the song's opening stanza: "The world changes / Revolutionaries die / And the children forget."

8   Kalundu's albinism was another site for my grandfather's cunning distortions. During World War I, my grandfather Ngũkũ would tell us, our village Kyamboo bordered Germany, and it is during one of those war days that a German mother left her child at the border while fleeing from the soldiers from Kyamboo. My grandfather, having been one of the soldiers, would then save the young German boy and bring him home. That German boy would later become his stepbrother, Kalundu.

9   I use *mother-in-law* rather than the often used heteropatriarchy-centered and loaded *female husband* because my grandmothers Mũkũta and Syondũrĩa were indeed mothers-in-law to the women they married and were seen as such.

10   See, for example, Cadigan 1998; Herskovits 1937; Krige 1974; Obbo 1976a, 1976b; O'Brien 1977.

11   I am not particularly interested in old philosophical debates about the normative authority of love and care or even volitional rationality.

Works Cited

Ahmed, Sara. 2010. *The Promise of Happiness*. Durham, NC: Duke University Press.

Amadiume, Ifi. 1987. *Male Daughters, Female Husbands: Gender and Sex in an African Society*. London: Zed Books.

Bakare-Yusuf, Bibi. 2003. "Determinism: The Phenomenology of African Female Existence." *Feminist Africa* 2: 8–24.

Cadigan, R. J. 1998. "Woman-to-Woman Marriage: Practices and Benefits in Sub-Saharan Africa." *Journal of Comparative Family Studies* 29, no. 1: 89–98.

Epprecht, Marc. 2013. *Sexuality and Social Justice in Africa: Rethinking Homophobia and Forging Resistance*. New York: Zed Books.

Glissant, Édouard. 1990. *Poetics of Relation*. Ann Arbor: University of Michigan Press.

Gqola, Pumla. 2017. *Reflecting Rogue: Inside the Mind of a Feminist*. Johannesburg: MF Books.

Herskovits, Melville. 1937. "A Note on 'Woman Marriage' in Dahomey." *Africa* 10, no. 3: 335–41.

Krige, E. J. 1974. "Woman Marriage with Special Reference to the Lovedu: Its Significance for the Definition of Marriage." *Africa* 44, no. 1: 11–36.

Macharia, Keguro. 2015. "Mbiti and Glissant." *New Inquiry*, March 9. www.thenewinquiry.com/blog/mbiti-glissant/.

Macharia, Keguro. 2017. "Queer African Studies: Personhood and Pleasure." *Gukira: Without Predicates*, May 3. www.gukira.wordpress.com/2017/05/03/queer-african-studies-personhood-pleasure.

Marechera, Dambudzo. 1978. *House of Hunger*. New York: Pantheon Press.

Margalit, Avishai. 2002. *The Ethics of Memory*. Cambridge, MA: Harvard University Press.

Mbembe, Achille. 2001. "African Modes of Self-Writing." *Identity, Culture and Politics* 2, no. 1: 1–39.

Mol, A. 2008. *The Logic of Care: Health and the Problem of Patient Choice*. London: Routledge.

Mupotsa, Danai. 2010. "If I Could Write This in Fire: African Feminist Ethics for Research in Africa." *Agenda Africa: (Re)imagining African Studies*, Postamble 6, no. 1: 1–18.

Nyeck, Sylvia, and Marc Epprecht. 2013. *Sexual Diversity in Africa: Politics, Theory, Citizenship*. Montreal: McGill-Queen's University Press.

Obbo, Christine. 1976a. "Dominant Male Ideology and Female Options: Three East African Case Studies." *Africa* 46, no. 4: 371–89.

Obbo, Christine. 1976b. "Is the Female Husband a Man? Woman/Woman Marriage among the Nandi of Kenya." *Ethnology* 19, no. 1: 69–88.

O'Brien, D. 1977. "Female Husbands in Southern Bantu Societies." In *Sexual Stratification: A Cross-Cultural View*, edited by A. Schlegel, 109–26. New York: Columbia University Press.

Sharpe, Christina. 2016. *In the Wake: On Blackness and Being*. Durham, NC: Duke University Press.

Steyn, M. V. M. 2009. *The Prize and the Price: Shaping Sexualities in South Africa*. Pretoria: HSRC Press.

Taylor, Janelle. 2010. "On Recognition, Caring and Dementia." In *Care in Practice: On Tinkering in Clinics, Homes and Farms*, edited by A. Mol, J. Moser, and J. Pols, 27–56. Bielefeld, Germany: Transcript Verlag.

Weston, Kath. 1991. *Families We Choose: Lesbians, Gays, Kinship*. New York: Columbia University Press.

Wynter, Sylvia. 1994. "No Humans Involved: An Open Letter to My Colleagues." *Forum N.H.I. Knowledge for the 21st Century, Knowledge on Trial* 1, no. 1: 42–71.

Zabus, C. 2013. *Out in Africa: Same-Sex Desire in Sub-Saharan Literatures and Cultures*. Woodbridge, U.K.: James Currey.

Patricia McFadden

Contemporarity
Sufficiency in a Radical African Feminist Life

Abstract: This essay theorizes contemporarity as a new framework for Black feminist resistances—personal and sociopolitical—and explores reimagined lived realities as a crucial site for the generation of new feminist epistemologies and alternative ways of living. Given the failures of neocolonial and neoliberal state regimes across the African continent and the globe to respond equitably to the imperatives of human emancipation, the paper argues for a return to and closer interrogation of personal politics and feminist relationships to the self and the ecosystems that nurture both. The challenge is to find new sources of creative imaginaries and resistance that will lead to the unfolding of discourses, practices, and ways of living that offer an alternative to neoliberal capitalism. From the experience of sustaining oneself through ecological balance, a respectful interaction with nature, and nonmarket practices of sufficiency, the paper proposes to glean the knowledge and inherent integrity embedded in such processes to create new radical social knowledge and practices.

. . . .

There are many kinds of open
how a diamond comes into a knot of flame
how sound comes into a word, coloured
by who pays what for speaking.
—Audre Lorde, "Coal," 1997
. . . .

Every now and then, as the result of a personal encounter that has brought me tremendous joy or sadness, or as the outcome of an intense struggle

MERIDIANS · feminism, race, transnationalism   17:2 November 2018
DOI: 10.1215/15366936-7176560 © 2018 Smith College

with some patriarchal institution or sociocultural force, I find myself at a conjuncture in my feminist consciousness and lived reality. I realize that I am in a new place in my creative imagination and social circumstances. This sense of consciousness, of having been part of the change in the aesthetic and material reality of my existence, is what I understand as being at "the cutting edge," consciously positioned in the shift as it occurs around one and within oneself.[1]

Over the years I have learned to read the signal to stop and take a careful, curious look inside my feminist self, to introspect and acknowledge that I am growing intellectually and politically, as well as to scrutinize the material and political terrains that encompass each particular moment. Learning to recognize the flutter of change inside one is always very rewarding in thinking and pleasuring terms.

It is this sense of consciousness about being in the contemporary moment which is a key element in my notion of becoming contemporary— of imagining and shaping the identity and political content of contemporarity, which is the pulse of contemporary African feminist theorizing and activism. Over the past decade, as a response to a sense of the inadequacy both of feminism as a universal politics of women's resistance to patriarchal repression and, more specifically, because of the "seepage" of nationalist ideology into feminist discourses on the continent, I have begun searching for an alternative sensibility of feminism within the African context.

Initially I entered this new journey through a critique of liberal declarations and practices of citizenship, which keep the majority of women outside the ambit of laws and protections that are supposed to be universal entitlements in all African constitutions. The realization that women would have to reinvent the notion and practice of citizenship was a spark that set me on a new journey toward thinking about how African women must become contemporary. The notion of the contemporary is run through by debates of modernity and Westernism on the one hand, and the inevitable backlash this elicits among African nationalists who are passionately searching for the authentic African male identity that lies at the heart of nationalism and neocolonialism. However, being critical of citizenship did not translate into a new and different consciousness. I needed to reimagine a different concept of rights, dignity, and eventually wellness and sufficiency, and how this can translate into real changes in all our lives.

Contemporarity is not conceived as the opposite of the "modern" or the "Western." It is about finding the innovative feminist energies and sensibilities that will enable each of us to live the new politics of this moment in African time. Therefore I found the notion of spatial intimacy both fascinating and illuminating in terms of my own positioning at the interface of new consciousness and radical living. I felt a visceral intellectual familiarity with Nthabiseng Motsemmi's (2004) reading of "violence and place," which helped me lean more closely toward the yearning for new spaces of intellectual feminist discourse and solidarity. Such radical thinking about the interactions of black femaleness with colonial and neocolonial infrastructures of patriarchal power, privilege, and dominance can enable creative conceptual terrains to open as possibilities of different explanations of hegemonic masculinist supremacy and practice.

Sometimes I become aware of the shift in my intellectual and organic feelings about a particular issue with which I have battled for as long as I came to feminist consciousness. Take, for example, the vexatious persistence and escalation of hetero-impunity and violation against mainly females of all ages. For many years in my activist writing and engagement with this expression of patriarchal supremacy, I felt the injustice of sexual impunity viscerally, in my human core, and my responses were largely reflective of an essentialist existentialism of outrage, accompanied by a sense of helplessness in terms of how effectively to respond to this enormously destructive social phenomenon. More recently, however, I have realized that my responses to heteropatriarchal violation—recounted daily in the media—have become habitual. One begins to expect to hear about patriarchal violation against women with each news bulletin. It becomes the norm within one's feminist hearing. One still feels the outrage, particularly when the incident is especially egregious, and one is overwhelmed by a sense of deep sorrow, but the seeming inevitability of women being violated creates a learned response which translates into a tendency to lean to the side so as to let the information pass by as the day moves on.

No doubt within the women's organizations that work to find adequate political responses to patriarchal violation, the struggle to protect women and demand accountability from the state and its representatives is an everyday challenge. However, not all radical women operate in the context of organizations and formal political structures. In this sense, I am reflecting on my own internal political stagnation and moments of growth as a feminist who has "stepped back" from the established sites of nationalist gendered women's movements and organizations.

My initial inkling that a gap had developed between my radical sensibilities regarding patriarchal violation and actively finding ways to resist such violation came while attending tribunals on women's narrations of hurt and grief about the patriarchal impunity they had experienced. I felt uneasy about being part of what seemed to be a kind of voyeurism that fed on women's pain, in spite of the insistence by other feminists that women should be able to expose violations within safe spaces that are created by and for women.[2] This initial sense of dis-ease has persisted, propelling me conceptually to examine its roots within my own experiences as a gendered female growing up in a deeply feudal society and working and living on a continent that is extensively precapitalist in economic, sociocultural, and political terms. Through this exercise in self-reflection on the events that have wounded me, as well as the adoption of a radically critical feminist perspective on heteroviolation, I realized that I had stimulated a shift in my own consciousness about violation, impunity, and supremacy. Making the personal political in an actively subjective manner that nurtures my political consciousness and sense of protectiveness signaled the enduring relevance of core feminist mantras and principles (hooks 1995).

By returning to these core notions of feminist theorizing about patriarchal power and privilege, I realized that, for example, publishing incidents of sexual violation had become a "business prop" for many newspapers. It keeps the circulation numbers up and provides a perverse form of voyeuristic entertainment for the public, who seem to have become inured to the horrors of brutality that little girls and older females endure, largely among working communities. On one level, we know that while the entertainment industry has mined violence and sexual violation in particular as a lucrative source of profit, egregious behavior has seemed to offend the most common moral sensibilities in most humans.

Certainly, while levels of moral indignation have increased everywhere, as evidenced by the outcries in various media forms, the sense of collective helplessness about how to "solve the problem of violence" hangs heavily between a moralistic outrage and the urgent need for a critical understanding of patriarchy as a brutal and dehumanizing system. Feminists know that bemoaning "the loss of culture" or the "impact of Westernization" will not answer the fundamental questions regarding impunity and misogyny. The critical thinking about the interfaces between heteropatriarchal supremacy and impunity, on the one hand, and the rampant plunder and mauling of any female body, on the other, will have to be imagined and located within key discursive and activist sites across the African continent. As Pumla Gqola (2012) succinctly put it during an interview, "I think we need to collectively re-invest in the value of critical thinking. It's not just nationally that there is a general consumerist, lazy, dumbing down and conformist culture. It is global, so we need to be quite mindful of this even as we cultivate critical thinking as valuable at the local level."

Increasing male activism around issues of violation seems to indicate a long overdue response on the part of men who are beginning to reimagine their masculinities and identities as Black men (Ouzgane and Morrell 2005; Ratele 2014). However, a large section of this activism is being influenced by sensibilities of shame and moral indictment driven by the twin right-wing forces of the Moral Re-Armament movement and Christian fundamentalism. These reactionary energies create a sense of "male exceptionalism" rather than leading to the kinds of political clarity and consciousness that are required to resolve the challenges presented by patriarchal supremacy, impunity, and male sexual privilege.

One of the most effective mechanisms that patriarchy deploys against femaleness is the claim that our creativity, imagination, and sensibilities of freedom and pleasure are taboo and must be suppressed. From childhood we are taught and we learn obedience—in a relative sense, of course, because none of us ever loses the natural instinct for autonomy and freedom. We learn how to suppress our uniqueness as female humans and to dress it up in all sorts of excuses and performances, so that we eventually become the unimagining custodians and gatekeepers of patriarchal privilege and power: "If women are in many ways socialized into submissiveness from the earliest age by rape and the threat of rape, whole peoples can be trained to intellectual passivity through invasive systems of knowledge" (Griffin 1996, 93). I am making the claim that we never lose our instinct to be free because I know that every time I draw on my childhood refusals to be engineered into a conforming female, I resuscitate an instinct that continues to infuse my feminist political consciousness, at the personal and larger political levels, with rebelliousness. Within the often overwhelming existence of being female in heteropatriarchal societies, everywhere, performing a radical action every day to remain outside the quagmire of

patriarchal conformity becomes a necessary tactic of human autonomy
and feminist resistance (Walker 2006).

As feminists, we know this narrative well, and many of us resent the
historical fact that we were taught how to become *patriarchalized* females.
We experience patriarchy's constraints and suppressions each day in intimate or public encounters, yet to a great extent we still allow this reality to
define our lives. This collusive stance remains a major challenge for all
women. Unlearning being patriarchal women is a difficult and daunting
task. So many women catch a glimpse of the possibilities of crafting new
identities for themselves that are based on a sense of freedom from the
control of males. But often, at some point during their lifetime, they revert
to being "good and decent" women, and sometimes it seems that they are
relieved at having returned to the fold of patriarchal "solace" and the
rewards of being acceptable. The fear of being unaccepted and therefore "inauthentic" functions as another leveler of women's political
imagination—all African women are still expected to aspire to be good
mothers, wives, daughters, sisters, and grandmothers. If they cannot be
totally self-sacrificing, then at least they should perform the parody of
being women in the "African cultural sense."

As a feminist who aspires to be as radical as possible in the deeply feudo-
patriarchal societies that I live in, I continue to be challenged by these
repressive forces and to struggle, often alone, to retrieve my instincts and
consciousness of freedom and well-being. In so doing I have come to
understand that being free of patriarchy in new ways is essential to my
dignity and well-being as a female person and that I cannot experience
pleasure as an intellectual and creative force without crafting and living a
life of feminist dignity. Generally I think that a compromise with African
feudo-patriarchy remains the most critical challenge and impediment to
the freedom and dignity of Black women everywhere. However, in this
context, I will not be speaking to women generally, because I have also
come to understand that indulging in the generalities of womanness is
another noose around the necks of radical women.

It is a conceptual and political essentialism that we have inherited from
nationalism, which has distracted us from the critical work that we owe to
ourselves, and because when we are free our communities and societies
benefit too. In my opinion, however, the latter is of less significance for a
contemporary feminism that is specific to the challenges Black women
currently face on the continent. Thinking, speaking, and undertaking

activism in terms of large, all-encompassing programs is not only dangerously idealistic—after all, women are differentiated by class, race, gender, age, social location, ability, sexual identity, and more—but it is also deeply nationalistic and reactionary. This is the ideological bridle that male nationalists have kept fastened over our political vocality and language. It is a deeply entrenched marker of learned patriarchality, of needing to save everyone as though our lives depended on it, which they do not.

Critically, in terms of imagining original, autonomously radical political forms and discourses, positioning our politics as wide-open platforms onto which everyone is welcomed feeds the altruism and self-abnegation that is an enduring hallmark of reactionary nationalist ideology. The debate over whether being feminist is elitist is one expression of the learned and politically internalized nationalist rhetoric of rescue and sociocultural acceptability that characterizes African women's politics. One can extend this argument to the issues of being African and feminist or whether men can be feminist. Invariably one gets caught up in the traps that nationalist ideology sets for us, through the construction of female politics as an extension of male interests and privilege.

Just the realization that the time for a different kind of feminism has arrived, which puts the individual Black woman at the center of its epistemology and lived aesthetic, creates a deep rupture with the ideological and often intimate hold that nationalism has had over Black feminist politics and activism. The ripple effects of our lived freedoms and dignity should not be a consequence from which we take incidental pleasure. It should be a deliberate act of self- nurturing. In appraising my sense of radical sensibilities, two main sources of propulsion seem to stand out: first, stepping away from the nationalist African women's movement a decade ago as a gesture of self-rescue from dangerous, reactionary essentialisms; second, redefining retrieval as the reclamation of Black female sexual and bodily integrity and the right to a life of dignity and wellness.

Retrieving the Feminist Imagination
In order to explain the importance of stepping away, I had to scrutinize the conceptual terrain around me more closely. I noticed that much of the thinking and activist language that women who name themselves feminist were using was in reality defined and controlled by gender activists who had mainstreamed feminist concepts and stripped them of their radical political content and meaning (Walby 2003). For example, GBV, the

acronym for *gender-based violence*, has systematically and insistently replaced concepts of heteropatriarchal violence, domestic violence, and sexual violence, let alone the more powerful notions of patriarchal impunity and violation in discussions regarding women's bodies and their integrity. As an outcome of the softer, less discomforting, conservative discourses of "gender-mainstreaming," the language women are using, which comes out of the technocratic vocabulary of the UN and other global status quo structures, is *gender-based violence*. What is politically astounding is the ease with which this new UNspeak has gained hegemony in the media, within the academy, in women's organizations, and across the various discursive sites of our social landscapes. The acronym has become so ubiquitous people do not even stop to consider what it actually means in conceptual and activist terms.

Over the past decade or so, this conceptually limited, theoretically ineffectual, neoliberal and reactionary linguistic technology has been able to systematically shut down the debates and the passions that had driven women's radical demands on the state and the United Nations system, transforming most women intellectuals into "gender activists." Women's bodily and sexual integrity has been replaced by structural and policy concerns through a language that does not enable women to acquire a consciousness of entitlements, rights, or protections. The main protagonists in terms of the response to violence against females have become the state and the UN system. Women's organizations and radical groups have been shunted to the edges of social engagement, and the radical agencies of women have been largely silenced. Language can either be an effective weapon in instilling conformity in people, especially in women, or it can serve as a wide-open doorway to intellectual and personal freedoms. What you say, and the tone you use, can still get you killed in many societies across the world. Language and words are importantly about power and access to financial and social resources. In the context of gender mainstreaming, the language a woman uses indicates whether or not she can get a lucrative consultancy, and in most instances, class and social reproduction trump any memory of radical thinking and activism against patriarchy.

Therefore, in this deeply problematic context, retrieving the powerful language and passion of feminist agency becomes a necessity for fulfilling the possibilities of the new imaginaries. Personally I refuse to use the conformist depoliticized linguistic technology of GBV in my writing or speech and instead take every opportunity to speak out against its hegemony in women's conversations and debates, one of a slew of reactionary appropriations of feminist political language. For African women, the persistent insertion of *cutting* or *surgery* to erase *mutilation* in the radical language of female genital mutilation presents another such dangerously reactionary strategy to change the meaning and content of the debate and silence the demand for bodily and sexual integrity by Black women (Thiam 1986).

A radical process of retrieval is thus critical to imagining differently, and it is by engaging in retrieval that we begin to redefine language as a feminist prerogative and initiate the new, contemporary African feminism. Imbuing the notion of *retrieval* with a deliberately feminist sense of ownership and agency is also a conceptual, personal, and intimate act that enables one to instigate alternative theoretical, activist, and existential trajectories, using the possibilities of this crucial time in the neocolonial conjuncture to redirect our lives. I say this deliberately because I know that such shifts in consciousness and personal reality come seldom during one's life. The personal opportunities that women have created through struggles against patriarchy—as feudalism, capitalism, settler and other colonialisms, and their ideological and exploitative infrastructures—will be lost if we do not anticipate the future in new ways. What tomorrow becomes depends on how we perceive it and what we do to define and live it differently.

Stepping Away to Lean Forward

In thinking about the challenges that face us as feminists in this neocolonial, neo-imperialist moment, I have found that the gesture of "stepping back"—in a personal and conceptual sense—enables one to understand more clearly the dominant hegemonies and their impacts on feminism as a theoretical framework and a personal politics. In clarifying the definition of the state in neo-imperial and neocolonial terms, M. Jacqui Alexander (2005, 4) argues, "While differently located, both neo-imperial state formations (those advanced capitalist states that are the dominant partners in the global 'order') and neo-colonial state formations (those that emerged from the colonial 'order' as the forfeiters to nationalist claims to sovereignty and autonomy) are central to our understandings of the production of hegemonies." This implies the need for the adoption of a very critical conceptual and activist stance in relation to nationalism and the state and toward Black men. For me, taking a step back from the subjectivities and surveillances of nationalism and gendered nationalist conservatism was essential in reimagining what being contemporary, African, and feminist could mean.

While I am aware of some of the lively, extensive debates around the notions and practices of nationalism, nation, third world feminism, and transnational feminism beyond the terrain of "the West" (Herr 2014), Aniko Imre's (2008, 255) definition of nationalism lies closest to my own critical theoretical stance toward this male-defined ideology and practice: "It has been well established that the **we** of nationalism implies a homosocial form of male bonding that includes women only symbolically, most prominently in the trope of the mother. . . . Nationalist discourses are especially eager to reassert the 'natural' division of labour between the sexes and to relegate women to traditional reproductive roles."

Many Black women of my generation found their voices and political sensibilities through resistance to white colonial patriarchy. We brought our resentment of African feudal and colonial patriarchal oppression to the broad platforms that male nationalists had created and crafted for their own masculinist political agendas. In the course of struggle, we learned to adapt and adjust our political imaginaries to the larger nationalist project of independence for all Africans. Later we retained the ideological infrastructures of nationalist politics and its compromises with Black feudo-patriarchy, as a means of reiterating our "Black femininity and Africanness, which remained deeply conservative and politically reactionary.

In this context, then, many women activists and scholars learned how to manipulate the opportunities that the neocolonial moment presented—structurally, through the organizations that composed what was called the African women's movement. This site became a deeply contested and often brutal terrain, where the radical agencies of feminists were conveniently applauded when it suited the agendas of the donors and the gender activists, or were vilified and driven out, often through reactionary, homophobic malice, outright lies, and malignant rumor-mongering. This "cat fight" signaled the profound ideological and structural crisis of women's collusive relationships with feudo-patriarchal state occupants at the national and continental levels.[3] The upward mobility of a small clique of Black women who fought ferociously to retain their middle-class status and the material wealth associated with gendered mainstreaming is one of the most significant expressions of the demise of gendered nationalist organizing. Most of those who fought against radical ideas in women's organizations have become well-paid functionaries in global state structures and donor-driven initiatives. For the majority of African women, however, life has remained basically what it has always been: precarious, vulnerable, and unjust.

Once again the lesson learned is a clearer understanding of nationalism as a masculinist ideology and identity, and its translation into Black ruling-class power in and outside the state. The more important illumination from this experience is realizing the necessity of "returning to the source" of feminist consciousness and thinking, thinking that is unencumbered by the conservative instincts and acquisitiveness of nationalism (Cabral 1973). As a collective ideology and mobilizing strategy, nationalism provided the public opportunity for women to leave the repressive intimacies of domesticity, albeit fleetingly—but it never professed to being the means for Black women's freedom on and beyond the continent. Feminists imbued nationalism with a radicalism it did not possess or aspire to, and we have paid a high price for that idealism in terms of not having built our own feminist organizations or conceptualizing an African feminism that is able to take us beyond the nationalist moment.

Alternative Lived Practice

For the past decade I have hidden away on one of the world's oldest mountains, living precariously in a tiny house crammed full of my clutter—the stuff of my life—as I sought to find myself in newly radical and invigorating ways. Thinking back, I intuit that my first steps toward becoming contemporary as a Black radical woman began with my sense of dis-ease about the tensions within the African women's movement associated with issues of LGBTIQ, sexuality, and pleasure, particularly in relation to a critical articulation of violation and the impacts of HIV/AIDS on women's sexuality, and heteronormative conformity. These four issues were particularly vexatious and eventually led to my expulsion from Zimbabwe and to being labeled a slut.[4] Raising the necessity of not only recognizing lesbian feminism and the political relevance of LGBTIQ struggles, but also the critical ideological and activist value of lessons to be drawn from the struggles of our sisters and the many groups of human beings who strive for dignity and rights in ways that are similar to those of women across all class and other divides, raised the ire of many reactionaries who had taken political cover under the broad umbrella of the African women's movement.

Stepping away from the sites of gendered nationalism signaled my personal retrospective on who I had become, as well as consciously constructing my self redefinition in personal terms (how I live in my middle-aged body), in theoretical terms (thinking about what it means to become contemporary), in political terms (interrogating my relationships with the infrastructures of political and state power), and in activist terms (how I would live my daily life in a radically transformational manner). These became the signposts of my journey toward a contemporary identity which I would craft at the theoretical, ideological, and practical levels.

Theoretically I have found that approaching notions such as citizenship, for example, with a critically feminist gaze transforms the entire discourse into a dynamic debate about women's personhood, entitlements, consciousness, rights, and the critical policy issues of accessibility and protection. The idea of citizenship becomes a very specific political process for African women who for centuries were located outside the most minimal recognitions of African personhood through colonial racist discourses and policies that colluded with long-entrenched feudal African notions and practices. The struggles of all politically and socioculturally excluded constituencies for a substantively inclusive notion and practice of citizenship are crucial to the imagining, formulation, and demand for a different kind of national belonging (Alexander 1994).

During the colonial period, Black men could imagine themselves becoming citizens in liberal, albeit limited ways. Black women were, in the despicable words of Verwoerd, "superfluous appendages," unseen and not heard. This construction of nonpersonhood for the majority of African women remains a daily lived reality across the continent, almost seventy years since the first African country became independent. In her critique of culture, religion, and tradition, and their impacts on women's sexuality in Nigeria, Charmaine Pereira (2009, 264) argues, "The balance of power at any one time shapes which group is excluded, marginalized, or exploited in the process. Understanding the context is thus crucial for discerning which spheres of activism may be invigorated by analytical as well as imaginative exploration of the conceptual dimensions involved and which strategies to adopt."

In exploring the possibilities of *contemporarity* partly as a recognition of the failure of nationalism for women and all those who will never have access to the largesse of the neocolonial moment, each one of us as feminists reinvigorates her relationship with radical concepts, their essential meanings and the paths these notions have traveled over the past century, the debates and conversations that have expanded or discarded them from the feminist lexicon and imbued the notions with the power and incisiveness that comes from living a radical life in a conscious and deliberate fashion.

I have chosen being vegan and living as an ecological feminist and herbal healer as my revolutionary landscape wherein I can reconfigure the core feminist principles of bodily, sexual, and spiritual integrity, wellness, and wholeness. This radical location also provides me a "room with a view," to riff on Virginia Woolf's (1929) A Room of One's Own, on the seemingly chaotic but deeply entrenched capitalist practices and policies that perpetuate class plunder and privilege across identities of race and heteronormativity, while enabling me to use the distance I have created between myself and gendered nationalists to scrutinize and interrogate their collusive tactics and strategies in relation to the neocolonial state, neoliberalism, and the various globalized structures of reactionary politics.

On a daily basis I have learned to translate what I feel and intuit in the field as I coax new seeds into life and maturity so that I can feed my body and nurture my soul from the wholeness and bounty that nature so graciously bequeaths us; from this generosity I have recognized the core of integrity as the source of nature's power. As women, we become invincible at the moment when we embrace and translate our sense of integrity into political and ethical discourses and activism (Lorde 1984; Walker 2006). Integrity infuses our demands and efforts for lives of dignity with an authenticity that cannot be denied. It might be resisted and rejected, but it cannot be disavowed. When we are born, we arrive with all the forms of integrity that are inalienable to the human experience of life. They are our heritage, and it is these sensibilities that undergird the politics and ethics of feminism as an ideology, an identity, and a way of living.

Locating myself as closely as possible to nature's power of life and generosity, I observed that the quality and the quantities of the crops I am growing increased with every season, despite being grown on the very same soil. With care and deep respect, I have carefully sought and begun to find the point of balance between the earth's nurturing capacities and my own abilities to live simply, quietly, and wholesomely (Harper 2009). This translates conceptually into sufficiency—the ability to feed and nurture ourselves, to have ENOUGH—through a balanced relationship with the earth and other living ecosystems.[5]

Beyond my personal experiences as I live a life that is attentive to the earth and its bounty, its boundless spiritual, nurturing, and aesthetic gifts,

I have also been able to initiate new relationships with some of my neighbors on the mountain. Over the past few years, I have supported and encouraged a neighbor who lives very precariously; she and her partner are living with HIV/AIDS, their son with Down Syndrome is in a wheelchair, and the only income they have is a measly, unpredictable social grant twice a year that barely suffices. One day I suggested to my neighbor that we clean out a little patch of land adjacent to her two-room house and rebuild the land so that she can grow some food. We spent a week removing the broken bottles, tins, and rubber, and slowly we brought in the manure, the compost, the seeds, and the love. It was magical. Today she looks forward to the rainy season, when she can put the seedlings down, and the joy on her face when she has a successful crop is irreplaceable. The family is able to live off that little piece of land for several months a year.

This initiative changed our relationship in several ways. She, a working-class woman with minimal education, and I have been able to build a bridge of solidarity between us based on a sense of integrity and self-exploration. We share knowledge about seed preservation, and she often teaches me about indigenous greens that have come back on that land—changing my own attitudes toward "weeds" and their immeasurable value to health and healing. She has planted a little corner with some of the basic herbs needed to control flu, pain, stomach upsets, and more. We have become these new women in ways that neither of us imagined.

In terms of class solidarities, this relationship has enabled me to step away from the prejudices that are inbuilt in relationships of class and social status. Initially we had to work our way through much of the baggage that constructs us as Black women in a feudal, patriarchal monarchy. We had to find a language in which to share this knowledge that has changed our lives. I watched her slowly let go of the fear that accompanies interactions between middle-class and working-class women. I also found a sense of ease with her abilities to transform her life without directing the process. It was a slow, caring, and rewarding journey. Now we discuss global warming and its impact on our crops—we grow mainly indigenous and drought-resistant crops—and what changes we will have to make in the next season. She is becoming more autonomous—to the ire of the locals who have more money than she does—and her sense of freedom has convinced me that such initiatives must form the core of the new contemporary African feminism.

Conclusion

I have chosen to locate the source of my new consciousness and experience of freedom in the process of growing organic food. Out of this new lived reality has also grown a deeper respect for healing and the use of medicinal herbs, which I grow around me and use for my own needs and to support my neighbors and friends within my community—in a society where allopathic medicine has a large and dominant presence and which systematically ridicules herbs even as the state claims to respect indigenous knowledge systems and practices.

This relocation into a site that has its challenges and joys provides me with bursts of insight and energy for contemplating what it means to live radically and to be engaged in this moment of neocolonial hegemony and blatant capitalist overconsumption. Certainly there are many sites of reinvigoration that each of us can relocate to, ideologically and physically. The larger challenge is how to bring new ideas, energies, agency, and shifts in consciousness to the process through which African feminists can begin crafting, articulating, and living an alternative future.

Speaking from my vegan and ecofeminist location, it is clear that the appropriation of new ideas around herbal healing and organic production, which in many ways have remained the bedrock of subsistence agriculture by most rural African women, is becoming an urgent political matter affecting the livelihoods of most African people.[6] It is these clarities from my lived experiences that have convinced me that the dialectical relationship between theory and praxis remains crucial in the imagining and articulation of a contemporary African feminism, which will be both revolutionary and essential to the making of new realities and life-scapes for us on the continent and beyond.

. . . .

Patricia McFadden is a radical African feminist who aspires to a life of freedom and joy. She is vegan and produces most of her own organic food on a mountain in eastern Swaziland. Her most recent publication is *Women's Freedoms Are the Heartbeat of Africa's Future: A Sankarian Imperative.*

Notes

1   Throughout my consciously feminist writing life, I have used my personal experiences and intimate thoughts as props either in articulating new ideas or in expressing sometimes controversial arguments, particularly around sexuality, pleasure, and black female identity. Very early on in my writing career I would

be reminded that using the personal was "subjective" and unscientific, sometimes by women who considered themselves quite radical. However, I have always taken license from the power of personal narration and its centrality as a uniquely feminist feature of women's writing to and for resistance. Interfacing both the personal and the formally political discourses of feminist existence and thought is a strategy that I have used in this piece.

2   See the work of the World Courts of Women NGO, led by Dr. Corinne Kumar, based in Tunis, together with that of the human rights advocacy group El Taller International.

3   Some supposedly progressive Black males who would argue that they are feminist derisively referred to these contestations as personal fights, exposing their own inability to acknowledge that women can and do engage in political contestation and struggles over ideology and power.

4   In a public conversation among a group of women, two sisters confronted me about my sexual behavior, implying that I was promiscuous and that I had an uncontrollable urge to have sex all the time. In Southern Africa there is a deep undercurrent of learned racial bigotry, which constructs mixed-race women as "sexually compulsive." Writing on sexuality and pleasure has tended to surface these prejudices in apparently unintended ways.

5   I was excitedly narrating to my dear friend Beverly Guy-Sheftall how my pantry was "bursting at the seams" with organic vegetables and fruits, and how astounded I was at this amazing process that I was part of—living off the earth in organically respectful ways. She wrote back to say "You have become SUFFI-CIENT," and the clarity of her response reinforced my understanding of how, when feminists share how we are living, we consolidate our collective ideas and expand our radical thinking.

6   The invasion of the African countryside by genetically modified organisms, as well as the push for title deeds to communal landownership is the new onslaught aimed at further commoditizing African rural societies and African biodiversity.

Works Cited

Alexander, M. Jacqui. 1994. "Not Just (Any) Body Can Be a Citizen: The Politics of Law, Sexuality and Postcoloniality in Trinidad and Tobago and the Bahamas." *Feminist Review* 48 (Autumn): 5–23.

Alexander, M. Jacqui. 2005. *Pedagogies of Crossing: Meditations on Feminism, Sexual Politics, Meditation, and the Sacred.* Durham, NC: Duke University Press.

Cabral, Amilcar. 1973. *Return to the Source: Selected Speeches of Amilcar Cabral.* New York: Monthly Review Press.

Gqola, Pumla. 2012. "Moving beyond Patriarchy." *MindMap–South Africa*, February 22. https://mindmapsa.wordpress.com/2012/02/22/pumla-gqola-moving-beyond -patriarchy/.

Griffin, Susan. 1996. *The Eros of Everyday Life: Essays on Ecology, Gender and Society.* New York: Anchor Books.

Harper, Breeze. 2009. *Black Female Vegans Speak on Food, Identity, Health and Society*. New York: Lantern Books.

Herr, Ranjoo. 2014. "Reclaiming Third World Feminism: Or Why Transnational Feminism Needs Third World Feminism." *Meridians: Feminism, Race, Transnationalism* 12, no 1: 1–30.

hooks, bell. 1995. "Some Home Truths on the Contemporary Black Feminist Movement." In *Words of Fire: An Anthology of African-American Feminist Thought*, edited by Beverly Guy-Sheftall, 254–68. New York: New Press.

Imre, Aniko. 2008. "Lesbian Nationalism." *SIGNS: A Journal of Women in Culture and Society* 33, no. 2: 255–82.

Lorde, Audre. 1984. "Uses of the Erotic: The Erotic as Power." In *Sister Outsider: Essays and Speeches by Audre Lorde*, 114–23. Freedom, CA: Crossing Press.

Lorde, Audre. 1997. "Coal." In *The Collected Poems of Audre Lorde*, 6. New York: Norton.

McFadden, Patricia. 2011. "Challenges for African Feminism in the Contemporary Moment." In *Harvesting Feminist Knowledge for Public Policy: Rebuilding Progress*, edited by Devaki Jain and Diane Elson, 293–306. Thousand Oaks, CA: Sage.

McFadden, Patricia. 2016. "Becoming Contemporary African Feminists: Her-stories, Legacies and New Imperatives." Paper read at the FES Conference, Maputo.

Motsemmi, Nthabiseng. 2004. "The Mute Always Speak: On Women's Silences at the Truth and Reconciliation Commission." *Current Sociology* 52, no. 5: 909–32.

Ouzgane, Lahouchine, and Robert Morrell, eds. 2005. *African Masculinities: Men in Africa from the Late Nineteenth Century to the Present*. New York: Palgrave Macmillan.

Pereira, Charmaine. 2009. "Setting Agendas for Feminist Thought and Practice in Nigeria." *SIGNS: A Journal of Women in Culture and Society* 34, no. 2: 263–69.

Ratele, Kopano. 2014. "Hegemonic African Masculinities and Men's Heterosexual Lives: Some Uses for Homophobia." *African Studies Review* 57, no. 2: 115–30.

Thiam, Awa. 1986. *Black Sisters, Speak Out: Feminism and Oppression in Black Africa*. London: Pluto Press.

Walby, Sylvia. 2003. "Gender Mainstreaming: Productive Tensions in Theory and Practice." Paper read at the ESRC Gender Mainstreaming Seminar, University of Leeds, May.

Walker, Alice. 2006. *We Are the Ones We Have Been Waiting For*. New York: New Press.

Woolf, Virginia. 1929. *A Room of One's Own*. London: Harvest Books.

About the Cover Artist

Gulshan Khan, For Black Girls Only (FBGO)

Artist Statement

For Black Girls Only (FBGO) is an image made during the inaugural For Black Girls Only event held in Johannesburg and is part of an ongoing project on women of color in spaces of activism and consciousness. I am moved by everything that deeply affects women. Social justice, identity, power, and belonging are overarching themes that drive my learning and direct my visual reflection of the human condition and the world around me. I am interested in diaspora and migrant groups, in the replication of origins, the reestablishment of communities, and the "organization of beliefs" that bind people together.

Creating imagery is speaking with light, shape, and form; it is a testimony of what you are seeing, bearing witness, and in every image, inextricably giving a little bit of yourself. Through it I find myself learning and connecting with people, and connecting more deeply with myself. It stretches me to see and feel more; it is a language that helps me make sense of this life. If even a little more than this happens, if in some tiny way one of my images shifts a perception, sheds light on an issue, inspires dialogue and understanding or moves someone toward a little kindness or a more impactful positive change, I am very grateful.

Keep up to date on new scholarship

Issue alerts are a great way to stay current on all the cutting-edge scholarship from your favorite Duke University Press journals. This free service delivers tables of contents directly to your inbox, informing you of the latest groundbreaking work as soon as it is published.

To sign up for issue alerts:

1. Visit **dukeu.press/register** and register for an account. You do not need to provide a customer number.

2. After registering, visit **dukeu.press/alerts**.

3. Go to "Latest Issue Alerts" and click on "Add Alerts."

4. Select as many publications as you would like from the pop-up window and click "Add Alerts."

read.dukeupress.edu/journals

Printed and bound by CPI Group (UK) Ltd, Croydon, CR0 4YY

25/03/2025